PHYSICS

for OCR A

FOR SEPARATE AWARD

Sandra Mitchell

Chris Sherry

Heinemann Educational Publishers
Halley Court, Jordan Hill, Oxford, OX2 8EJ
Part of Harcourt Education

Heinemann is the registered trademark of
Harcourt Education Limited

First published 2001

ISBN 0 435 58294 1

05 04
10 9 8 7 6

Edited by Donna Evans

Designed and typeset by Oxford Designers & Illustrators

Illustrated by Oxford Designers & Illustrators

Printed and bound in Great Britain by Bath Colourbooks

Photo research by Ginny Stroud-Lewis

Acknowledgements
The authors and publishers would like to thank the following for permission to use photographs:
Cover photo: Images
TB1: Fig 19, Allsport. TB2: Fig 2, Corbis. Fig 6, Sheena Verdun-Taylor. Figs 14, 22,
Popperfoto/Reuters. Fig 33, Sheena Verdun-Taylor. Figs 40, 41, Shout Pictures. Fig 42, Actionplus.
Fig 46, Sheena Verdun-Taylor. Figs 47, 48, Shout Pictures. Fig 49, Highway Code. Fig 53, Peter
Gould. Fig 54, Corbis. Fig 61, Sheena Verden-Taylor. Fig 72, Actionplus. TB3: Figs 1, 2, Corbis.
Fig 7, Peter Gould. Fig 8, Redferns. Fig 10, Corbis. Fig 32, Peter Gould. Fig 43, Shout Pictures.
Fig 48, Skyscan. TB4: Fig 4, SPL. Fig 9, Sheena Verdun-Taylor. Fig 10, Ginny Stroud Lewis. Fig
12, Ginny Stroud Lewis. Fig 18, Radarsales. Fig 19, SPL. Fig 21, SPL. Fig 29, University of Iowa.
Fig 33, SPL. Fig 35, Popperfoto/Reuters. Fig 51, SPL. TB5: Fig 1, SPL. Fig 3, SPL. Figs 5, 9,
Corbis. Fig 15 (left) NRPB, (right) Chris Sherry. Fig 19, Chris Sherry. Fig 22, SPL. Fig 23 (top)
Sheena Verdun-Taylor, (left) SPL, (right) Sheena Verdun-Taylor. Figs 24, 25, Corbis. Fig 26, SPL.
Fig 27, Chris Sherry. Fig 28, Department of Information and Public Affairs. TB6: Figs 5, 6, 11,
NASA. Fig 13, SPL. Fig 14, NASA. Figs 15, 16, SPL. Fig 18, NASA. Fig 19, Shout Pictures. Fig
22, SPL. Fig 24, SPL. Fig 24, Kobal. Fig 26, SPL. Fig 28, Popperfoto/Reuters. TB7: Fig 1, Corbis.
Fig 2, Sheena Verdun-Taylor. Fig 15, Corbis. Fig 17, Popperfoto. Fig 19, Peter Gould. Fig 35,
Sheena Verdun-Taylor. Fig 42, SPL. TB8: Fig 1, SPL. Fig 14, Sheena Verdun-Taylor. Fig 27, Peter
Gould. Fig 30, SPL. Fig 34, Sheena Verdun-Taylor. Fig 36, Ace Photo Library. Fig 41, SPL.
SPL = Science Photo Library. TBA2: Fig 19, www.viewimages.com. Fig 21, Chris Sherry. Fig 38,
www.acs.appstate.edu.html. Fig 49, http://store.corbis.com. Fig 51, Eric Whitehead Photography.
Fig 56, www.polarshades.com. TBA3: Fig 19, Jeremy Davy, Mach 1.02 Ltd.

The publishers have made every effort to trace the copyright holders, but if they have
inadvertently overlooked any, they will be pleased to make the necessary arrangements at the first
opportunity.

p186 fig 1, MEG Nuffield Coordinated Sciences; Double award paper 1772/9, June 96,
question 8; **p195 fig 21**, Longmans; Double award paper 1772/6, Central tier paper 6, 11 June 96

Introduction

This book provides coverage of OCR Physics (1982). The first examination of these specifications is in June 2003. It concentrates on Extension Block A only. Further information about the alternative Extension Block B is available from OCR.

The book has been written by examiners who have been involved in the writing of the new specifications. It is supported by other materials published by Heinemann including a Homework book, a Teacher's Resource pack and a CD-ROM.

The book is divided into two parts.

Material common to the Physics of Double Award is covered by the first eight Teaching blocks. This reminds you of what you should already know from Key Stage 3. It also gives a quick Check-up test. If you feel there are things you do not remember, your teacher should have a Summary sheet to help you.

Extension A material is covered by three additional Teaching blocks, A1–A3. These also have an introductory spread so that you can check what you already know from Double award. Remember that this material can only be tested on Paper 3 or 4.

Throughout the book there are:

Key Points

Each Teaching block is split into double-page spreads. Each double-page spread starts by listing the key points it covers.

Higher tier material

If you are taking the Higher tier papers (1982/2 and 1982/4) you will be expected to know and understand all the material in this book. If, however, you are taking Foundation tier, you can miss out the parts that are shown in pink tinted boxes. This is Higher or H material.

Thinking further

At the end of each double-page spread there are questions to test your understanding. They are at two levels. The easier questions are shown by a ■ and the harder questions by a ◆.

Ideas and evidence

In the new specifications there will be questions about how scientists worked in the past and how they work today. Throughout the book there are Ideas and evidence boxes and questions.

Taking it further

Taking if further boxes include interesting facts which are not on the specification. You will not be examined on the material in these boxes.

Key words

Key words are important scientific terms that you need to know. They are emboldened in the text, listed at the end of the double-page spread and explained in the Glossary. Key words for Higher only are shown in pink.

Key facts and formulae

These are indented and shown in blue tinted boxes throughout. It is important that you remember these.

Questions

At the end of each Teaching block there are examination-type questions. Questions with symbols ● and ■ are similar to those found on Foundation papers; those with (square) and (diamond) are similar to questions found on Higher papers.

Skills sections

At the back of the book are sections to help you improve your skills in particular areas.

We hope that this book will help you throughout your course.

Contents

Electric circuits

Electric circuits are an important part of many pieces of equipment that we use every day. The simple circuits, comprising batteries and lamps, that you have probably set up have been developed to include more and more components, some of which we shall investigate.

Circuit components have become smaller and smaller so that now millions of components can be assembled on one tiny circuit board, or chip. Think about a modern computer – it's small and fast. Earlier computers worked very slowly and could perform fewer tasks, but were enormous! Mobile phones are becoming smaller and smaller and have more and more features.

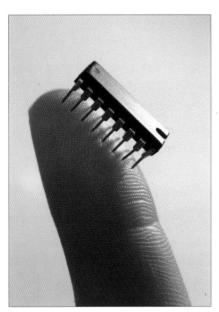

fig 1

New discoveries in electronics are made every day. Can you imagine what electrical items will be in production in 50 years time?

This Teaching block helps you to understand more about electric circuits.

Check-up

Have a go at the following questions. They will remind you what you should already know about electric circuits.

a Look at the three circuits shown in fig 2. In which circuit would you see:
   • the brightest lamp(s)
   • the dimmest lamp(s)?

Give reasons for your choice.

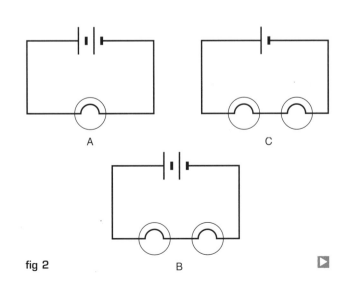

fig 2

▶ Check-up (continued)

b Which circuit in question **a** has the largest current? Explain your answer.

c What instrument is used to measure electric current? What unit is it measured in?

d What instrument is used to measure voltage? What unit is it measured in?

e Name two materials that are good conductors of electricity and two materials that are bad conductors.

f Draw a circuit to show how you would connect two lamps and one cell so that the lamps are as bright as possible.

g Christmas tree lights are connected in series. Give one advantage and one disadvantage of connecting them in this way.

h Draw a diagram to show how to connect two lamps so that they can be switched on and off independently.

i Write down the readings on the ammeters in fig 3.

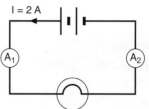

fig 3

j In fig 4, which switch must be closed for the lamp to light? What would happen if *both* switches were closed?

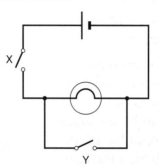

fig 4

If you have difficulties, your teacher has a Summary sheet you can have.

Contents of the Teaching block

This Teaching block is divided into three double page spreads.

1.1 Circuit components

We look at how energy is transferred to make things happen in an electric circuit – to light a lamp, to ring a bell, and many more! We also consider some circuit components that you may not have met before.

1.2 Measuring resistance

Current and voltage are two basic quantities that we often measure in electric circuits. We see how these measurements can be used to calculate resistance.

1.3 More about resistance

We consider resistance in more detail and look at how it varies with current and voltage in various components.

Links with other Teaching blocks

1.1 Circuit components

Key points

- Energy is transferred from cells and other sources to make things happen in a complete electrical circuit.
  Circuit components dissipate this energy, producing heat, light, sound or movement.
- Resistors become hot when charge flows through them.
- Variable resistors alter the current in a circuit.

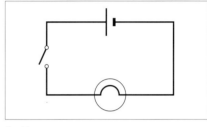

fig 5

Energy transfer in a circuit

The circuit diagram shows a cell being used to light a lamp. When the switch is closed, **energy** in the cell produces light and heat in the lamp. We say that energy is **dissipated** in the lamp.

In general, energy is dissipated in the components placed in the circuit. Examples of circuit components, in addition to lamps, are motors, bells and buzzers.

There *must* always be an electrical source – a cell, battery or generator, or a power supply connected to the mains.

a A power supply is connected to a buzzer. How is energy dissipated when the power supply is turned on?

Circuit components and symbols

The electrical symbols for the components you will meet are shown in fig 6. These are standard symbols used worldwide, so you must learn them.

A **diode** only allows a current to pass through it in one direction, which is shown by the direction of the arrow on its symbol. A **light emitting diode (LED)** emits light when it conducts a current. LEDs can be used to tell the direction of a current.

b Will the LEDs P, Q, R and S light in the circuits in fig 7?

The resistance of a **light dependent resistor (LDR)** varies with the intensity of the light

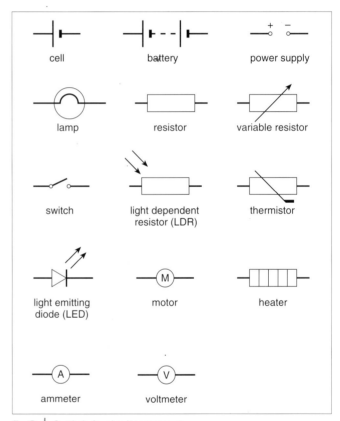

fig 6 | Symbols for circuit components

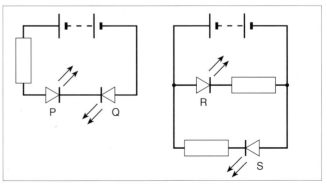

fig 7

shining on it. This alters the current in the circuit. LDRs can be used to switch lights on when it gets dark.

A **thermistor** is a temperature sensitive resistor. The resistance of a thermistor decreases when it becomes warm.

The action of the other components is clear from their names.

Resistors

Energy from the cell reaches the lamp in fig 5 because charged particles move in the copper connecting wires. The charged particles are **electrons**. Connecting wires are very good conductors of electricity and hardly impede the flow of electrons. However, the wire filament resists the flow of electrons. Electrons collide with the atoms in the filament, losing kinetic energy. The kinetic energy makes the atoms in the filament vibrate faster, and the filament gets hotter.

If the **resistance** in a circuit *increases*, the **electric current** *decreases*. A **variable resistor** can be used to alter the current in a circuit, for instance by altering the length of wire connected into a circuit.

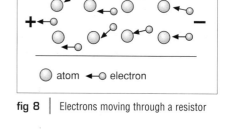

fig 8 | Electrons moving through a resistor

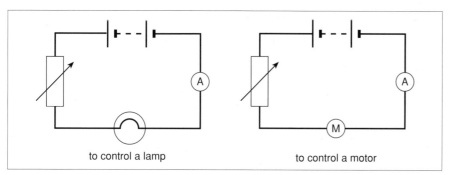

to control a lamp   to control a motor

fig 9

Look at the lamp circuit in fig 9. Increasing the resistance decreases the current and the lamp is *dimmer*.

Look at the motor circuit in fig 9. Increasing the resistance decreases the current and the motor turns more *slowly*.

Thinking further

■ **1** LEDs are damaged if too large a current passes through them. How can you make sure that the current remains low?

■ **2** What will happen to a resistor if the current in it is increased? Explain your answer.

◆ **3** Draw a circuit diagram to show how two LEDs can be connected to indicate current direction. Why are *two* LEDs necessary?

◆ **4** Tungsten is used to make the filament in a lamp that reaches a very high temperature when in use. Suggest some properties of tungsten which make it suitable.

┌─ **KEY WORDS** ─────────────────────────────────────
│ diode • dissipated • electric current • electrons • energy • light dependent resistor (LDR) •
│ light emitting diode (LED) • resistance • thermistor • variable resistor
└───

Resistors connected in a series.

1.2 Measuring resistance

> ### Key points
>
> - An electric current is a flow of charge. It is measured using an ammeter placed in series in a circuit.
> - Voltage is a measure of the energy transferred in a component. It is measured using a voltmeter placed in parallel.
> - Resistance can be found by finding the current through a resistor and the voltage across it.
> - Voltage divided by current gives the resistance value.

Electric current

Energy is transferred in a circuit by a flow of charge; this is an electric current. Electric current is measured in **amperes** (usually shortened to amps or A) using an **ammeter**. An ammeter is connected in **series** in the circuit.

The current is always the same in all parts of a series circuit. In **parallel** circuits the current splits. The smaller the resistance the easier the path and the bigger the current in it. If the current I is split into I_1 and I_2 then $I = I_1 + I_2$

a In fig 10 the current is measured at P, Q and R. What is the current at each point?

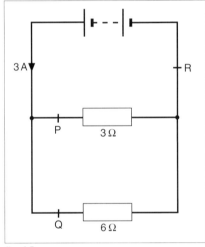

fig 10

Voltage

The battery (or power supply) provides energy. The higher its voltage the more energy it supplies. The **voltage** across a component is a measure of the work done, or energy transferred to other forms, when taking the current through the component.

Voltage is measured in **volts** (V) using a **voltmeter**. Voltmeters are always connected in parallel across the component.

In series circuits the supply voltage is shared between the components in the circuit. The greater the resistance of a component the greater the voltage across it.

In fig 11 V_1 is less than V_2 and $V = V_1 + V_2$.

b What are the missing voltmeter readings, V_1 and V_2, in fig 11?

The voltage is the same across all components connected in parallel.

c What would a voltmeter read if it were connected between the points P and Q in the circuit shown in fig 10?

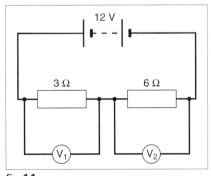

fig 11

Measuring resistance

resistance (in **ohms**) = $\dfrac{\text{voltage across the resistor (in V)}}{\text{current through the resistor (in A)}}$

We can write $R = \dfrac{V}{I}$

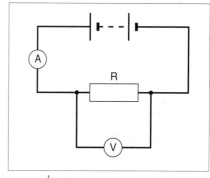

fig 12 | Circuit diagram to measure resistance

Resistance can be measured using the circuit shown in fig 12. The ammeter measures the current in the resistor. Ammeters have a very low resistance so that they do not greatly increase the resistance of the circuit.

The voltmeter measures the voltage across the resistor. Voltmeters have a very high resistance so that there is hardly any current through them.

If the voltmeter reads 10 V and the ammeter 2 A, the resistance is

$R = \dfrac{V}{I} = \dfrac{10}{2} = 5\,\Omega$

Circuit calculations

We have seen that resistance is given by $R = \dfrac{V}{I}$

Rearranging this we can write $V = IR$, or $I = \dfrac{V}{R}$

d An 8 Ω resistor has a current of 3 A in it. What is the voltage across it?

Thinking further

■ **1** Copy and complete the table.

voltage in V	current in A	resistance in Ω
	0.5	24
24	4	
12		48

fig 13

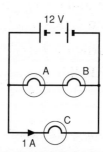

fig 14

■ **2a** If all the lamps in fig 14 are similar, write down the current in lamps A and B. Hence find the current through the battery.

b What is the voltage across each of the lamps A, B and C?

◆ **3** Draw a circuit to show how the starter motor, lights and wipers on a car can be switched *separately* using the 12 V car battery. If the car is started with the lights on the lights may go dim. Explain.

◆ **4** Design circuits to light two lamps so that

a one lamp is brighter than the other

b one has constant brightness, the other has variable brightness.

KEY WORDS

ammeter • ampere • ohms • parallel • series • volt • voltage • voltmeter

---

🖳 *IT application – measurement of resistance using data logger.*

1.3 More about resistance

Current and voltage variation

Look again at the circuit used to measure resistance (see fig 12). If a variable power supply is used, or a variable resistor is included in the circuit, several pairs of current and voltage values can be obtained. The results can be plotted on a graph of current against voltage (see fig 15).

If the resistor is a *metal wire* the graph will be a straight line passing through the origin, as long as the temperature does not change too much. This shows that the resistance of the resistor is constant; it is said to be **ohmic** because it obeys **Ohm's Law**.

Ohm's Law states that the voltage across a conductor is proportional to the current in it as long as the temperature does not change.

a How can you keep any temperature changes small?

If the resistor experiment is repeated using a **filament lamp** in place of the wire the graph is curved, fig 16.

b The lamp filament is a fine metal wire (usually tungsten). Why is the graph in fig 16 not a straight line?

c Use the graph to estimate the resistance of the lamp filament when the voltage is 2 V, 4 V and 6 V. What do you notice?

A silicon diode can be substituted for the metal wire in the original experiment. The diode is damaged if there is too high a current in it, so a large resistor is included in the circuit. The current is then in **milliamps** (mA) (1 mA = 1/1000 A).

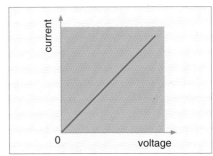

fig 15 | Graph of current–voltage variation for a wire

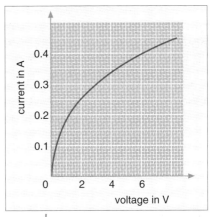

fig 16 | Graph of current–voltage variation for a lamp

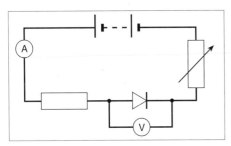

fig 17 | Circuit to show current–volatge variation for a diode

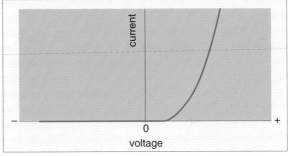

fig 18 | Graph to show current–volatge variation for a diode

If the battery terminals are reversed, it can be shown that there is no current.

Light dependent resistor

A light dependent resistor (LDR) is made of cadmium sulphide. This **semiconductor** (a very poor electrical conductor) has a very high resistance in the dark (several million ohms), but when light is shone on it, its resistance falls to a few hundred ohms.

Thermistor

A thermistor is a resistor whose resistance changes considerably with temperature. The resistance of a semiconductor, such as silicon, decreases by a large amount when it is heated. This is because the extra thermal energy releases more electrons from the semiconductor atoms, so the current increases.

d As it gets hotter, the resistance of a thermistor changes in the opposite way to the resistance of a filament lamp. Suggest a reason for this.

Factors affecting resistance

If the voltage across a wire is kept the same while the length of the wire increases, the current decreases. It is found that the resistance of a wire is proportional to its length. Although there are more vibrating positive ions in a longer wire to impede electron flow, there are also more free electrons, so the effects should cancel out. But, at constant voltage, less energy is available to the electrons to move through each centimetre of wire. This means that the electrons move more slowly, so fewer pass a given point in one second. Hence the current, which is rate of flow of charge, is reduced and the resistance increases.

e A thicker wire has less resistance than a thin one. Explain why.

fig 19 LDRs are found in light meters used by photographers and umpires

> **LDR** – resistance is low in the light, high in the dark.

> **Thermistor** – resistance is low when hot, high when cold.

Thinking further

■ **1** Sketch the I–V graph for a lamp. Add to your graph the line you would get if a more powerful lamp were used.

■ **2** Use the I–V graph for a diode (fig 18) to help you to describe how the resistance of the diode changes with voltage.

■ **3** A milliammeter is placed in series with a battery and a LDR. How will the milliammeter reading change as it gets dark?

◆ **4** A thermistor is used to protect the filament of a TV tube from a current surge as it is switched on.
  a Why does a current surge occur?
  b How does the thermistor prevent it?

◆ **5** Using the correct symbols draw a circuit diagram of a 12 V power supply in series with a protective resistor and a conducting LED. If it is not to be damaged, the maximum voltage allowed across the LED is 2 V and the maximum current through it is 20 mA. Calculate the resistance of the protective resistor.

— **KEY WORDS** —
filament lamp • milliamp (mA) • ohmic • Ohm's Law • semiconductor

Current-voltage graph for a metallic conductor.   *I–V graphs for diode and thermistor using data logger.*

Questions on electric circuits

● **1** Copy and complete the sentences below. Use words from the list; you can use them more than once.

ammeter · amperes · current · light · ohms · parallel · series · thermal · voltage · voltmeter

- In an electric fire energy is dissipated as _____ energy and _____ energy.
- The electric current in a component is measured in _____ using an _____ connected in _____ with the component.
- If there is a current in a component there must be a difference in _____ across it. This is measured using a _____ connected in _____ across the component.
- Resistance is found by dividing _____ by _____.
- Resistance is measured in _____. *(11)*

● **2** Draw a circuit diagram to show how you would connect two similar lamps in series with a 6 V battery. Add a voltmeter to measure the voltage across one of the lamps. What would you expect the voltmeter reading to be? *(4)*

3 Apeksha did an experiment to measure the current through and the voltage across a resistor. These are her results.

voltage in V	current in A
0	0.00
1	0.10
3	0.13
5	0.52
7	0.72
9	0.87

fig 20

● **a** Draw a graph of current against voltage. *(4)*
● **b** What does it tell you about the resistor? *(2)*
■ **c** Use your graph to estimate
   i the current when the voltage is 2 V *(2)*
   ii the voltage when the current is 0.60 A. *(2)*

4 Look at the circuit in fig 21.

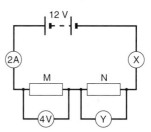

fig 21

● **a** What type of meter is X and what will it read? *(2)*
● **b** What type of meter is Y and what will it read? *(2)*
■ **c** Calculate the resistance of the resistors M and N. *(4)*

■ **5** Look at the circuit in fig 22.

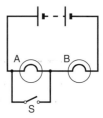

fig 22

What would you notice about the brightness of lamps A and B with
  i switch S open
  ii switch S closed.
Give reasons for your answers. *(6)*

6 Paul has a small filament lamp marked 2.5 V 0.3 A.

■ **a** Calculate the resistance of the lamp when working normally. *(3)*
◆ **b** Paul measured the current through the lamp and the voltage across it as he increased the voltage across it from zero to 3 V.
  i Draw a suitable circuit to do this. *(3)*
  ii Sketch the graph he would get if he plotted current against voltage. Explain the shape of the graph. *(5)*

Paul wants to light the lamp to normal brightness using a 6 V supply. He decides to add a resistor to the circuit.

◆ **c** Draw the circuit he should use now and calculate the value of the resistor needed. *(5)*

7 Gary is 17 years old and has just got his first car. He has bought a fog lamp and wants to wire it into the headlamp circuit. The circuit in fig 23 shows how he did it.

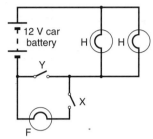

fig 23

■ **a** Gary closed switch (X) to test the fog lamp (F). The headlamps (H) came on as well but all the lamps were dim. Explain why this happened. *(3)*

■ **b** When Gary turned on the headlamp switch (Y) as well the fog lamp went out. Why? *(1)*

◆ **c** Sketch the circuit Gary *should* have connected to make the headlamps and fog lamp work properly. *(3)*

8 Look at the circuit in fig 24 (a).

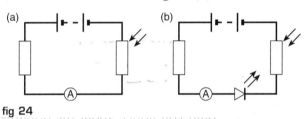

fig 24

■ **a** What happens to the ammeter reading when light shines on the LDR? Explain. *(3)*

An LED is added to the circuit (b) but does not light up, even when a bright light is shone on the LDR.

◆ **b** Suggest a reason for this. What can be done to make the LED light? *(2)*

9 The graph in fig 25 shows how the resistance of a thermistor changes with temperature.

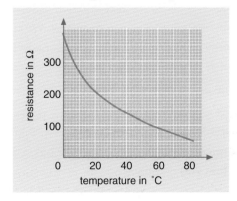

fig 25

■ **a** Estimate the resistance of the thermistor at 30 °C. *(1)*

The resistance increased from 100 to 250 ohms.

■ **b** Estimate the temperature change that occurred. *(3)*

◆ **c** At what temperatures would the thermistor be most sensitive? Explain how you decided. *(2)*

◆ **d** Suggest a use for this thermistor. *(1)*

─── **IDEAS AND EVIDENCE** ───

10 We have seen that the resistance of a metal increases with temperature. Conversely, if a metal is cooled, its resistance decreases. In some materials this continues until a critical temperature is reached, when the resistance suddenly drops to zero. This means that a current flows with no energy wasted as heat. This effect has been known since 1911, but no practical use could be made of it because the critical temperature for metals is very low indeed – only a few degrees above absolute zero (–273 °C). More recently special ceramic materials have been developed with much higher critical temperatures, well above the boiling point of liquid nitrogen (–196 °C), which is readily available for cooling. Scientists dream of producing a material that is a superconductor at 'normal' temperatures.

In medicine, superconductors are used to produce the very powerful magnets needed for magnetic resonance imaging. When cooled below its critical temperature a superconductor will repel a magnet so that the magnet floats. In the future this could be used to propel a train that would float on air.

a Explain why the resistance of a metal decreases if it is cooled. *(2)*

b Why does a superconductor never become hot? *(2)*

c What is meant by 'critical temperature'? *(1)*

d Superconductivity has been known since 1911. Why has it not been made use of until quite recently? *(2)*

e What use is already made of a superconductor? *(1)*

f What would be the advantage of 'a train that would float on air'? *(2)*

g Why do scientists want to produce a material that is superconducting at 'normal' temperatures? *(2)*

h Suggest another application for 'normal' temperature superconductors. *(1)*

Forces and energy

Forces and energy are a fundamental part of any study of Physics. A force can be a push or a pull; it can change the shape, the speed or the direction of motion of an object. There are contact forces, like friction, and non-contact forces such as gravity. Isaac Newton developed the idea of gravity when, so the story goes, he wondered why an apple fell from a tree. Now we always measure force in newtons (N). The weight of an average eating apple is 1 N.

Energy is needed to do work. In Physics work has a special meaning; work is only done when a force *moves*. The energy that enables us to run comes from the food we eat. A car moves because petrol provides the energy required. Energy cannot be made or lost; it can only be changed from one form to another. For example, the energy of the petrol is changed into kinetic energy in the engine; heat and sound are also produced. A more efficient engine produces less non-useful energy. The less non-useful energy produced, the more efficient the car engine. Engineers constantly try to design more efficient machines so that we do not waste our valuable energy resources.

fig 1

fig 2

Check-up

Have a go at the following questions. They will remind you what you should already know about forces and energy.

a Name three things a force can do.

b What unit do we use to measure forces?

c A car travels 800 m in 40 s. What is its average speed?

d What is the weight of a 1 kg bag of sugar?

e Sam hangs a 2 kg bunch of onions from the kitchen ceiling by a string. What is the tension in the string?

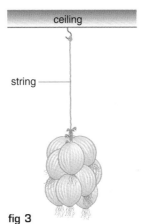

fig 3

f Why does a car slide about when the road is icy?

g A plank is balanced at its mid-point. A 4 N weight is hung at one end as shown in fig 4. Where must a 6 N weight be placed if the plank stays balanced?

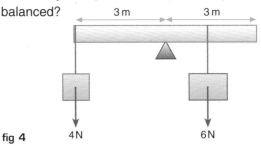

fig 4

h Jane holds a ball above her head. What sort of energy does it have? What happens to this energy when she drops the ball?

i What is the difference between temperature and heat?

j Name four ways in which heat can be transferred.

If you have difficulties, your teacher has a Summary sheet that you can have.

Contents of the Teaching block

This Teaching block is divided into twelve double page spreads.

2.1 Turning forces

The turning effect (or moment) of a force depends on the size of the force and its perpendicular distance from the pivot. It is the principle behind all sorts of things from seesaws to spanners.

2.2 Motion graphs

Speed–time and distance–time graphs are useful ways of describing motion. They give more detail and are easier to understand than any number of words.

2.3 Displacement and velocity

Displacement is distance moved in a particular direction.
Velocity is speed in a particular direction.

2.4 Acceleration

Acceleration is the rate of change of velocity. We see how to find acceleration from a velocity–time graph.

2.5 Forces

There are various types of force. We consider the forces acting between objects, even when they are not in contact.

2.6 Force and motion

We see how the size and direction of the forces acting on an object affect the way it moves.
If there is an unbalanced force on an object it will accelerate (or decelerate).

2.7 Force and acceleration

Newton showed that the resultant force acting on an object equals its mass multiplied by its acceleration. We apply this to car seat belts and crumple zones, as well as to several sporting activities.

2.8 Force and energy

Energy is needed to do work. The energy transferred is equal to the work done. We see how to calculate work, energy and power.

2.9 On the road

We apply the ideas learned earlier to road safety. We see that the total stopping distance is not only the distance travelled while braking, but also the distance you travel in the time your brain takes to react – thinking distance.

2.10 How things fall

Every object is attracted towards Earth due to gravity. We look at the forces acting on falling objects and consider the effect of air resistance.

2.11 Keeping warm

We see how energy losses due to conduction, convection and radiation can be kept to a minimum in our houses and consider the cost effectiveness of various methods.

2.12 Energy efficiency

All energy transfer processes waste energy. We see how to calculate the energy efficiency of several processes, both large and small.

Links with other Teaching blocks

2.1 Turning forces

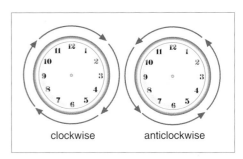

fig 5

Moments

Think about opening a door. The handle is usually as far away from the hinges as possible. This makes it easy to open. The further away you are from the hinges (or **pivot**) the smaller the **force** needs to be to open the door. Try opening a door by pushing in the middle, or close to the hinges; you have to push much, much harder!

fig 6

To calculate the turning effect, or **moment**, of a force we use

$$\text{moment (in Nm)} = \text{force (in N)} \times \frac{\text{perpendicular distance}}{\text{from pivot to force (in m)}}$$

Moments are measured in **newton metres** (written as Nm). Moments are clockwise or anticlockwise, depending on which way they turn.

a Fig 7 shows a spanner used to undo a nut. Using the equation above, calculate the moment of the force.

A **couple** is two equal turning forces acting in opposite directions a distance apart. You apply a couple when you turn on a tap or open a jar. The moment of a couple is also called a **torque**.

In fig 8, the moment of the couple = $F \times d$

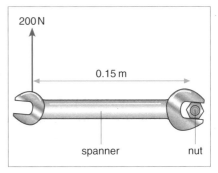

fig 7

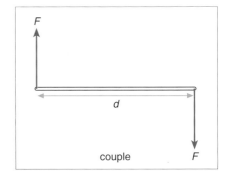

fig 8

Balancing

Fig 9 shows Priya and Dan on a seesaw.

b Calculate the moment of Priya about the pivot.

c Calculate the moment of Dan about the pivot.

d Which way will the seesaw move?

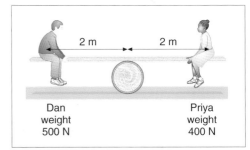

fig 9

The seesaw balances when

the sum of the anticlockwise moments	=	the sum of the clockwise moments

When the seesaw is balanced, we say it is in **equilibrium**.

e How could they make the seesaw balance? (Think of as many ways as you can.)

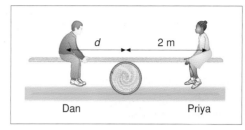

fig 10

They decide Dan should move nearer the pivot. To find out where he should sit to balance the seesaw, we equate their moments.

$500 \times d = 400 \times 2$ so $d = 1.6$ m

Dan must sit 1.6 m away from the pivot.

Dan moves back to the end of the seesaw. Little Alex, of **weight** 250 N, joins Priya and Dan. How can he help to balance the seesaw? Alex must sit on the same side as Priya.

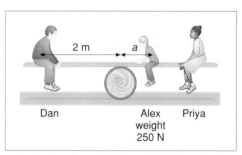

fig 11

Equating moments:

$500 \times 2 = (250 \times a) + (400 \times 2)$ so $a = 0.8$ m

Alex must sit 0.8 m from the pivot on the same side as Priya.

f Ali is carrying bricks in a wheelbarrow. The total weight is 800 N. What force, F, does he need to apply?

We use the idea of balanced moments:
- to lift a heavy load with a small force using a crowbar
- to open a can of paint with a screwdriver.

We call this use of moments **leverage**.

g Draw diagrams to help to explain why the force needed is less.

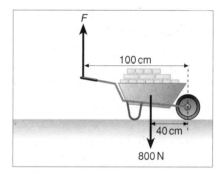

fig 12

Thinking further

1 You want to undo a tight nut on your bicycle. Would you choose a long or a short spanner? Explain your choice.

2 Priya's Dad, who weighs 800 N, sits on the seesaw in fig 10. What will happen if he sits

  a above the pivot

  b at the end on the left-hand side?

3 Fig 13 shows a lorry on a light bridge. Calculate the upward force on the bridge at

  a A   **b** B.

  What assumption have you made?

  c Sketch a graph to show how the force at A changes as the lorry moves from A to B.

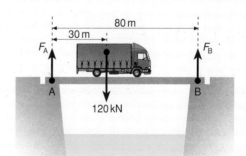

fig 13

4 You are provided with a metre rule pivoted at its mid-point and a 1 N weight.

  a Show how you could use them to weigh accurately a metal block weighing approximately 2 N.

  b How could you adapt the system to measure a 12 N weight?

  c Why is your machine very sensitive?

KEY WORDS

couple • equilibrium • force • leverage • moment • newton metre • pivot • torque • weight

 Balancing metre rules.

2.2 Motion graphs

Key points

- Speed = $\dfrac{\text{distance travelled}}{\text{time taken}}$
- A distance–time graph shows how the distance travelled varies with time.
- The gradient of a distance–time graph is equal to the speed.
- A speed–time graph shows how the speed varies with time.
- The area under a speed–time graph is equal to the distance travelled.

fig 14

Average speed

If you travel 200 km along the motorway in 2 hours you have an *average* **speed** of 100 km/h.

a Why is this an *average* speed?

average speed = $\dfrac{\text{distance travelled}}{\text{time taken}}$

Speed is measured in km/h or m/s.

b The British Men's coxless fours rowing crew won an Olympic gold medal in Sydney by rowing 2000 m in 5 min 56.24 s. What was their average speed?

Distance–time graphs

We know the speed is constant in graph (a) (fig 15) because the distance travelled in each second is always the same.

The **gradient** of the graph is constant and is equal to the speed.

c Calculate the speed from graph (a).

d How do you know the speed is *increasing* in graph (b) and *decreasing* in graph (c)?

In graphs (b) and (c) we can find the speed at any particular time by finding the gradient of the **tangent** to the curve at that time. In graph (b), after 3 s the gradient of the tangent = $\frac{15}{5}$ = 3. So the speed after 3 s is 3 m/s.

e Find the speed after 4 s for graph (b).

f Find the speed after 2 s and 4 s for graph (c). What do you notice?

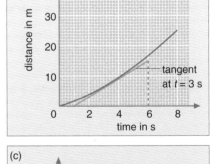

fig 15

Speed–time graphs

The *distance travelled* is equal to the area under a speed–time graph. So in fig 16, the distance travelled in 5 s = 10 × 5 = 50 m.

Since the speed is constant, this is the same as saying

distance = speed × time = 10 × 5 = 50 m.

g Find the distance travelled in 5 s in figs 17 and 18.

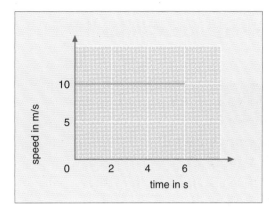

fig 16

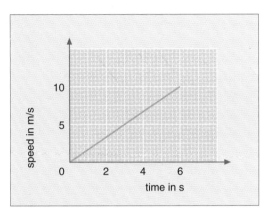

fig 17

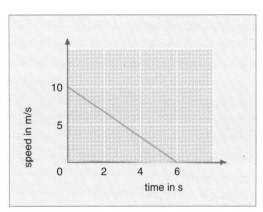

fig 18

Thinking further

■ **1** Ben lives 12 km from school. The journey to school takes 20 minutes. Find his average speed in km/h. He averages 48 km/h on the return journey. How long does he take to get home?

■ **2** Use the values in the table to plot a distance–time graph for a car over a 10 s period.

time in s	0	1	2	3	4	5	6	7	8	9	10
distance in m	0	20	40	60	80	100	100	100	100	130	160

fig 19

a Describe the motion as fully as you can.

b What was the average speed over the 10 s period?

◆ **3** The table shows how far a car travels during a journey from Luton to Birmingham.

time	distance from Luton in km
8.00 a.m.	0
8.30	30
9.00	60
9.30	110
10.00	110
10.30	130

fig 20

a Draw a distance–time graph for the journey.

b Calculate the average speed for the whole journey.

c Another car leaves Birmingham at 9.00 am and reaches Luton at 10.30 am, without stopping. Show this journey on your graph and estimate the time when the two cars pass each other. Why is your answer only an estimate?

KEY WORDS
gradient • speed • tangent

How speed affects stopping distance.

2.3 Displacement and velocity

Displacement

Displacement refers to distance in a particular direction.
Displacement is a **vector** as it has size and direction.
Distance is a **scalar** as it only has size.

Fig 21 shows a displacement-time graph for a train running a shuttle service between three stations, A, B and C, each 8 km apart. It goes from A to B to A to C to A. Its displacement is zero as it ends up at its starting point. But the total distance travelled is 32 km.

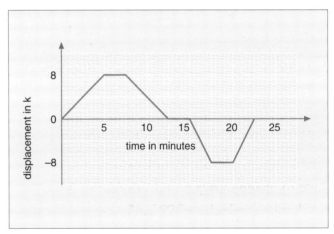

fig 21

Velocity

Speed is how fast you are going.

$$\text{speed} = \frac{\text{distance}}{\text{time}}$$

Velocity is how fast you are going *and* in what direction.

$$\text{velocity} = \frac{\text{displacement}}{\text{time}}$$

For example, a Formula One racing car may go along a straight track at a *speed* of 300 km/h but its *velocity* is 300 km/h *due North*. The car may have a *constant speed* around a gentle bend, but its *velocity changes* because its *direction is changing*. Velocity is a vector, but speed is a scalar.

fig 22

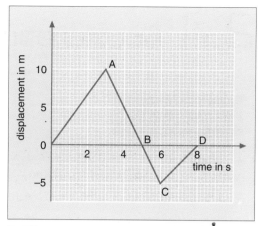
fig 23

The gradient of a displacement–time graph is equal to velocity.

a Describe the motion for each part of the displacement–time graph in fig 23. Does the object return to its starting point?

If the gradient changes, the velocity changes.

b Sketch a displacement–time graph to show increasing and decreasing velocities. Label these parts of your graph.

Units

We measure speed, and velocity, in different units depending on how fast the object is moving. Car, train and aircraft speeds are usually given in km/h, but the speed of a snail is very small, perhaps 1 mm/s.

If we use velocity in equations and formulae it *must* be in m/s.

$$1\,\text{mm/s} = \frac{1}{1000} \text{ or } 0.001\,\text{m/s}$$

fig 24

A train speed of 180 km/h is not as easy to change to m/s.

- 180 km/h = a distance of 180 km in a time of 1 h
- 180 km in 1 h = 180 000 m in 1 h
- 1 h = 60 × 60 = 3600 s
- 180 000 m in 1 h = 180 000 / 3600 = 50 m in 1 s

So a speed of 180 km/h = 50 m/s.

Rule to change km/h to m/s: divide by 3.6.

c Change a velocity of 90 km/h to m/s.

fig 25

Thinking further

■ **1** A racing car completes a 5 km lap in 100 s. After this lap what is its

  a displacement

  b average speed

  c average velocity?

■ **2 a** The speed limit on a French motorway is 130 km/h. Express this in m/s.

  b The speed of sound in air is about 330 m/s. Express this in km/h.

◆ **3** Draw a velocity–time graph for the train in fig 21. Use your graph to find

  a the total distance travelled

  b the displacement of the train.

Show your working clearly.

Compare your answers with the values given in the text.

◆ **4** The London Eye is a large vertical wheel of radius 60 m that rotates at a steady speed of 0.20 m/s.

  a How long does it take to make one revolution?

  b What is the change in a passenger's velocity as she travels from the highest to the lowest point of the wheel's path?

KEY WORDS

displacement • scalar • vector • velocity

Using a data logger to measure displacement and velocity.

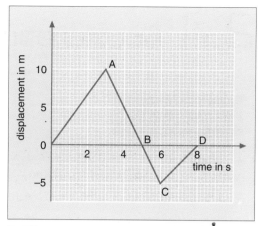

2.4 Acceleration

Acceleration

Acceleration occurs if the velocity of an object changes.

$$\text{acceleration} = \frac{\text{change in velocity}}{\text{time taken}}$$

If velocity is in m/s and time in s, acceleration is in m/s².

When the velocity is getting smaller, the object is slowing down. We say the object has negative acceleration. It is also called **deceleration**, or **retardation**.

a The velocity of a car increases from 8 to 12 m/s in 4 s. What is its acceleration?

Velocity–time graphs

Velocity has direction so you must remember to decide which direction is positive when drawing a velocity–time graph. If the direction of motion changes the velocity becomes negative.

The gradient of a velocity–time graph gives the acceleration. If the graph is a straight line the velocity changes regularly and so the acceleration is constant. The gradient of a velocity–time graph is negative when the object is slowing down *or* accelerating in the opposite direction.

The area under a velocity–time graph gives the displacement. (Compare this with the speed–time graphs studied in spread 2.2.)

b Describe the motion at each stage of the graph in fig 26. Does the object return to its starting point?

We often refer to the acceleration of an object when its *speed* changes, but strictly we should always refer to changes in *velocity*.

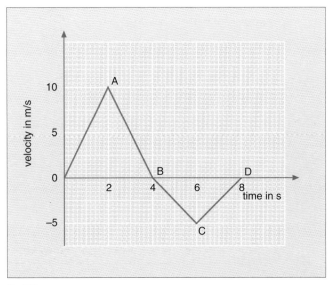

fig 26

Acceleration of a falling ball

Every object is attracted towards the Earth due to **gravity**

It is said that in the sixteenth century Galileo, an Italian scientist, dropped a small iron ball and a large cannon ball from the top of the Leaning Tower of Pisa. To everyone's surprise they landed almost simultaneously.

Gravity gives all falling objects close to the Earth an acceleration of 10 m/s² (as long as the force due to air resistance can be ignored – see spread 2.10).

c A ball is dropped from the top of a tall tower. Find its velocity after
i 1 s, **ii** 2s, **iii** 5 s.

When a ball is thrown up it has a deceleration of 10 m/s². Its velocity decreases until it becomes zero. Gravity then accelerates the ball back to the ground. The greater the velocity given to the ball, the further it will rise before its velocity becomes zero.

d A ball is thrown vertically upwards and returns to its starting point after 3 s. With what velocity was it thrown?

fig 27 | The Leaning Tower of Pisa

Thinking further

■ **1** A cyclist travels around a circular track at a constant speed of 10 m/s. Explain why he is accelerating.

■ **2** A car advertisement states '0 to 130 km/h in 12 seconds'. What is the acceleration of the car?

◆ **3** A car starts from rest and accelerates uniformly to 20 m/s in 16 s. It travels at this velocity for 60 s and decelerates uniformly so that it stops 116 s after starting. Sketch a velocity-time graph and use it to find

a the acceleration

b the retardation

c the total distance travelled.

◆ **4** What can you say about the motion of the object in the velocity-time graph shown in fig 28? Does it return to its starting point? Suggest a situation the graph could represent.

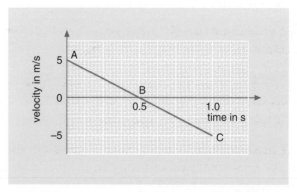

fig 28

KEY WORDS

acceleration • deceleration • gravity • retardation

 Use a data logger to measure acceleration.   *Use a data logger to plot velocity-time graphs.*

2.5 Forces

reaction force from table on computer

weight

Types of force

A force is essentially a push or a pull. Some useful examples are:

- weight – a force due to the attraction between an object and the Earth
- **reaction** force – an object resting on a surface has an upward force on it perpendicular to the surface
- **tension** – force in a rope or cable
- **lift** – upward force on the wing of an aeroplane
- **friction** – a force that slows down moving things
- **air resistance** (or **drag**) force – a friction force that slows down an object moving through the air
- **thrust** – push or pull due to a rocket engine.

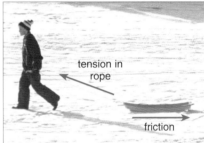

tension in rope

friction

fig 29

thrust

drag

lift

fig 30

Forces between objects

Forces always occur in pairs. When Jo pushes against the wall, the wall pushes back against her with an equal force but in the opposite direction.

a What happens to Jo if she is on roller skates?

In general, the force on an object A due to an object B is equal and opposite to the force on object B due to A. These pairs of forces:

- are of equal size
- are the same type of force
- act in opposite directions
- act on different objects (one on A and one on B).

This is Newton's Third Law.

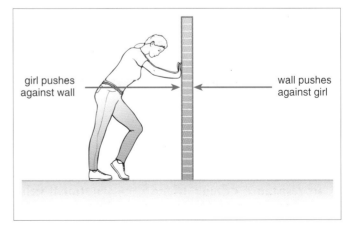

girl pushes against wall

wall pushes against girl

fig 31

Newton's Third Law helps to explain why the Moon orbits the Earth. There is a force on the Moon due to the gravitational attraction of the Earth, and an equal and opposite force on the Earth due to the gravitational attraction of the Moon. The Earth is more massive than the Moon, so the Moon orbits the Earth.

b Use the idea of gravitational attraction to explain the Solar System.

Gravity

Newton said that every mass in the Universe attracts every other mass with a gravitational force. The size of the force between you and the person sitting next to you is too small to notice.

When one, or both, of the objects is a planet or other large mass, the gravitational attraction becomes large.

Newton said that an apple is attracted to the Earth and the Earth is attracted to the apple with equal and opposite forces. The mass of the apple is much less than the mass of the Earth so the apple moves towards the Earth. We call this force of attraction gravity.

fig 32

Weight

On Earth a mass of 1 kg is attracted to the Earth with a force of 10 N. We say that the **gravitational field strength** (g) is 10 N/kg.

On the Moon the gravitational field strength is 1.6 N/kg, about $\frac{1}{6}$th of its value on Earth. The force on an object due to gravity is called its weight.

> weight (W) = mass × gravitational field strength = mg

c Fig 33 shows a boy of mass 45 kg holding an apple of mass 100 g and a 1 kg bag of sugar. Find the weight of the boy, the apple and the bag of sugar
i on Earth, **ii** if they were on the Moon.

fig 33

Thinking further

■ **1a** Friction occurs when two surfaces rub together. It causes wear in machinery with moving parts. How can it be reduced?

   b Give two examples when friction is useful.

■ **2** Find the weight of an astronaut having a mass of 72 kg,

   a on Earth

b on planet Zeus where the gravitational field strength is 20 N/kg.

c What is his mass when he is on planet Zeus?

◆ **3** Amy is sitting on a chair. She weighs 450 N. There is a downward force on her of 450 N. Explain why she does not move.

◆ **4** Use your ideas about forces to explain the structure of the atom.

KEY WORDS

air resistance • drag • friction • gravitational field strength • lift • reaction • tension • thrust

 Friction.

2.6 Force and motion

Balanced forces

When the forces on an object are **balanced** – equal in size but opposite in direction – the object is *either*

- stationary (not moving), *or*
- moving at a constant velocity.

This is Newton's First Law. We say that the **resultant** (or net) force on the object is zero.

fig 34

Unbalanced forces

When the forces on an object are **unbalanced** – bigger in one direction than the other – the object *accelerates* or *decelerates*.

If the object *starts from rest*, it accelerates in the direction of the bigger, or resultant, force.

fig 35

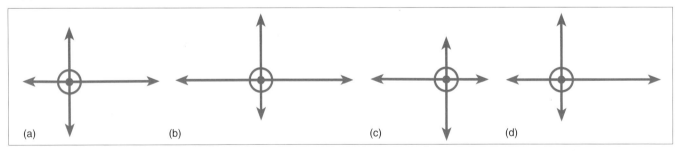

(a) (b) (c) (d)

a Describe the motion, if any, in each diagram in fig 35.
(The objects are not moving before the forces are applied.)

If the object is *moving* when the unbalanced force occurs, it will:

- accelerate if the bigger force is in a forward direction
- decelerate if the bigger force is backwards.

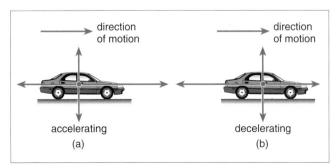

fig 36

Going fast

Things that go very fast, such as racing bikes, cars and speedboats, are designed to keep their resistance to motion as small as possible. Their shape is **streamlined**. Many animals have a streamlined shape to enable them to move quickly.

Objects with a large cross-sectional area displace more molecules as they move and so have a bigger resistance to motion. Pointed objects pass through air and water more easily. Ships designed to go fast are usually narrow with pointed bows.

b Why do cyclists crouch down when racing?

c Why do athletes often wear tight fitting clothing?

The faster a car is travelling the greater the resistance to motion. This means the car has a top speed when the resistance to motion is equal to the forward thrust. To increase its top speed a more powerful engine must be used, or the design must be changed to make it more streamlined.

fig 37

Thinking further

■ **1** An aeroplane is flying horizontally at a *constant velocity* of 300 m/s. Draw a diagram to show the forces acting on it. Name each force. (Remember to make the arrows represent the size of the forces.)

   a The forward force increases. How does this affect the motion of the aeroplane?

   b The backward force increases. How does this affect the motion of the aeroplane?

   c How must the forces change when the aeroplane starts to climb?

■ **2** Ben is pushing a box across the floor at a steady speed. He pushes it with a force of 200 N. How big is the friction force? Ben gets tired and only pushes the box with a force of 150 N. What happens to the motion of the box?

■ **3** A spacecraft is travelling to a distant planet. There are no forces acting on it. What can you say about its motion?

◆ **4** The first stage rocket motors of a spacecraft produce a thrust of 3.5×10^7 N. The complete spacecraft has a mass of 2.8×10^6 kg.

   a Calculate the resultant force on the spacecraft at take-off.

   b How will the resultant force change in the first few minutes of the flight? Explain your answer.

   c How will this affect the motion of the spacecraft?

◆ **5** Sam's car is towing a trailer of mass 1000 kg at a steady speed along a level road. The tension in the tow-rope is 400 N.

   a Sam expected the tension to be zero. Explain why it is not.

   b What is the forward thrust of the car engine?

   c Name and give the value of the forces acting on the trailer.

— KEY WORDS —
balanced • resultant • streamlined • unbalanced

2.7 Force and acceleration

F = ma

Newton's Second Law states that the resultant force on an object is proportional to its mass times its acceleration.

The acceleration of a trolley when pulled by various known forces can be measured using ticker tape or light gates, perhaps connected to a data logger as shown in fig 38.

The ramp is **friction compensated**; it is raised slightly so that the effect of the trolley's weight *down* the slope is exactly equal to the friction force *up* the slope. The trolley now runs down the ramp at a constant speed if no other force acts on it. Any acceleration must be due to the known force pulling it.

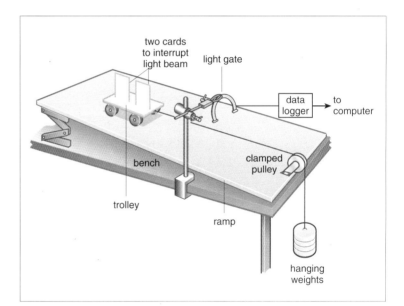

fig 38

A graph of acceleration *a* against force *F* is a straight line through the origin, showing that *a* is proportional to *F*.

If the acceleration is measured for various trolley masses *m*, keeping the pulling force constant, it can be shown that *a* is inversely proportional to *m*.

a The ramp needs to be re-compensated for friction each time the trolley's mass is changed. Why?

b What would you plot to show the relationship between *a* and *m*? Sketch the graph you would expect.

Combining these two results: *a* is proportional to $\frac{F}{m}$ or $F = kma$,

where *k* = a constant. If *m* is in kg and *a* in m/s², the newton is defined so that we can write

$$F = ma$$

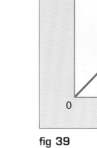

fig 39

c Find the force needed to give a mass of 3 kg an acceleration of 20 m/s².

Car seat belts and crumple zones

In any collision, $F = ma$ shows that the smaller the deceleration, a, (the car is slowing down) the smaller the force, F.

d Davina says 'a is negative because the car is slowing down, so F will be negative'. What does the negative force mean?

$$\text{deceleration} = \frac{\text{change in velocity}}{\text{time}}$$

To make the deceleration small the time must be large.

Seat belts are designed to stretch slightly so that you stop more slowly. This reduces your deceleration and also the force on you.

Crumple zones are sections at the front and back of a car that are designed to crumple in a collision. The crumpling increases the time of the collision so that the deceleration, and hence the force on you, is less.

fig 40

fig 41

Sporting examples

- Gymnasts, high jumpers and parachutists bend their knees as they land so that they stop more slowly – their deceleration is less. This reduces the force on their knees to a safe level.

- In games such as golf, tennis and football you '**follow through**'. This means that you keep your club, racquet or foot in contact with the ball for as long as possible so that it gains the greatest possible speed.

e Explain why the ball gains a high speed.

fig 42

fig 43

Thinking further

◆ **1** A force of 20 N acts on a 4 kg mass. What is its acceleration?

◆ **2** A car's engine provides a thrust of 5000 N. The total resistance to motion is 1400 N. The mass of the car is 1200 kg. Find its acceleration.

◆ **3** Designers keep the mass of Formula 1 racing cars as small as possible. Suggest why.

◆ **4** The motors of a rocket of mass 8×10^5 kg give it a thrust of 1×10^7 N. What is its acceleration at lift-off?

KEY WORDS

crumple zone • follow through • friction compensated • seat belt

 To investigate a factor which affects the distance travelled by a projectile.

2.8 Force and energy

- Work done = force × distance moved in the direction of the force.
- Energy is the ability to do work.
- Work done = energy transferred by a force.
- Power = $\dfrac{\text{work done (or energy transferred)}}{\text{time taken}}$
- Change in gravitational potential energy = mass × gravitational field strength × height moved (mgh)
- Kinetic energy = $\frac{1}{2}$ mass × (velocity)^2 = $\frac{1}{2}mv^2$

Work done

Work is done when a force *moves*. Paul is pushing the car in fig 44, but he only does work when he succeeds in *moving* the car against the opposing friction force. The further he moves it the more work he does.

work done = force × distance moved in the direction of the force

If the force is in **newtons (N)** and the distance in metres (m), the work done is measured in **joules (J)**. 1 J is the work done when a force of 1 N moves a distance of 1 m. This means 1 J = 1 Nm.

a In fig 44 Paul manages to move the car 5 m against a friction force of 300 N. How much work does he do?

Paul can only do this work if he has some **energy**. He gets his energy from the food he eats (chemical energy). He transfers an amount of energy equal to the work he does on the car. Energy is also measured in J.

work done = energy transfer

b How much energy does Paul transfer to the car?

Power

Power is the *rate* of doing work.

power = $\dfrac{\text{work done (or energy transferred) (in J)}}{\text{time taken (in s)}}$

Power is measured in **watts (W)**, or kilowatts (kW) (1 kW = 1000 W).

c Paul pushes the car 5 m in 20 s. Pat takes 60 s to move it the same distance. Compare their power.

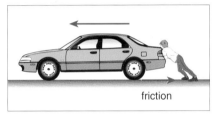

friction

fig 44

fig 45

Gravitational potential energy

Sarah holds a ball 1.8 m above the ground. It has potential, or stored, energy due to gravity; we call this **gravitational potential energy** (GPE). When she lets it go gravity pulls it down to the ground. The ball has more GPE

* the greater its mass (m)
* the higher it is raised above the ground (h).

Change in GPE = mass × gravitational field strength × height moved

change in GPE = mgh

d Sarah's ball has a mass of 0.5 kg. How much GPE does it gain when she lifts it 1.8 m?

e Use the equation for work done to calculate how much work Sarah did in lifting the ball. What do you notice?

fig 46

Kinetic energy

Sarah's ball moves so it has gained **kinetic energy** (KE). As it falls it loses GPE and gains an equal amount of KE. The *total* amount of energy remains constant.

The more KE the ball gains, the faster it moves. If it has a velocity, v, its kinetic energy is $\frac{1}{2}mv^2$.

KE = $\frac{1}{2}mv^2$

f What is the KE of Sarah's ball just before it hits the ground?

g How fast is it moving just before it hits the ground?

h How much GPE and KE does it have when 0.9 m above the ground?

Thinking further

1 A car has a mass of 800 kg. Find its kinetic energy when travelling at a speed of 15 m/s.

2 Suzy has a mass of 50 kg. When she is on holiday in Paris she decides to climb the Eiffel Tower. It is 300 m high and there are 1792 steps. It takes her 15 minutes.
 a What is her weight?
 b How much work does she do?
 c Calculate her power.

3 Darren has a mass of 60 kg. He is skateboarding. Find his kinetic energy if he is going at 12 m/s. Meera has a mass of 30 kg. How much kinetic energy does she have if she also goes at 12 m/s? What do you notice about your answers?

4 Ben is a pole-vaulter. His mass is 70 kg.
 a How much gravitational potential energy does he gain if he *just* clears the bar at 5 m?
 b Find his speed on landing.

— KEY WORDS —————————————————————

energy • gravitational potential energy • joule • kinetic energy • newton • power • watt • work

2.9 On the road

Thinking distance

Thinking distance is the distance a vehicle travels between the driver seeing a hazard and applying the brakes; in other words, while the brain reacts. The time the brain takes to react is called the **thinking time** or **reaction time**. It is increased by:

- tiredness
- drugs and alcohol
- old age
- not concentrating properly (e.g. using a mobile phone)
- weather conditions which may make hazards harder to spot.

Normally a person's reaction time is about 0.7 s.

a If the driver's reaction time is 0.7 s, calculate the thinking distance for a car travelling at **i** 10 m/s, **ii** 30 m/s.
iii Sketch a graph of thinking distance against speed.

Braking distance

Braking distance is the distance a vehicle travels while stopping *after* the brakes are applied. Braking distance depends on:

- the mass of the vehicle and its load
- the speed of the vehicle
- how good the brakes are
- how good the grip is – tyres, road surface, weather conditions.

b Discuss how you think each of the above factors affects the braking distance.

The braking distance increases rapidly as the speed increases. This is because the kinetic energy of a vehicle is proportional to its (velocity)², so if the speed doubles the KE is *four* times bigger.

fig 47

All the KE of the vehicle must be transferred in stopping, mainly to thermal energy in the brakes and tyres.

KE transferred = work done by the brakes

$$\frac{1}{2}mv^2 = \text{maximum braking force} \times \text{braking distance}$$

(1)

So if the speed doubles, the KE is four times bigger and hence the braking distance is also four times bigger. This is why reducing speed is an important factor in road safety.

c A car of mass 1000 kg is travelling at 20 m/s when the driver brakes to a standstill in 40 m. Find the braking force.

Stopping distance

Stopping distance = thinking distance + braking distance

Look at equation (1) and your answers to question **a** above. They show that:

- the *thinking* distance and speed are proportional
- the *braking* distance is proportional to (speed)^2.

So both parts of the equation for stopping distance increase as the speed increases.

d Find the total stopping distance for the car in question **c**.

e How would the stopping distance change if the mass of the car and its load in **c** were doubled?

f Goods vehicles above 7.5 tonnes (7500 kg) have a lower speed limit on our roads than cars and light goods vehicles. Suggest a reason for this.

fig **48**

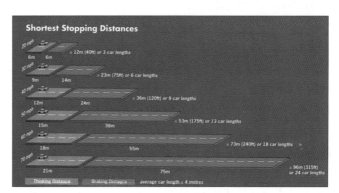

fig **49**

Thinking further

1 Copy and complete the table.

speed in m/s	thinking distance in m	braking distance in m	stopping distance in m
15	9	20	
20	12	35	
25		55	
30			

fig **50**

What do you notice about the values in the table?

2 A drunk driver has a reaction time of 2 s. Compare his thinking distance when driving at 20 m/s with a 'normal' value of 0.6 s. How does this affect his stopping distance? (Use the table in question 1 to help you.)

3 Tyres should have a minimum tread depth of 1.6 mm. Suggest a reason for this.

4 A car has a mass of 1000 kg. Calculate its kinetic energy when travelling at 15 m/s. Use the table in question 1 to estimate the braking force at this speed.

KEY WORDS

braking distance • reaction time • stopping distance • thinking distance • thinking time

 Discussing road safety and the increase in heavy lorries on our roads. *Measuring reaction time.*

2.10 How things fall

> ### Key points
>
> - When falling through a fluid (liquid or gas) the molecules of the fluid resist the motion so the acceleration is less.
> - The greater the speed, the greater the resistive force.
> - When the resistive force is equal to the weight of the object its velocity becomes constant; this is called terminal velocity.

Forces on a falling ball

Gravity gives all falling objects close to the Earth an acceleration of $10 \, \text{m/s}^2$, as long as the force due to air resistance can be ignored. Look at the ball in fig 51. The forces acting on the ball are:

- its weight, $W \, (= mg)$ • air resistance, R.

The force making the ball accelerate is $(mg - R)$. Using $F = ma$ we can write $(mg - R) = ma$, so the acceleration of the ball is *less than* $10 \, \text{m/s}^2$.

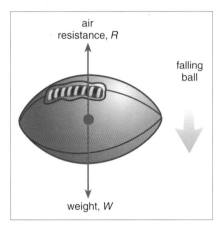

fig 51

The force due to air resistance, R, is *not* constant.

- As the speed of the ball increases it pushes more air molecules out of the way each second so R *increases*.
- This means the acceleration *decreases*.
- R may increase until it is *equal* to the weight of the ball.
- The forces on the ball are then balanced.
- The acceleration of the ball is zero.
- The ball travels at a constant speed called its **terminal velocity**.

a A ping-pong ball reaches its terminal velocity when dropped from a much lower height than a golf ball. Explain.

Air resistance also increases as the surface area increases. You can see this by dropping a small ball and a feather simultaneously in a tall glass tube. The feather falls more slowly than the ball because it has a very small weight (small force down) and a large surface area (big force up). If most of the air is pumped out of the glass tube both take the same time to fall.

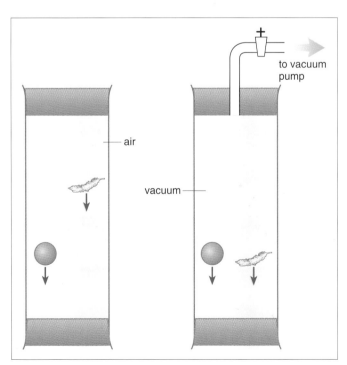

fig 52

Air resistance depends on speed and surface area.

If the ball falls in a liquid the resistive force is greater, so it has a lower terminal velocity and reaches it more quickly.

b Explain why the terminal velocity is lower and reached more quickly.

Parachuting

Look at fig 54.

- When the parachutist drops from the aircraft she accelerates at 10 m/s^2.
- As her speed increases so does air resistance until the forces are balanced and she reaches terminal velocity.
- When she opens her parachute the air resistance force increases suddenly so she decelerates rapidly.
- Eventually the air resistance force is the same as her weight again so she falls at a new, lower, terminal velocity until she reaches the ground.

c A parachutist weighs 600 N. How big is the air resistance force when she reaches terminal velocity?

d How would the parachutist's fall differ if she fell in an upright position?

e Sketch a speed–time graph for the parachutist from the moment she leaves the aircraft until she reaches the ground.

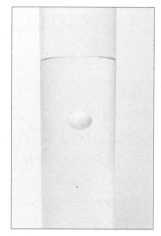

fig 53

fig 54

Thinking further

■ **1** A marble is falling in a tall cylinder of oil. What could you do to show that it reaches a terminal velocity?

■ **2** Maria measured the bounce height (*b*) of a ping-pong ball when dropped from various heights (*d*).

d in cm	0	20	40	60	80	100	120
b in cm	0	15.0	29.0	44.7	59.2	68.2	73.2

fig 55

a Plot her results on a graph of *b* against *d*.

b Explain the shape of her graph.

◆ **3** Use the equation $F = ma$ to explain why objects near the Earth's surface fall with an acceleration of 10 m/s^2. (You may ignore the effect of air resistance.)

◆ **4** Two balls, of the same diameter but of masses 0.1 kg and 1 kg, are falling through the air. Calculate their acceleration when the air resistance force on each of them is 1 N.
What can you say about their speeds at that time?

┌─ **KEY WORDS** ─────
│ **terminal velocity** │   *Dropping steel ball bearings in oil.*   *Velocity–time graphs for falling balls.*

2.11 Keeping warm

Conduction

Conduction is the way in which thermal energy is transferred in solids. Metals are good conductors of heat as they allow energy to spread through them quickly. Non-metals are thermal **insulators** – they do *not* allow energy to spread through them quickly.

Energy is transferred from a hotter to a cooler part *without any movement of the object itself.*

a What does this suggest about the structure of insulators?

Convection

Convection is the way in which thermal energy is transferred in fluids – liquids and gases.

b In fig 56 why is the hot water outlet at the top of the tank?

c Why can't convection take place in solids?

Radiation

Radiation is the transfer of thermal energy by waves. These waves can travel through a vacuum; it is how heat reaches us from the Sun. All objects emit and absorb radiation. The hotter the object the more energy it radiates.

Good emitters are also good absorbers of radiation. In general:

- black surfaces are better emitters and absorbers than white surfaces
- matt surfaces are better emitters and absorbers than shiny surfaces.

d A central heating radiator is misnamed because radiation is *not* the main way in which heat is transferred throughout a room. Explain how a radiator heats a room.

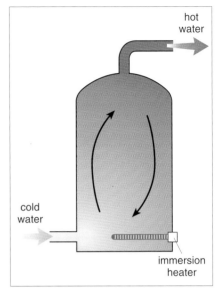

fig 56

Conduction

Energy is transferred by:
- atoms bumping into other atoms, passing on KE
- free electrons moving through the metal.

Convection

As the fluid is heated, its particles move faster, so:
- it expands
- becomes less dense
- rises up and is replaced by colder, denser fluid.

This is a **convection current**.

Domestic insulation

Energy is lost from our homes in many ways. We use a variety of insulating materials designed to keep heat losses to a minimum. These include:

- loft insulation
- carpets and curtains
- double glazing
- cavity wall insulation
- draught proofing
- lagging of hot water tank and pipes.

The materials used are all thermal insulators. The materials used trap air, a bad conductor of heat, between their fibres, making them even more effective. The tiny pockets of trapped air only allow a small amount of convection. An air-filled cavity in exterior walls for example, allows large convection currents to circulate, transferring a lot of energy. When the cavity is filled with insulation, only small convection currents can circulate, reducing energy loss.

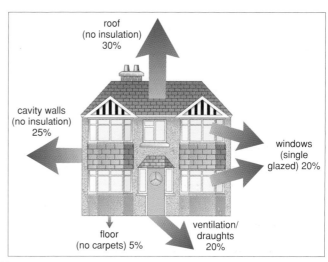

fig 57

Pay-back period

Pay-back period is the time it takes to pay for the insulation from the savings made on fuel bills. Here are some examples.

insulation	cost in £	annual saving in £	pay-back time in years
cavity wall insulation	600	30	20
double glazing	3000	60	?
draught-proofing	?	220	2
loft insulation	400	?	5
jacket for hot-water tank	15	15	?

fig 59

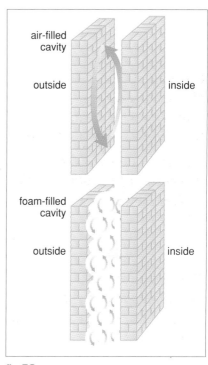

fig 58

e Copy and complete the table. What improvement would you make first?

Thinking further

■ **1** Explain why the freezing compartment of a refrigerator is usually placed at the top.

■ **2** Stopping draughts saves on fuel bills, but for safety there should be a complete change of air in a room every hour. Why?

■ **3** Why is it cheaper to heat a terraced house than a similarly constructed detached one of the same size?

◆ **4** For each of the insulation methods mentioned in the list above, state the types of heat transfer that are reduced.

◆ **5** The Green family wants to reduce their heating bills. Suggest what they could do, in addition to the ways already mentioned.

--- **KEY WORDS** ---
conduction • convection • convection current • insulators • pay-back period • radiation

 *What difference does a lid make?*

2.12 Energy efficiency

Key points

- Energy efficiency = $\dfrac{\text{useful energy output}}{\text{total energy input}}$

- All machines waste energy, often as heat due to friction, but good design should make them as efficient as possible.

- Energy becomes degraded when it is spread over such a large area that no further use can be made of it.

- It is important to heat buildings efficiently so that little energy is wasted and fuel bills are kept as low as possible.

Energy efficiency

When devices transfer energy only some of it is in the form required; the rest of it is in a non-useful form and so is wasted.

$$\text{energy efficiency} = \frac{\text{useful energy output}}{\text{total energy input}}$$

$$or = \frac{\text{useful power output}}{\text{total power input}}$$

Energy efficiency is often given as a percentage by multiplying this fraction by 100.

Machines

A **machine** is a device that changes one form of energy into another. No machine is 100% efficient. Energy is always wasted as heat and/or sound. In machines with moving parts friction leads to energy wastage as heat.

a How can energy loss due to friction be reduced?

A 100 W light bulb produces 8 W of light and 92 W of heat. This means that in 1 s the light bulb transfers 100 J of energy into 8 J of light and 92 J of heat.

b Calculate the efficiency of the light bulb.

c A 25 W low-energy light bulb only produces 10 W of heat.
  i How much light is produced?
  ii Calculate its efficiency.

d An electric hoist supplies 7500 J of energy when it raises a 600 N load 5 m. How efficient is it?

Degraded energy

All energy is eventually transferred to the surroundings making them warmer. This energy is **degraded**; it becomes so spread out

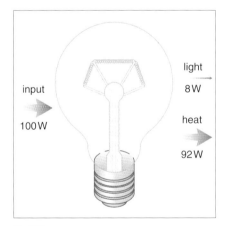

fig 60

fig 61 | Low-energy light bulb

that it cannot be transferred into other useful forms. For instance, a certain amount of energy may be sufficient to boil a cupful of water but the same amount of energy would only raise the temperature of a bathful of water by a fraction of a degree. As the energy is spread out more and more it becomes less and less useful.

	rate of heat loss		
	before in W	after in W	power saved in W
ceiling	3000	500	2500
walls	4000	2000	?
floor	1000	400	?
windows	3000	1500	?

fig 62

Heating buildings

Buildings that are not **insulated** are very expensive to keep warm. Energy must be provided to replace the energy lost to the surroundings if the temperature is to remain constant.

The table compares the rate of heat loss from a house before and after insulating it.

e Copy and complete the table by calculating the power saved in each case.

f What is the total power saved?

Combined heat and power (CHP) power stations use the thermal energy left over from generating electricity to heat homes or offices directly. Normally this energy is wasted, so CHP power stations are much more efficient *overall* than conventional power stations. The power station is usually run at a slightly lower efficiency so that the water used for heating is hotter.

g What is the efficiency of the conventional and CHP power stations in fig 63?

fig 63

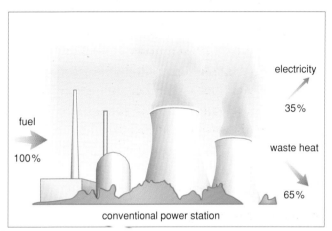

conventional power station

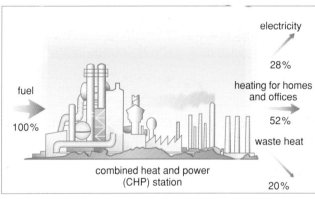

combined heat and power (CHP) station

Thinking further

■ **1** A 1000 MW wood-burning power station is 10% efficient. What input power is required?

■ **2** A diesel engine does 3000 J of useful work for every 10 000 J of energy supplied to it.

   a Calculate its efficiency.

   b What happens to the rest of the energy supplied?

◆ **3** Dean is in the gym. He is strengthening his arms by doing pull-ups. His body is using energy at a rate of 500 W. He weighs 800 N and lifts his body 0.5 m each time. He manages to do 20 pull-ups in a minute. Calculate his efficiency.

◆ **4** Bill and Katy are having a new house built. They want it to be energy efficient. What features should their architect include?

─ **KEY WORDS** ─────────
combined heat and power (CHP) • degraded • energy efficiency • insulated • machine

Questions on forces and energy

1 Use words from the list to complete the sentences that follow.

efficient • energy • force • gravitational potential • gravity • heat • joules • kilograms • kinetic • light • mass • newtons • power • sound • watts • weight

_____ is the amount of matter in an object. It is measured in _____.

_____ is due to the pull of _____ on an object. It is measured in _____.

An object has the same _____ anywhere in the Universe but its _____ is different.

_____ is needed to do work. It is measured in _____.

As a ball falls _____ energy is converted into _____ energy.

No energy transfer is 100% _____ . Energy is often wasted as _____ and _____.
(14)

2 A metre rule weighs 0.90 N. It is hung from the 30 cm mark. Where does a 1.00 N weight need to be placed to balance the ruler? Sketch a diagram of the arrangement. (5)

3 The aircraft shown is flying horizontally at 300 m/s.

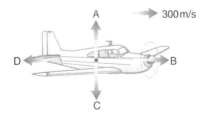

fig 64

a Identify the forces A, B, C and D. Choose from **drag • lift • tension • thrust • weight** (4)

b Write down two pairs of equal forces. (2)

c The aircraft starts to accelerate and climb. What happens to each of the forces A, B, C and D? (4)

4a Give two examples of situations where friction is an advantage. (2)

b Why does friction result in energy being wasted? (2)

5 A crane lifts a 1000 N load at a constant speed.

a As the load is rising it has two main forms of energy. Name them. (2)

b Do these forms of energy increase, decrease or stay the same as the load rises? (2)

c How big is the tension in the cable? (1)

6 Fig 65 shows a section of a roller-coaster ride.

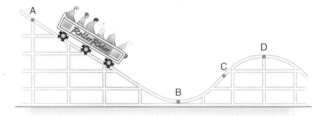

fig 65

a i Where does the car have the greatest gravitational potential energy? (1)

ii Where does the car have the greatest kinetic energy? (1)

b Is the car accelerating or decelerating at C? Explain. (2)

7 The way in which the velocity of a car varies with time over a 60 s period is shown in the table.

time in s	velocity in m/s
0	0
5	5
10	10
15	15
20	15
25	15
30	15
35	15
40	15
45	11
50	7.5
55	3.5
60	0

fig 66

a Draw a velocity–time graph for the car. (4)

b Use your graph to find
  i the acceleration of the car from 0 to 15 s
  ii the deceleration of the car
  iii the total distance travelled. *(9)*

c What can you say about the forces acting on the car between 15 s and 40 s? *(1)*

■ **8a** What is meant by energy efficiency? *(2)*

◆ **b** When power stations generate electricity they also heat large amounts of water. This energy is usually wasted. Some power stations use this hot water to heat buildings such as schools and hospitals.
  i Explain how this increases the energy efficiency of the power station. *(2)*
  ii Give one disadvantage of using hot water from power stations in this way. *(1)*

◆ **9** Molly is riding in the back of her father's car when he has to brake suddenly. She is not wearing a seat belt.

a Explain *carefully* what is likely to happen. *(3)*

b Explain what would have happened if Molly had been wearing a seat belt. *(2)*

10 The diagram shows a ball at various stages after it is dropped from A, 1 m above the ground, and rebounds to D, 0.2 m above the ground. The ball has a mass of 50 g.

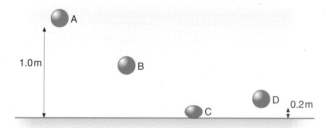

fig 67

● **a** The ball has gravitational potential energy at A. In what forms is this energy at B, C and D? *(4)*

■ **b** **i** Calculate the gravitational potential energy of the ball at A and D. *(5)*
  ii Hence find the energy 'lost' during the impact. *(2)*
  iii What has happened to this 'lost' energy? *(2)*

11 Two spheres of similar size are released together in a vertical tube which has had the air

removed from it. They reach the bottom of the tube together. The mass of A is 100 g and the mass of B is 300 g.

■ **a** What is the value of the gravitational force
  i on A
  ii on B? *(2)*

◆ **b** How does the acceleration of A compare with that of B? *(1)*

◆ **c** The spheres are now released together when the tube contains air. Explain why B reaches the bottom before A. *(3)*

12 The diagram shows the forces acting on a car as it travels along a level road.

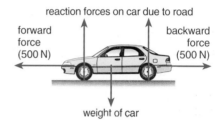

fig 68

● **a** Describe the motion of the car. *(1)*

■ **b** The speed of the car is 25 m/s. Calculate the work done by the forward force in 1 s. *(3)*

■ **c** What is the useful power output of the engine? *(1)*

■ **d** The petrol supplies 50 000 J of energy to the engine in 1 s. Calculate the efficiency of the engine. *(3)*

■ **e** The forward force on the car is increased to 700 N. Why does the car accelerate? *(1)*

◆ **f** The forward force remains at 700 N. Explain why the car does not continue to accelerate. *(2)*

■ **13** An electric motor is used to lift a crate through a vertical height of 15 m. The crate weighs 400 N.

a What is the smallest force needed to lift the crate at a steady speed? *(1)*

b Calculate the work done in lifting the crate through a height of 15 m. *(3)*

c What is the useful output energy of the motor? *(1)*

d The input energy to the motor is 10 000 J. Calculate the efficiency of the motor. *(3)*

e What extra information is needed to calculate the power of the motor? *(1)*

Continued ▶

Questions on forces and energy (continued)

14 A house built in 1900 has solid brick walls. A house built in 1950 has cavity walls – two brick walls with air between. A house built in 2000 also has cavity walls but the cavity is filled with mineral wool (an insulator). All have similar heating systems.

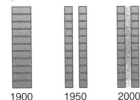

fig 69   1900   1950   2000

● **a** Explain why the 1950 house is warmer than the 1900 house in cold weather. *(3)*

■ **b** Explain why the walls in the 2000 house are even better at keeping the house warm. *(2)*

■ **c** Apart from being more comfortable, what are the other advantages of the 2000 house compared to the older ones? *(2)*

15 A train usually takes 5 hours to travel from London to Edinburgh, a distance of 650 km.

■ **a** Calculate the average speed
  i in km/h
  ii in m/s.
  iii Why is this an average speed?

◆ **b** The mass of the train and passengers is 300 000 kg. Find the force needed to accelerate it out of a station at 0.5 m/s². *(3)*

◆ **c** The same force is used to accelerate the train when it is less crowded and has a total mass of only 250 000 kg. What is the acceleration then? *(3)*

◆ **d** One day the train reaches Doncaster, 250 km from London, in 2 hours but is then delayed there for 12 minutes. What speed must it average for the rest of the journey if it is to reach Edinburgh on time? *(4)*

16 A child runs into the road 60 m in front of a car travelling at 20 m/s. The driver's reaction time is 0.7 s. Once he applies the brakes the car stops in 4 s.

■ **a** Calculate the driver's thinking distance when travelling at 20 m/s. *(3)*

■ **b** Sketch a speed–time graph for the interval between the child running into the road until the car stopped. *(4)*

◆ **c** Calculate the deceleration of the car. *(3)*

◆ **d** Does the driver stop in time? Explain how you decided. *(4)*

◆ **e** What difference would it have made if the driver had been travelling at 25 m/s? Explain, showing any necessary working. *(3)*

◆ **17** The diagram shows the rocket ship ride at a fairground.

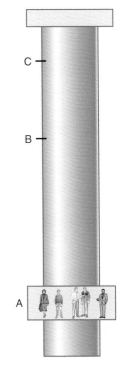

fig 70

The carriage and passengers are accelerated from the bottom of the column for a few seconds.

a The total weight of the car and passengers is 30 000 N. The force used to accelerate them upwards is 90 000 N.
  i Find the acceleration of the car. *(4)*
  ii Find the velocity of the car after 3 s. *(3)*

b At B the upwards force is switched off. The car stops at C. What is the car's acceleration between B and C? *(1)*

18 The table gives some data on the stopping distances for a car travelling at different speeds.

speed in m/s	thinking distance in m	braking distance in m	stopping distance in m
10	6	6	12
15	9	14	
20		24	
25		38	
30		55	
35		74	

fig 71

■ **a** Calculate the thinking time. (3)

■ **b** Copy and complete the table. (5)

■ **c** What happens to the thinking distance as the speed of the car increases? (2)

■ **d** What do you think would happen to the thinking distance if the driver was tired or had been drinking alcohol? Explain. (2)

■ **e** How would the braking distance change if the road were icy? Explain. (2)

◆ **f** Two cars are following each other at a speed of 30 m/s. Suggest, with reasons, a minimum safe distance between the cars. (3)

◆ **g** The car has a mass of 600 kg.
　　i Calculate the KE of the car at each speed in the table. (6)
　　ii Plot a graph of KE against braking distance. (4)
　　iii What does your graph show? Explain. (2)
　　iv Use your graph to find a value for the braking force exerted on the tyres. (6)

IDEAS AND EVIDENCE

19 Read the following passage adapted from an article in *The Times*, 9 September 2000 and then answer the questions that follow.

fig 72

A former French Army major is in training for a death-defying attempt to become the first man to break the sound barrier in free-fall through the sky. If successful Michel Fournier, 56, will not only shatter sky-diving records for the highest and longest jumps, but will also become the highest-flying balloonist in history. He aims to jump from an adapted weather balloon at an altitude of 45 km.

A skydiver jumping from a normal altitude never approaches the speed of sound (330–340 m/s). Terminal velocity is usually reached at about 53 m/s. Its exact value depends on whether the skydiver is stretching out his arms or is diving head first.

At the extreme altitude planned by Fournier the air is thin, but the force of gravity is virtually unchanged. This means that he should be able to reach a much higher terminal velocity and, if his scientific team is right, will comfortably exceed the speed of sound after falling for 30 s.

The air temperature will be extremely low, at −60 °C, but friction will raise the surface temperature of his insulated suit to high temperatures, perhaps as high as 65 °C.

One of the uncertainties is what will happen to Fournier if he exceeds the speed of sound. His view is that there will be no effect; the air at this altitude is so thin that the effect will be no greater than putting a hand out of a car window at 18 m/s.

The estimate is that it will take Fournier 51 s to reach his maximum speed, in the near-vacuum at the edge of space. Then, as the air thickens, he will slow. His parachute will open after 6 min 25 s when he will be at about the height of Mount Everest.

a What is meant by *terminal velocity*? (2)

b Why does the value of the terminal velocity depend on whether the skydiver is stretching out his arms or diving head first? (3)

c **i** What does the passage mean when it says 'the air is thin'? (1)
　　ii How does this affect the terminal velocity? Explain (2)

d Why will Fournier's suit get very hot although the air temperature is very low? (2)

e Suggest two physical properties his suit should possess. (2)

f There is a large build up of pressure if an aircraft exceeds the speed of sound at lower altitudes. Why is this not likely to be a problem for Fournier? (2)

h Why will he slow down as the air thickens? (3)

i Describe how his speed will change once his parachute opens until he reaches the ground. (3)

Wave properties

Energy is often moved from one place to another by waves. Whenever we hear a sound or see an object energy has been moved to our ears and eyes.

We can only hear sounds because the sounding object vibrates and causes vibrations to be transmitted to our ears. We can only see things because they are luminous or because they reflect light into our eyes.

Check-up

Have a go at the following questions. They will remind you what you should already know about wave properties.

a Fig 1 shows an orchestra playing. What does the sound from the orchestra do to the eardrum of a person in the audience?

fig 1

b What could happen to a pop-fan who listened to very loud music for a long time?

c Fig 2 shows the night sky. What is the difference between the way in which we see light from the stars and light from the moon?

fig 2

d Fig 3 shows a girl in front of a pinhole camera. Copy the diagram and draw rays from the top of her head and the bottom of her head to show how the image is formed in the camera.

fig 3

e Fig 4 shows a periscope. Copy and complete the diagram by adding the path of the light from the footballer to the observer's eye.

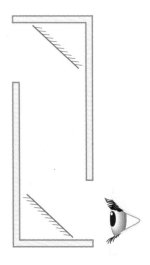

fig 4

If you have difficulties, your teacher has a Summary sheet you can have.

Contents of the Teaching block

This Teaching block is divided into seven double page spreads.

3.1 What are waves?

Waves are produced by vibrations which may be mechanical (as in water waves and sound waves) or electromagnetic (as in light). Waves can be longitudinal or transverse depending on the nature of the vibration.

3.2 Wave characteristics

We know that there are different types of wave but they do have certain characteristics in common. In this spread we examine the characteristics of these waves.

3.3 Water waves

The ripples produced by water waves are an easy way to examine the behaviour of waves in the laboratory.

fig 5

3.4 Reflection of light and sound

You already know how light is reflected, but in this spread we will examine the reflection of light in more detail and look at the reflection of sound.

3.5 Refraction

When a wave passes from one material into another, its speed changes. This usually causes the wave to change direction.

3.6 Images

You probably see your reflection every day. We examine how images are formed by reflection and refraction.

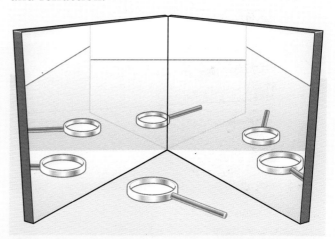

fig 6

3.7 Diffraction

We can hear round corners, but we cannot see round corners. In this spread we examine the reasons why.

Links with other Teaching blocks

3.1 What are waves?

Vibrations

A loudspeaker is a cone that is made to **vibrate**. As it vibrates, the layer of air next to it vibrates, which in turn causes the next layer to vibrate and so on. The air does not move from the loudspeaker to the ear of the listener. It is the air which passes on the vibration.

In a guitar the vibrating strings make the air start to vibrate.

fig 8

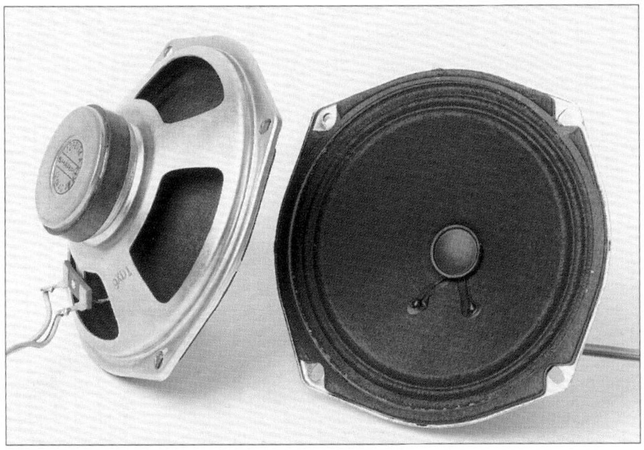

fig 7

a What makes the air start to vibrate when a piano is played?

b What makes the air start to vibrate when a drum is played?

c What makes the air start to vibrate when a clarinet is played?

In these examples, the air vibrates in the same direction as the direction in which the wave moves. We can show this with the aid of a slinky spring. This type of wave is called a **longitudinal** wave.

The region where the layers of the spring are pushed closer together is called a **compression**; where the coils are further apart is called a **rarefaction**.

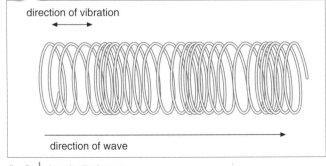

direction of vibration

direction of wave

fig 9 | Longitudinal wave

fig 10

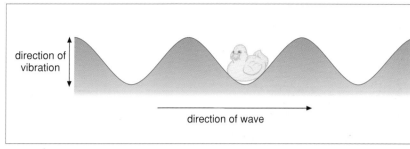

direction of vibration

direction of wave

fig 11 | Transverse wave

A duck is sitting in the middle of the lake. If a boat passes the duck and causes waves, how does the duck move? Does it bob up and down or does it move to the edge of the lake with the wave? In this example, the duck vibrates up and down while the wave moves across the surface of the lake.

Next time you watch a football match, look at a Mexican wave. How do the people move? How does the wave move? This type of wave is called a **transverse wave**.

d What type of wave is made by the string of a guitar when it is plucked?

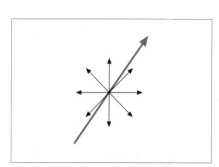

fig 12 | Vibrations are always at right angles to the direction of the wave

Light is another example of a transverse wave caused by **electromagnetic** vibrations at right angles to the direction in which the light is travelling.

Energy transfer

No-one can be in any doubt about the tremendous amount of energy that can be transferred by waves. In some parts of the world, scientists are investigating ways in which they can extract energy from the waves and use it to produce electricity.

fig 13

Thinking further

■ **1** Tom and Jerry have lost their toy yacht in the middle of the lake. Tom says 'If we throw stones into the lake so they land just beyond our boat, the waves will push the boat back to us.' Explain why this is not a good idea.

◆ **2** A long vertical spring is suspended from a crane 25 m above the ground. A weight hangs on the other end. When the weight is raised up it stays still for a few seconds before falling back. Suggest a reason for this behaviour.

─ **KEY WORDS** ─
compression • electromagnetic • longitudinal wave • rarefaction • transverse wave • vibration

3.2 Wave characteristics

> ### Key points
>
> - Amplitude is the maximum displacement of a particle in a wave from its rest position.
> - Frequency is the number of complete waves passing a point in one second.
> - Wavelength is the distance between two successive points on a wave of similar displacement.
> - Speed is a measure of how fast a wave is travelling.

Amplitude (a)

The **amplitude** of a wave is the maximum displacement of a particle in the wave from its rest position. In a transverse wave this is very easy to see.

In a longitudinal wave, it is more difficult. Fig 15 represents a longitudinal wave pattern after different time intervals. The red layer is vibrating backwards and forwards. The arrow shows a compression moving to the right. If **R** is the rest position and **A** the maximum displacement, then the distance from **R** to **A** is the amplitude.

If the amplitude of a sound wave is increased, the sound becomes louder.

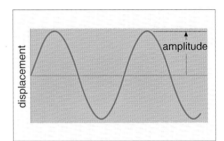

fig 14 | Transverse wave amplitude

Frequency (f)

The **frequency** of a wave is the number of complete waves passing a point in one second. Frequency is measured in **hertz** (Hz). Frequency is related to pitch. If the frequency of a sound wave is increased, the pitch of the sound gets higher.

a Shahjhan counts the water waves as they reach the edge of a lake. He counts 30 waves in one minute. Calculate the frequency of the waves.

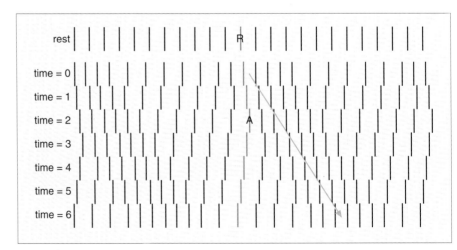

fig 15 | Longitudinal wave amplitude

Wavelength (λ)

The **wavelength** of a wave is the distance between two successive points having the same displacement. The symbol used to represent wavelength is the Greek letter lambda (λ).

Fig 16 shows the wavelength of both a transverse and a longitudinal wave.

b What is the basic unit used when measuring wavelength?

c Measure the amplitude and the wavelength of the transverse wave in fig 16.

d Measure the wavelength of the longitudinal wave in fig 16.

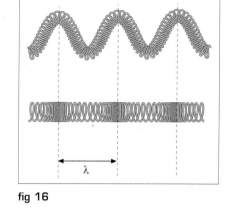

fig 16

Speed (v)

The **speed** or **velocity** of a wave is a measure of how fast it is travelling.

$$\text{speed} = \frac{\text{distance travelled}}{\text{time taken}}$$

e A wave takes 20 seconds to travel 100 metres. Calculate its speed.

The speed of a wave is also related to its wavelength and frequency.

$$\text{wave speed} = \text{frequency} \times \text{wavelength}$$
$$v = f\lambda$$

Thinking further

■ **1a** What happens to the pitch of a note if its frequency changes from 256 Hz to 512 Hz?

b What happens to the wavelength of the note when its frequency changes from 256 Hz to 512 Hz?

■ **2** A water wave has a wavelength of 20 cm and a frequency of 7 Hz. Calculate its speed.

◆**3 a** Jane is watching a forester cutting down a tree with an axe. She hears the axe hit the tree 0.75 seconds after she sees the axe hit the tree. Sound travels at a speed of 300 m/s. How far away is she from the forester?

b In part **a**, what assumption have you made about the speed of light compared to the speed of sound?

KEY WORDS

amplitude • frequency • hertz • speed • velocity • wavelength

 Demonstrating waves in springs.

3.3 Water waves

- Water waves are an example of transverse waves.
- In the laboratory, water waves can be seen with the aid of a ripple tank.
- The water waves in a ripple tank model the behaviour of other types of wave.

Ripple tank

The **ripple tank** consists of a shallow, transparent-bottomed tray containing water. Light is shone from above the tank onto a white screen below the tank. Sometimes the ripple tank can be mounted on an overhead projector.

A circular **pulse** can be produced by dipping a finger into the water once. A straight pulse can be produced by rolling a dowel rod. A vibrating bar or round dipper produces continuous waves.

The wave pattern produced can be looked at with the help of a **stroboscope**. This has the effect of 'freezing' the wave pattern.

Plane waves at a straight barrier

Straight waves are sometimes called **plane** waves. The **wavefront** is perpendicular to the direction of the wave. When a plane wave is incident at a straight barrier, the wave behaves in the same way as light behaves when it is reflected.

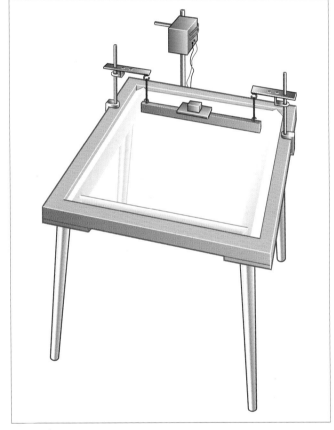

fig 17 | A ripple tank with an overhead light source

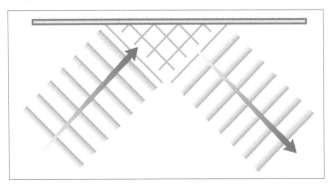

fig 18 | Plane waves reflecting off a straight barrier

a What is the relationship between the angle of incidence and the angle of reflection?

Straight waves at a curved barrier

When a plane wave is incident at a curved barrier, the wave behaves in the same way as light behaves when it is reflected at a curved mirror. The same rules of reflection apply. The curved reflected waves appear to **converge** to or **diverge** from a point called a **focus** (**F**).

b The curvature of the reflected waves is greater than the curvature of the barrier. Suggest why.

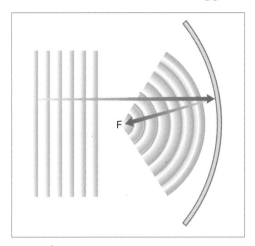 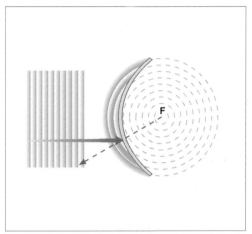

fig 19 | Plane waves reflecting off a concave barrier   **fig 20** | Plane waves reflecting off a convex barrier

Curved waves at a straight barrier

When a curved wave is incident at a straight barrier, the reflected wave is also curved. The waves appear to start at a point behind the barrier. This point is the same distance behind the barrier as the source of the waves is in front of the barrier.

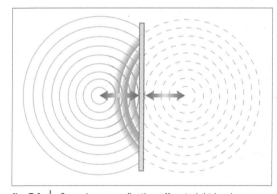

fig 21 | Curved waves reflecting off a straight barrier

Thinking further

■ **1** A plane wave with a wavelength of 2 cm is travelling towards a straight barrier. The angle between the wavefront and the barrier is 30°.

   a What is the value of the angle of incidence?

   b Draw an accurate diagram to show three wavefronts travelling towards the barrier and three wavefronts after reflection at the barrier.

◆ **2** A series of circular waves of wavelength 2 cm and frequency 1 Hz are produced at a point 8 cm in front of a straight barrier.

Draw an accurate, full size diagram showing how all of the waves appear 6 s after the first wave is produced.

KEY WORDS

concave • converge • convex • diverge • focus • plane • pulse • ripple tank • stroboscope • wavefront

3.4 Reflection of light and sound

Reflection of light

Surfaces reflect light, which is why we can see things. A plane mirror allows us to study the law of reflection.

Any line drawn at right angles to a surface is called a **normal**. The **incident ray** is travelling towards the mirror and the **reflected ray** travels away from it. Angles of incidence and reflection are always measured between the rays and the normal. The angle between the incident ray and the mirror is termed the **glancing angle**.

  angle of incidence = angle of reflection

a A ray of light strikes a plane mirror so that the angle between the ray and the mirror is 25°. What is the angle of reflection?

When a beam of light strikes an uneven surface, the reflected light is scattered, but at each point of incidence the law of reflection is obeyed.

At a concave mirror, a parallel beam of light is reflected back to a focus.

b The reflectors in torches and car headlamps are concave. Where should the filament of the bulb be to produce a parallel beam of light?

c Draw a ray diagram to show how a parallel beam of light is reflected from a convex mirror.

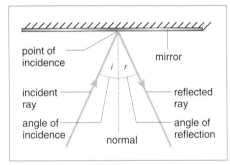

fig 22 | Regular reflection from a plane mirror

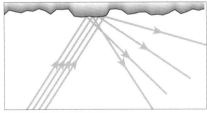

fig 23 | Diffuse reflection from an uneven surface

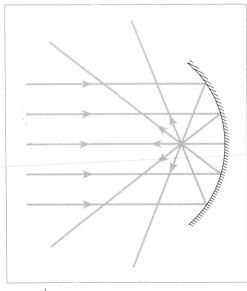

fig 24 | Reflection from a concave mirror

Uses of mirrors

As well as using a mirror to look at yourself every morning, mirrors have many other uses.

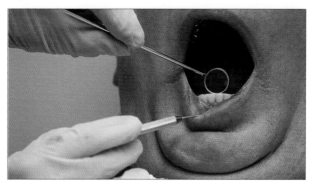

fig 25

fig 26 | A mirrored panel reflects the Sun's rays toward an energy collecting tower at a solar power plant in Almeria, Spain

Reflection of sound

In just the same way as light is reflected, sound is reflected from a solid surface. This is called an **echo**. In large rooms, loud sounds may keep on reflecting off the walls and ceiling. The sound seems to continue for a few moments. We call this **reverberation**.

Some softer surfaces absorb sound, which is why lecture theatres, cinemas, theatres and large restaurants have drapes or special acoustic boards on the walls. An audience too helps to absorb sound because they are wearing clothing of soft material.

fig 27 | Reflection of sound

Thinking further

■ **1** Mirrors at the top of the stairs in double-decker buses, roadside mirrors at dangerous junctions and the rear view mirrors in some cars are convex. Suggest why.

■ **2** Fig 28 shows a school hall. Look carefully at the ceiling. Describe and explain what is there.

◆ **3** Isaac tried to test the law of reflection using a ray box. He found that the incident ray got wider as it got closer to the mirror (fig 29).

  a What effect does this have on the reflected ray?

  b How does this make the experiment less accurate?

fig 28

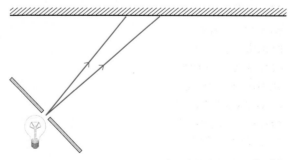

fig 29

┌─ **KEY WORDS** ─────────────────────────────
diffuse • echo • glancing angle • incident ray • normal • reflected ray • reverberation
└──

 Reflection of a light by a plane mirror.

3.5 Refraction

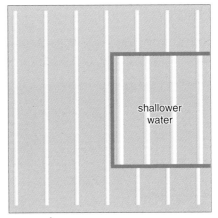

fig 30 | Refraction of water waves in a ripple tank

Key points

- The speed of a wave changes when the wave passes from one material to another.
- This change in speed causes a change in wavelength and hence can cause a change in direction.
- This is called refraction.

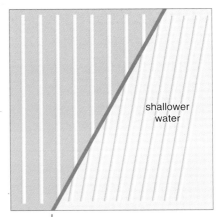

fig 31 | Refraction of waves in a ripple tank

Refraction in water

If you have looked closely at waves on the beach, you realise that as the water gets shallower the distance between the waves (wavelength) decreases. This is because the wave slows down.

a Explain why the wavelength gets shorter if a wave slows down.

You can see the slowing effect in a ripple tank if a sheet of glass is placed in the tank to make the water shallower.

If the wave is at an angle to the boundary, then the wave changes direction as it crosses the boundary. This is known as **refraction**.

Refraction of light

Using a ray box, you can see the path of a light ray as it passes through a glass block (fig 33).

fig 32 | Refraction through a glass block

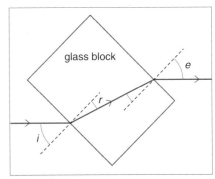

fig 33 | Refraction as light passes through a glass block

There is a normal, angle of incidence i, angle of refraction r and angle of emergence e.

When light passes into a more dense material, the angle of refraction is less than the angle of incidence. When light passes into a less dense material, the angle of refraction is greater than the angle of incidence.

b With a rectangular glass block, what is the relationship between the angle of incidence and the angle of emergence?

Scientists often use familiar objects or ideas to explain difficult situations. We call this modelling. Fig 34 shows one model of refraction.

As a toy car moves from a hard, tiled floor onto a carpet, it changes direction. This is because the first wheel onto the carpet is slowed down. The toy car moves more slowly on the carpet than on the hard tiled floor.

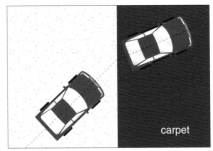

fig 34

Refraction of sound

Refraction is not as important with sound as it is with light but bending of sound waves does occur and is an interesting phenomenon.

The people most likely to be familiar with refraction of sound are early morning fishermen. Sound travels in all directions from a source. Normally, only sound directed toward the listener can be heard, but refraction can bend sound downward. It can add some additional sound, effectively amplifying the sound. Sounds which come from too far away to be heard under normal circumstances are quite audible. The cool water keeps the air near the water cool, but the early sunshine has begun to heat the air higher up, creating a thermal inversion. The fact that the speed of sound is faster in warmer air bends some sound down towards the listener.

fig 35

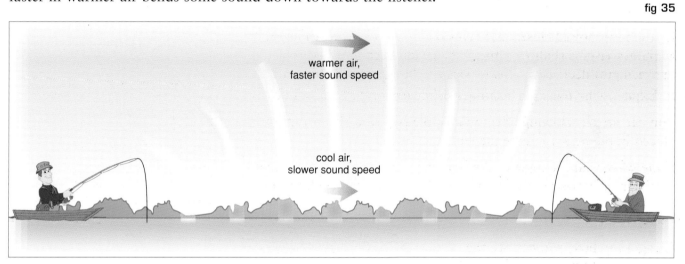

warmer air, faster sound speed

cool air, slower sound speed

Thinking further

■ **1** Fig 36 shows wavefronts heading towards an area of deeper water. Copy and complete the diagram to show what happens to the wavefronts as they travel in the deeper water.

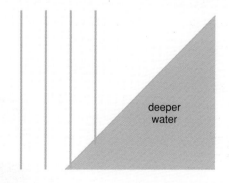

deeper water

fig 36

◆ **2** Edward did an experiment to measure angles of incidence and refraction as light entered a glass block. The table shows his results.

angle of incidence, i in degrees	10	20	30	40	50	60	70
angle of refraction, r in degrees	7	13	19	25	31	35	39

fig 37

a Plot a graph of angle of refraction against angle of incidence. Comment on its shape.

b Plot a graph of sine r against sine i. Comment on its shape.

─ **KEY WORDS** ─
refraction

 Refraction of light by a perspex block.   *Using a spreadsheet to find the relationship between i and r.*

3.6 Images

> ### Key points
> - Images can be real or virtual.
> - An image is formed when light is reflected or refracted.

Real or virtual?

A **real image** is one which can be produced on a screen.
A projector or camera produces real images.

A **virtual image** is one which is not really there. An image is produced at a point from which light *appears* to come. No light actually passes through a virtual image and it cannot be projected onto a screen.

a Where is the image in a camera produced?

Images in plane mirrors

When you look at yourself in a plane mirror, your **image** appears to be behind the mirror. If you ask someone to look behind the mirror, your image is not there. It is virtual. The image looks almost the same as you. It is

upright
the same size
on the same normal
as far behind the mirror as you are in front

b What does your image in a plane mirror do if you raise your right hand?

The eye sees the image of an object in a plane mirror by looking along the paths of the reflected rays to the point from which they seem to come.

When trying to find the position of an image in a plane mirror, try placing a tall pin behind the mirror at the position of the image of a similar pin in front of the mirror. As you move your head from side to side, the top of the pin behind the mirror and the bottom of the image of the pin in front of the mirror appear to move together as one pin. This is called **no-parallax**.

c Suggest why some ammeters and voltmeters have plane mirrors in the scale beneath the needle.

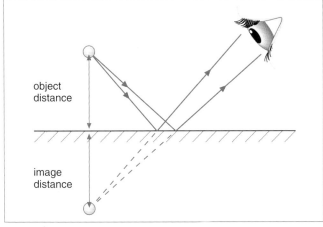

fig 38 | How the eye sees an image in a plane mirror

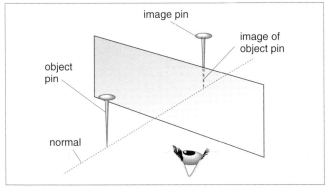

fig 39 | No-parallax in a plane mirror

Images in inclined mirrors

If two mirrors are inclined to one another, multiple images are obtained. A kaleidoscope has two mirrors at 60° to one another. The two mirrors produce five images. Two mirrors at right angles produce three images.

d Suggest why two mirrors at right angles produce three images. Hint – think about the angles between the mirror and the angles in a circle.

e Try to explain how many images are produced with two parallel mirrors facing one another.

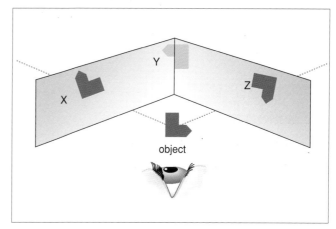

fig 40

Images caused by refraction

If you look into a swimming pool, the pool appears to be shallower (**apparent depth**) than it really is (**real depth**). An image of the bottom of the pool is formed because the light from the bottom is refracted at the pool's surface.

For the same reason, a drinking straw appears bent in a glass of liquid.

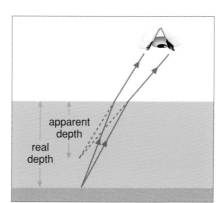

fig 41

fig 42

Thinking further

■ **1** Fig 43 shows the front of an emergency vehicle. Explain why the writing is the way it is.

fig 43

■ **2** Fig 44 shows a fisherman trying to catch a fish in a traditional manner. Explain where he should aim to hit the fish.

fig 44

◆ **3** If the object in fig 40 is a person, explain what happens to image Y when the person raises his right hand.

KEY WORDS

apparent depth • image • no-parallax • real depth • real image • virtual image

3.7 Diffraction

Diffraction of water waves

Diffraction can easily be seen using a ripple tank and straight waves heading towards a gap. If the gap is large, there is little spreading of the waves as they pass through the gap.

If the size of the gap is reduced, the waves spread out more.

If the size of the gap is similar to the wavelength of the wave, there is a lot of diffraction.

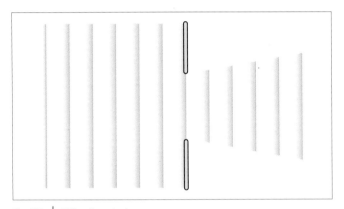

fig 45 | Diffraction at a large gap

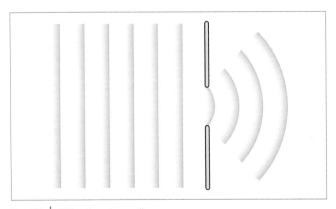

fig 46 | Diffraction at a smaller gap

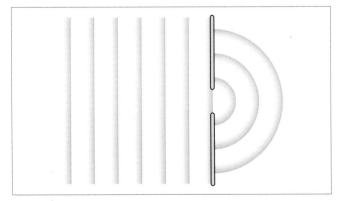

fig 47 | Diffraction at a gap similar in size to wavelength

Fig 48 shows an example of water waves diffracting as they enter a harbour.

a A water wave travels at 2 m/s with a frequency of 4 Hz. Calculate its wavelength.

b Sound travels at 300 m/s. A typical frequency for sound is 250 Hz. What is an approximate value for a typical wavelength?

c Radio 4 broadcasts at 200 kHz and Radio 5 at 909 kHz. Radio waves travel at the speed of light. What are approximate values for the wavelengths of Radio 4 and Radio 5?

d Visible light has a typical frequency of about 10^{14} Hz. What is a typical wavelength for visible light?

e Richard is in the lounge watching television. Judy is in the hall. She can hear the television through the open door but she cannot see it. Explain why.

Diffraction of sound

The sounds we hear have wavelengths of between a centimetre and about fifteen metres. The 'gaps' we normally hear sound through are about a metre or so wide. The wavelengths of sounds are therefore of a similar **order of magnitude** to the gap. This is why we can hear round corners.

Diffraction of light and radio waves

Light has a very small wavelength so 'gaps' have to be very small before light is diffracted. The wavelength of radio waves is much larger so the diffraction is greater. The fact that light can be diffracted is evidence that supports the idea of light being a wave.

Transmission masts usually have many aerials on them. The different aerials are used to transmit long, medium and short wave radio, VHF radio, television and microwave signals.

fig 48 | Water waves diffract at harbour entrance

fig 49

Thinking further

■ **1** Fig 50 represents a radio mast situated on the top of a hill. In the next valley there are four houses.

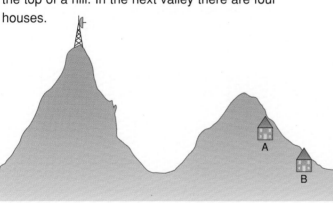

fig 50

House **A** has poor long wave reception and nothing else.
House **B** has good long wave reception, poor medium wave reception and nothing else.
House **C** has good long and medium wave

reception, poor short wave reception and poor mobile phone reception.
House **D** receives all radio stations and has good mobile phone reception.

a Explain these observations.

b What action can be taken to improve radio reception?

◆ **2** A parallel beam of light is shone through a hole in some black card onto a screen.

Describe in as much detail as you can what you would expect to see on the screen if the hole in the card is

a 1 cm in diameter   **b** a *very* small pin hole.

─ KEY WORDS ─
diffraction • order of magnitude

Questions on wave properties

● **1** Which of the following statements are true and which are false?

   a Sound waves are longitudinal waves.

   b Water waves are longitudinal waves.

   c Light is a transverse wave.

   d Transverse waves have compressions and rarefactions.

   e Light waves vibrate at right angles to their direction of travel. *(5)*

● **2** Fig 51 shows a loudspeaker placed near to some plastic film stretched over a wire circle. The loudspeaker is vibrating at 600 Hz.

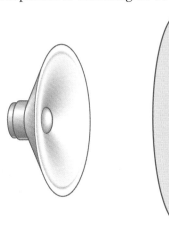

fig 51

   a Describe how sound from the loudspeaker reaches the film. *(2)*

   b Describe what happens to the plastic film. *(2)*

● **3** Fig 52 shows three wave patterns. They were produced by

   A dropping a marble into a shallow trough from a height of two centimetres

   B rolling a wooden rod backwards and forwards in a shallow trough

   C vibrating a vertical rod up and down in a shallow trough.

   Match each pattern with how it was produced. *(3)*

fig 52   X   Y   Z

● **4** Emma writes her name and looks at the reflection in a mirror as shown in fig 53. What does the image look like? Choose A, B, C or D.

fig 53

   A *ɒmmƎ*

   B *Ǝmmɒ*

   C *Emma*

   D *Ɛwwɒ* *(1)*

● **5** When Sharon looks into her swimming pool, she has the impression that it is 1.50 m deep. What is its real depth? Choose **A, B, C** or **D**.
   A 1.00 m
   B 1.25 m
   C 1.50 m
   D 2.00 m *(1)*

■ **6** Copy and complete the table by calculating the values which should be in the empty boxes. *(5)*

speed in m/s	frequency in Hz	wavelength in m
	150	3
	20	0.25
600	150	
1000		25
2500		1500

fig 54

7 Nadia is 1.7 m tall. She is 3 m away from, and walking in a northerly direction towards, the front of a vertical, plane mirror. She waves her right hand.

Describe, in as much detail as possible, the image she sees of herself in the plane mirror. *(7)*

8 Ben is watching a thunderstorm. He sees the lightning and hears the thunder five seconds later. He knows that sound travels at 330 m/s. How far away is the storm? *(3)*

fig 55

9 Steven is playing snooker. He has to hit the last red ball, but is snookered (the blue and black balls are in the way).

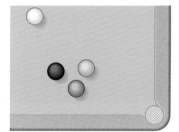

fig 56

a Describe how he could use two mirrors and a torch with a narrow beam to help him decide where to aim the white ball. *(4)*

b Explain why this method works. *(2)*

10 Joe did an experiment to find out how many images were formed when he had two inclined mirrors. He set the mirrors at different angles and counted the images.

This is his results table.

angle between mirrors in degrees	number of images seen in degrees
90	3
60	5
45	7
30	11
20	17

fig 57

a Plot a graph of number of images against angle between mirrors. *(2)*

b Use the graph to find out the angle between the mirrors so that four images can be seen. *(1)*

c How many images can be seen when the angle between the mirrors is 40°? *(1)*

d How many images can be seen when the angle between the mirrors is 80°? *(1)*

e Explain why this answer is not the value read from the graph. *(2)*

11 Fig 58 represents the trough of a ripple tank. The side **CD** is raised slightly so that the water is shallower than on the other side **AB**. A single wave pulse is produced at **M** the middle of the tank. Copy the diagram of the tank and show clearly the wave pattern produced by the pulse. *(1)*

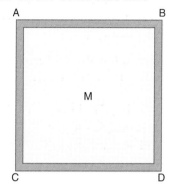

fig 58

12 As light passes from water into air, how are the following affected

a its speed *(1)*

b its frequency *(1)*

c its wavelength? *(1)*

13 Paula is watching the waves produced by boats as they pass through the narrow entrance to a harbour.

The first boat she sees is a small motor boat travelling quite quickly. The second boat is a large yacht travelling very slowly.

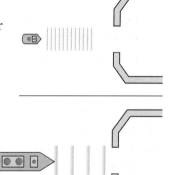

fig 59

a Copy the diagram of the small motorboat entering the harbour and continue to add wavefronts towards the entrance and into the harbour. *(3)*

b Copy the diagram of the large yacht entering the harbour and continue to add wavefronts into the harbour. *(2)*

c Explain why the patterns of the wavefronts are different. *(3)*

Using waves

Waves transfer energy from one place to another. Most of us make use of this every day as we look at and listen to the things which surround us.

Different types of wave have different properties and these allow us to use the wave to do a particular job.

Check-up

Have a go at the following questions. They will remind you what you should already know about using waves.

fig 1

a Fig 1 shows a rainbow. What are the seven colours which form a rainbow? Write them down in order.

b Red, blue and green are known as primary colours in light. Copy and complete the table to show what happens when these colours are shone onto the same area of a white screen.

colours shone onto screen	colour of screen
red and blue	
blue and green	
green and red	
red and blue and green	

fig 2

c Objects appear to be different colours depending on the colour of light shone on them. Copy and complete the table below to show what colour everyday objects appear in different coloured light.

object	colour of light	colour object appears
red tomato	red	
blue car	green	
yellow daffodil	red	
white paper	yellow	

fig 3

If you have difficulties, your teacher has a Summary sheet you can have.

Contents of the Teaching block

This Teaching block is divided into eight double page spreads.

4.1 The electromagnetic spectrum

The electromagnetic spectrum is a family of transverse waves, all of which travel at the speed of light. They differ in their wavelengths and energies. Visible light is in the middle of the spectrum.

4.2 Infrared and ultraviolet

Next to the red end of the visible spectrum can be found infrared waves and next to the violet end, ultraviolet waves. We examine the properties, uses and dangers of these waves.

fig 4

4.3 Opposite ends

Next to infrared can be found a band of waves known as radio waves. Included within this band are microwaves as well as radio and television waves.

Beyond ultraviolet we find the X-ray band which includes gamma rays. Both X-rays and gamma rays have their uses in medicine and industry, but they can be very harmful.

4.4 Total internal reflection

When light is incident at a boundary between a more dense and a less dense material, it can become trapped inside the more dense material. We are able to send messages over very long distances or look inside the body by using total internal reflection.

4.5 Ultrasound

Sound with a frequency beyond human hearing allows us to monitor an unborn baby or clean golf balls!

4.6 Seismic waves

Whenever an earthquake occurs, vibrations are felt all over the Earth. Different waves travel in different ways through the Earth; this allows us to find out what is inside the Earth.

4.7 The structure of the Earth

We examine more closely the inside of the Earth and how the Earth has changed during its history.

4.8 Plate tectonics

Theories, which are less than 40 years old, are starting to explain how the Earth has changed over the past 200 million years.

Links with other Teaching blocks

4.1 The electromagnetic spectrum

Key points

- Electromagnetic waves are transverse waves.
- All waves in the electromagnetic spectrum travel at the speed of light $300\,000\,000$ m/s (usually written as 3×10^8 m/s).

The spectrum

Waves in the electromagnetic **spectrum** are grouped in broad bands according to their wavelength.

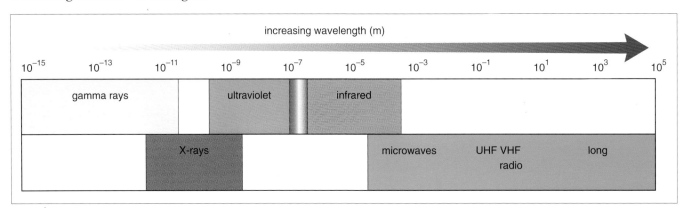

fig 5 | The electromagnetic spectrum

The wavelengths vary from as small as 10^{-15} m (gamma rays) up to 10^5 m (radio waves).

a The wavelength of Radio 4 is 1500 m. What is the frequency of a Radio 4 broadcast?

b An X-ray source has a frequency of 10^{18} Hz. What is the wavelength of the X-ray source?

The energy of the waves also depends on the wavelength. The shorter the wavelength, the more penetrating the wave.

The visible spectrum

When Isaac Newton was at Cambridge, he discovered that white light could be split into the colours of the rainbow using a glass prism. He probably held a prism in front of a small hole in a blind, and saw the visible spectrum on the opposite wall.

Taking a Prisme, (whose angle fbd was about 60gr into a darke roome into wch ye sun shone only at one little round hole k in such manner yt ye rays, being equally refracted at (n & h) their going in & out of it, cast colours rstv on ye opposite wall.

fig 6 | Newton discovers the colours of the rainbow

The colours should have beene in a round circle were all ye rays alike refracted, but their length to about 7 or eight inches, & ye centers of ye red & blew, (q & p) being distant about 2¾ or 3 inches. The distance of ye wall trsv from ye Prisme being 260 inches.

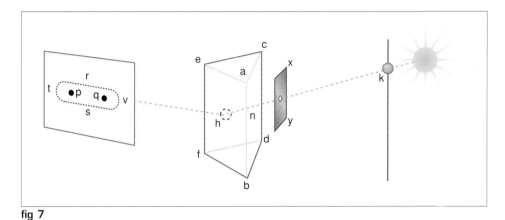

fig 7

Fig 8 shows the visible spectrum with its wavelengths.

| | | | |
|0.4|0.5|0.6|0.7|

wavelength in μm

fig 8 | Wavelengths of visible light in air

c Which colour of visible light has the highest frequency?

Visible light sources

Light originates from stars such as our Sun, hot bodies such as a filament in a lamp, **fluorescent** materials such as the coating on a television screen, LEDs and lasers.

Thinking further

■ **1** Visible light will not pass through flesh. X-rays pass through flesh but not bone. Gamma rays pass through flesh, bone and even lead. Explain these observations.

◆ **2** Use the information in fig 5 to calculate approximate frequency ranges for the gamma ray, X-ray, ultraviolet, infrared and radio wavebands.

KEY WORDS ─────────────────
fluorescent • infrared • radio • spectrum • ultraviolet • visible light • X-rays

 The visible spectrum.

4.2 Infrared and ultraviolet

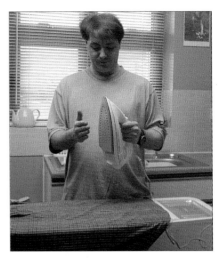
fig 9

> ## Key points
>
> - Infrared radiation has wavelengths longer than visible light, up to nearly 1 mm.
> - Infrared radiation is produced by warm or hot objects.
> - Ultraviolet radiation has wavelengths shorter than visible light, typically 10^{-8} m.
> - Ultraviolet radiation is produced by very hot objects.

Infrared radiation

Invisible infrared radiation is produced by objects at temperatures up to 500 °C. At hotter temperatures, red light is visible as well. An iron emits invisible infrared radiation, but a coal fire burns with a red glow as well.

a Blue flames are hotter than red flames. Suggest why.

The human body is not very hot, but the infrared radiation it emits can be detected with a special camera or a **thermistor**. As a result, search parties can find missing persons by taking a **thermograph** of an area from a low-flying helicopter.

Fig 11 shows a street scene taken with a thermal imaging camera in a helicopter. The white areas are the hottest. Notice the white areas from the person, the car engines and the tyres.

fig 10

fig 11

Devices linked to burglar alarms in our homes and offices detect the infrared radiation that our bodies emit. Also at home we use infrared radiation for the remote control of our televisions, video recorders and hi-fi systems.

b A baked potato emits infrared radiation. It is wrapped in aluminium foil. Explain how this helps to keep the potato hot.

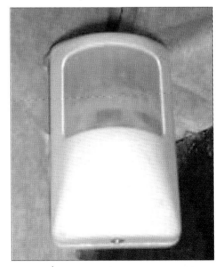
fig 12 | An infrared detector

Ultraviolet radiation

Ultraviolet radiation is produced by very hot objects, such as the Sun, and mercury lamps. It causes fluorescent materials to glow by absorbing the energy from the ultraviolet radiation and then re-radiating it as visible light. This is what happens in fluorescent tubes.

You can use pens with fluorescent ink to mark a security code on your possessions. The code is invisible unless ultraviolet radiation is shone onto it. A signature in invisible ink is often written into savings account books. This means your signature can be checked with ultraviolet light whenever you use your savings book.

Some washing powders contain fluorescers. These cause the clothes to look much whiter in ultraviolet radiation. You may have noticed this at discos.

It is the ultraviolet radiation from the Sun which causes us to have a suntan, but too much exposure to the Sun can result in sunburn or in extreme cases skin cancer. People with darker coloured skins have more melanin pigment. This filters out more ultraviolet radiation. They can still get sunburned, but not as easily as people with fairer skin. Ultraviolet radiation can also be very damaging to the eyes.

You should always use sunscreen when sunbathing. Every sunscreen product has a 'factor' printed on the container. The factor is a number that tells you approximately how long you can stay in the sun without burning. Using a sunscreen with factor 4 means that you can sunbathe four times as long without burning than if you did not wear a sunscreen. Young children and people with fair skin should use sunscreen with high numbered factors.

fig 13

c A sunscreen has a factor of 20. The normal burn time on a hot sunny day is given as 15 minutes. How long can someone using the sunscreen stay in the sun without burning?

Other practical uses of ultraviolet radiation are in the purification of water and in our bodies, which use ultraviolet radiation to convert natural fats below the skin into vitamin D.

Thinking further

■ 1 Welders always wear special goggles with dark filters. Suggest why.

■ 2 In the past, coal miners often suffered from vitamin D deficiency. Explain why.

◆ 3 The police had been following a stolen car through the night streets when it turned into a large, full car park. The police officers did not see where the car parked.

A helicopter fitted with a special camera took a thermograph of the car park some minutes later. Describe in detail all of the evidence on the thermograph which allowed the police to identify the car.

KEY WORDS

thermistor • thermograph

4.3 Opposite ends (1)

Key points

- At one end of the electromagnetic spectrum, next to infrared, are radio waves.
- Radio waves have wavelengths that range from a few centimetres to nearly two kilometres.
- Within the radio waveband are microwaves, radar and the more familiar radio and television waves.
- At the opposite end of the spectrum, next to ultraviolet, is the X-ray waveband.
- X-rays have wavelengths which are shorter than 10^{-9} m.
- The X-ray waveband includes very penetrating, energetic gamma rays with even shorter wavelengths.

Microwaves

Radio cookery

Microwaves have the shortest wavelengths within the radio waveband. This means they are able to transfer the most energy.

In a microwave oven, this energy is transferred to the water molecules in the food. The water molecules absorb this energy and increase their vibrations. This energy is passed on to neighbouring molecules so the food becomes heated.

The modern microwave oven has a source of microwaves which are reflected by a 'stirrer' into the oven. The highly polished walls and the metal grid on the door also reflect the microwaves. A turntable ensures that the food is heated evenly. Microwaves are able to penetrate several centimetres into foodstuffs.

a Suggest why it is important to reflect the microwaves from the door of the oven and not let them pass out into the kitchen.

Getting the message across

The BT Tower in London is one of many tall buildings that have microwave **aerial** dishes. These are used for transmitting and receiving telephone signals. Your mobile phone works because of microwaves.

b Look back at spread 3.7. Explain why microwave transmission needs aerials to be in 'line of sight'.

Signals sent to **satellites** and other spacecraft use microwaves. Goonhilly Earth Station, in Cornwall, is the largest satellite station on Earth. With the ability to cover more than two-thirds of the

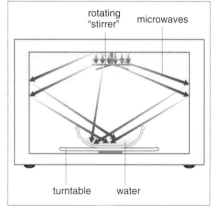

fig 14

fig 15

Earth, Goonhilly simultaneously handles hundreds of thousands of international phone, fax, video and data calls. The site is capable of handling 600 000 worldwide phone calls at any one time.

Merlin is the largest dish on the site, with a diameter of 32 metres and a mass of just 395 tonnes. It is one of the most sophisticated aerials in the world. Opened in 1985, it carries four times as many transatlantic calls as any other route. This aerial carried the Live Aid Concert in 1985 to over 2 billion people in about 100 counties throughout the world.

fig 16 | Goonhilly Earth Station

Radar

Traditionally, **radar** is associated with tracking aircraft or boats, or checking the speed of moving cars. A radio beam is transmitted and reflected off the object back to a receiver. A display appears on a screen showing either the position of the aircraft or boat or a readout of the car's speed. Today, radar guns measure the speed of athletes, cricket balls and baseballs.

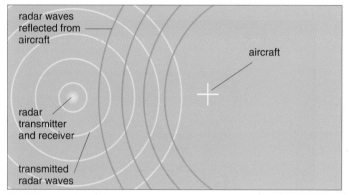

fig 17

fig 18

Some car manufacturers are using radar to ensure cars automatically keep safe distances from the car they are following.

The Magellan spacecraft used radar from 1991 to 1992 to map the surface of Venus. Venus is obscured by dense clouds of sulphuric acid, but by using radar, three-dimensional maps were generated with the aid of computers.

Radio

Radio waves are divided into wavebands. The shortest wavelengths are in the ultrahigh frequency (UHF) band. Television is transmitted in the UHF band. Very high frequency (VHF) is the next band and this is used by local radio transmitters. The range is limited by the power of the transmitter.

fig 19 | Computer generated surface view of Venus

c Suggest another reason why VHF transmitters only transmit locally. (Look back at spread 3.7 to help you.)

d Most home owners will have television aerials as high as possible above the roof, but satellite dishes mounted much lower on the wall of the house. Explain why.

continued ▶

4.3 Opposite ends (2)

The other wavebands are known as short wave, medium wave and long wave. As their names imply, the wavelength increases from one band to the next. The longer the wavelength, the better the radio reception. Short, medium and long waves can also be reflected by charged particles in the upper atmosphere (the **ionosphere**). Microwaves, UHF and VHF do not reflect in this way.

X-rays

At the other end of the electromagnetic spectrum, next to ultraviolet, we find X-rays. These vary in their energy. Less energetic waves are capable of penetrating soft materials such as flesh, but not denser materials such as bone. In medicine, X-rays are used to detect broken bones or to examine teeth. In airports, X-rays are used to scan luggage.

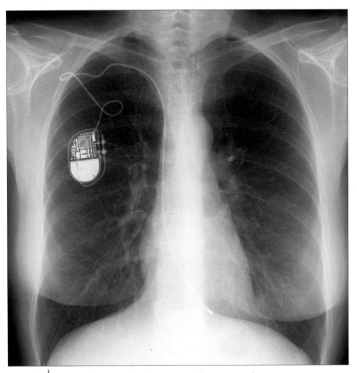

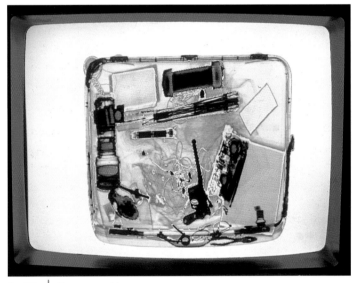

fig 21 | X-ray scan of luggage

fig 20 | Chest X-ray showing heart pacemaker

More energetic waves are used in medicine to treat cancers and in industry to examine welds and joints in metals.

All X-rays can be harmful. They can cause cancer.

e When the nurse at the dentist takes an X-ray of your teeth, she leaves the room to operate the X-ray machine. Explain why.

f What does the dental nurse place across your chest when she takes the X-ray of your teeth? Explain why.

Gamma rays

Gamma rays are very similar to X-rays. They have similar wavelengths and are used for similar jobs. Their main difference is in their source. Gamma rays originate from the nucleus of radioactive atoms. X-rays are produced when high-speed electrons (typically travelling at one-third the speed of light) hit a metal target and are slowed down very quickly. Some of their kinetic energy is transferred into electromagnetic radiation.

g What is the approximate speed of electrons travelling in an X-ray generator before they are slowed down by the target?

Gamma rays have more energy than X-rays and are therefore more penetrating. Like X-rays, they are used in medicine to treat cancers and in industry to examine metal joints. They are also used in sterilisation processes for food and medical equipment. The uses of gamma rays are discussed in more detail in spread 5.4 and 5.5.

Thinking further

■ **1** Jack, in London, phones his Uncle Sam in America. The microwave telephone signal via a satellite in space travels 90 000 km. Calculate the time delay from when Jack says 'Hello' to when his uncle hears him.

■ **2** A long-wave transmitting aerial and the aerial on Tom's radio at his home are 50 km apart. The curvature of the Earth means that the two aerials are not in 'sight' of each other. The long wave reception on Tom's radio is very good. Explain why.

◆ **3** Fig 22 shows a car travelling along the road. It is fitted with cruise control. This means that once the driver has selected a speed, the car continues at that speed until the driver changes it.

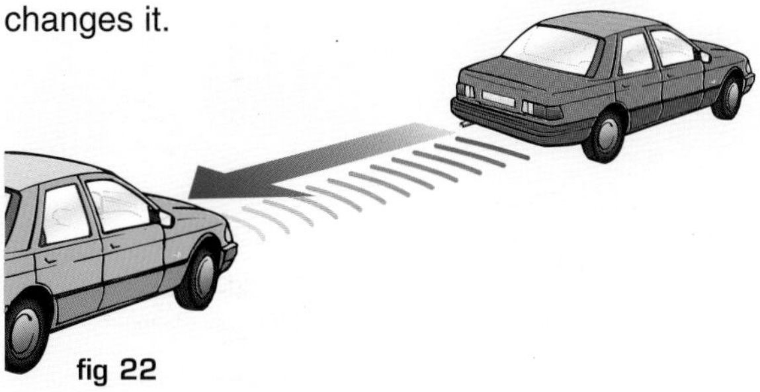

fig 22

This car also has radar fitted. This allows a measurement to be made of the distance to the car in front. If this distance is too small, the cruise control speed is reduced automatically to a safe speed.

Nicola has set the cruise control on her car at 60 mph (100 km/h). A pulse of radio waves is sent out from the car, reflected from the car in front and the signal is received back 6×10^{-7} s later.

a Calculate the total distance travelled by the radio wave.

b What is the distance between the two cars?

c The stopping distance quoted by the Highway Code for a car travelling at 60 mph (100 km/h) is 73 m. Discuss whether the on-board computer will make any adjustments to the cruise control speed.

◆ **4** Modern technology allows us to look right inside materials at the way in which atoms and molecules are held together. Explain which part of the electromagnetic spectrum would allow us to do this by examining how the electromagnetic wave behaves in the gaps between atoms and molecules.

--- KEY WORDS ---
aerial • gamma ray • ionosphere • microwave • radar • satellite •

■ *Looking at the evidence for locating mobile phone masts.*

4.4 Total internal reflection

Key points

- When light passes from a more dense into a less dense material the angle of refraction is greater than the angle of incidence.
- At some larger angles of incidence, the angle is too large for refraction to take place. The light remains in the material by reflecting off the boundary.
- Total internal reflection is used, among other things, for telecommunications and endoscopy.

Boundary conditions

When light passes from a more dense material, such as glass or water, into a less dense material, such as air, the angle of refraction is greater than the angle of incidence. A small amount of light is reflected. This means that it is possible to have an angle of refraction of 90°. When this happens, the angle of incidence is called the **critical angle**.

If the angle of incidence is larger than the critical angle, the light is not refracted, but instead obeys the laws of reflection. The light remains in the more dense material. This is known as **total internal reflection**.

a When the angle of incidence is the same as the critical angle, the refracted light often forms a spectrum. Explain why.

In the laboratory you can look at total internal reflection with the aid of a semicircular glass or perspex block. Light from a ray box is aimed at the centre of the semicircle and the angle of incidence gradually increased.

b Explain why there is no refraction when the incident ray enters the semicircular block.

Total internal reflection in prisms

The critical angle between glass and air is about 42°. We can use this property to reflect light in **prisms**.

c The angles of incidence at the reflecting boundaries of the prisms shown in fig 25 are all the same. What is the value of this angle? Why does total internal reflection take place?

Binoculars are really two telescopes 'folded up'. The optical path length is increased by having prisms which reflect the light along three times the length of the binoculars.

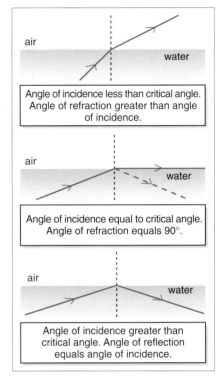

Angle of incidence less than critical angle. Angle of refraction greater than angle of incidence.

Angle of incidence equal to critical angle. Angle of refraction equals 90°.

Angle of incidence greater than critical angle. Angle of reflection equals angle of incidence.

fig 23

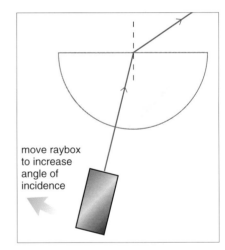

move raybox to increase angle of incidence

fig 24

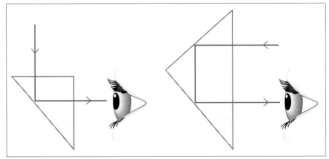

fig 25

One advantage of using prisms instead of mirrors in periscopes and binoculars is the clarity of image produced. Mirrors give a blurred image because of multiple reflections and refraction which occurs. Most reflection takes place at the silvered surface on the back of the mirror, but there is partial reflection at the air/glass boundary as well (fig 27). Another advantage of prisms is that because all the light is reflected, the image is brighter.

Optical fibres

Optical fibres are very fine lengths of glass or plastic along which light is shone. Being fine they are able to bend easily. When the fibres bend, the light reflects from the surface and remains trapped inside the fibre (fig 28).

Optical fibres are used instead of copper cable for the transmission of telephone communications over large distances. They are, by comparison, low maintenance and the quality of signal is much better. A pair of copper wires is needed for each telephone call. By encoding a **digital signal**, many more calls can be sent by pulses of laser light down an optical fibre. The latest fibre optic cable, linking the UK to America, can handle 320 000 simultaneous telephone calls. Digital signals are affected by interference but this can be removed by the receiver. Analogue signals, such as electric current, cannot have the interference removed.

d Telephone signals sent through copper cables need to be amplified every 0.5 km. A fibre optic cable only needs to amplify the signal every 15 km. Explain the difference.

An **endoscope** is an instrument that allows doctors to look inside the body without the need for surgery. It can be inserted through an orifice (such as the mouth to look at the stomach) or a small incision (to examine a joint). One bundle of optical fibres transmits light and a second bundle carries the reflected light back to either an eyepiece or to a camera.

Some delicate internal operations are now performed without the need for major surgery and general anaesthetic.

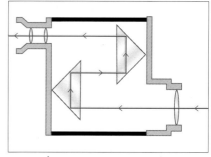

fig 26 | Binoculars

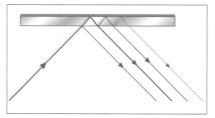

fig 27

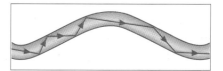

fig 28

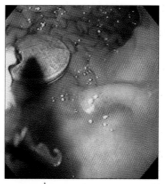

fig 29 | In this patient, two coins have been in the stomach for one month

Thinking further

■ **1** Information between computers is usually transmitted by means of a fibre optic cable. Explain why.

◆ **2** The fibres in an endoscope, which transmit the light to the inside of the body, are arranged randomly in the bundle.

The fibres which transmit the reflected light back to the viewer are arranged in the same pattern at both ends of the bundle. Explain the reason for these differences.

KEY WORDS

critical angle • digital signal • endoscope • optical fibres • prism • total internal reflection

Endoscope images on the Internet.

4.5 Ultrasound

> ### Key points
>
> - There is a sound spectrum just as there is an electromagnetic spectrum.
> - Ultrasound is very high frequency sound with a pitch too high for us to hear.

The sound spectrum

Waves in the sound spectrum are grouped in broad bands according to their wavelength.

The frequencies vary from as small as 10^{-4} Hz up to 10^{10} Hz. **Ultrasound** is sound with a frequency above 20 000 Hz.

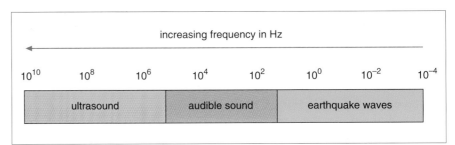

increasing frequency in Hz

| 10^{10} | 10^8 | 10^6 | 10^4 | 10^2 | 10^0 | 10^{-2} | 10^{-4} |

| ultrasound | audible sound | earthquake waves |

fig 30

Sonar – echolocation

To detect what is below a boat, pulses of ultrasound are transmitted into the sea. The ultrasound is reflected from submerged objects and the reflection is picked up by special microphones. The time taken for the pulse to return provides information about the depth of the submerged object. This technique is known as **sonar**.

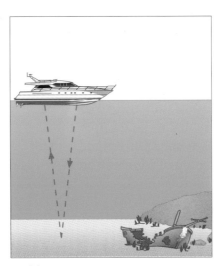

fig 31

a What difference will be noted when the boat passes over the sunken wreck?

b Sound travels at a speed of 1500 m/s in water. The time taken for the pulse to travel to the sea bed and back is 0.4 s. Calculate the depth of the sea bed.

c The picture shows a boat looking for a wreck. What other uses are there for sonar?

Dolphins, piranha, rats and bats use ultrasonic **echolocation** for navigation and/or to find food. The frequency used by dolphins is 150 000 Hz. This means the wavelength is very small.

d Suggest why bats have quite large ears.

fig 32

To help them detect objects around them, some blind people wear spectacles that transmit an ultrasonic pulse. Electronic circuits convert the reflected signal into different frequencies depending on the distance travelled.

When estate agents measure the size of rooms in houses, they often use ultrasonic tape measures.

e Describe how an ultrasonic tape measure works.

Ultrasonic scanning

Ultrasound is often used in medicine in preference to X-rays. Provided the power is low, no damage is done to body cells by ultrasound. Pictures are built up as the sound reflects off the boundaries between different body tissues. Pregnant women are routinely scanned to see how the fetus is developing in the womb. Other parts of the body often examined by ultrasound include the heart and liver. Ultrasound can also be used to detect tumours.

Ultrasonic vibrations

Other uses of ultrasound rely on the high frequency of vibrations.

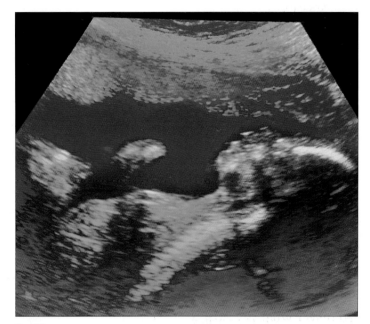

fig 33

- Opticians use ultrasound to vibrate water in a tank. Spectacles placed in the tank have the dirt on them shaken loose. Jewellery and electronic components are cleaned in a similar way.
- Dentists direct beams of ultrasound onto your teeth. The dirt and plaque are loosened by the vibrations.
- Old buildings and statues have the dirt removed from them with ultrasound.
- Older people sometimes have stones in their kidneys. The stones are smashed by ultrasonic vibrations into small pieces and pass out of the body in urine.

Thinking further

■ **1a** A dolphin emits an ultrasound signal of 150 kHz. Calculate the wavelength of the sound.

b The dolphin is following a boat. It receives a large echo from the boat 1.5 s after sending a pulse. A second pulse produces an echo 1.0 s later. How does the boat's speed compare to the dolphin's?

c There is another small echo from a fish 0.05 s after sending a pulse. How far away is the fish?

◆ **2** Why can dolphins find small fish by emitting high frequency ultrasound, but could not do so if the frequency was in the audible range?

KEY WORDS

echolocation • sonar • ultrasound

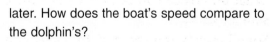 *Research on uses of ultrasonics.*

4.6 Seismic waves

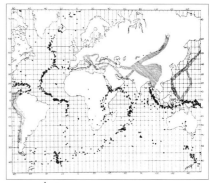

fig 34 | Sites of major earthquakes

Earthquake – surface waves

An **earthquake** is caused when rocks break suddenly at a **fault**. Minor earthquakes occur every day, but major ones, which cause severe damage and loss of life, are rare.

The origin of an earthquake is called the **focus.** The point on the Earth's surface immediately above the focus is known as the **epicentre.**

From the focus of the earthquake three types of **seismic wave** are transmitted. **L waves** (an abbreviation for Love waves) move outwards from the epicentre as surface waves. They travel more slowly than the other waves and are responsible for damaging buildings.

fig 35

Earthquake – body waves

The earthquake also produces longitudinal **P waves** (primary or pressure waves) and transverse **S waves** (secondary or shake waves). These waves travel through the Earth and it is their different properties which allow us to find out what is inside the Earth.

P waves are the faster moving wave and can travel though all parts of the Earth. S waves are slower moving and cannot travel through liquids. As these waves travel through the Earth, they are partially reflected at the boundaries between different materials and partially refracted as the density of the material changes. The waves are detected on the surface by **seismometers.**

a How are seismic waves similar to sound waves?

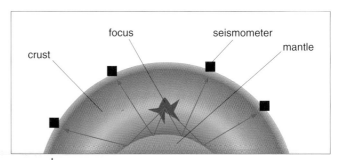

fig 36 | Reflection from the mantle

In some areas, only P waves are detected. The shadow cast by the absence of S waves means that the outer core must be liquid. The size of the shadow allows us to deduce that the size of the outer core is about 7000 km in diameter.

Earthquakes cause the Earth to reverberate for a long time afterwards. These reverberations are quite slow, so we don't normally notice them. From these vibrations we can also learn that inside the liquid outer core there is a solid inner core about 2400 km in diameter.

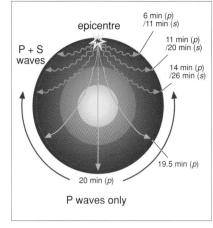

fig 37

Seismometer

A seismometer consists of a solid base secured to rock. A pen on the bottom of a heavy mass is suspended above a rotating drum on which is graph paper. As the Earth moves in an earthquake, the heavy mass stays still and a jagged trace is drawn on the paper.

The different traces produced are analysed and deductions made about the structure of the Earth. The time delay between the earthquake and the vibrations received allows scientists to calculate the velocities of the seismic waves.

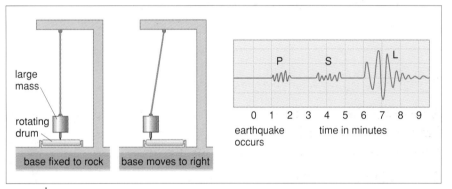

fig 38 | A seismometer

Thinking further

◆ **1** Look at the map showing major earthquakes, fig 33. Find a map of the world's most densely populated cities. Compare the two maps, what do you notice?

◆ **2** Fig 39 represents the position of an earthquake, Q, and two seismometers S, T.

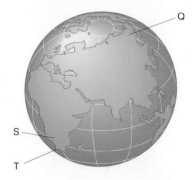

fig 39

Fig 40 shows the traces produced from the two seismometers.

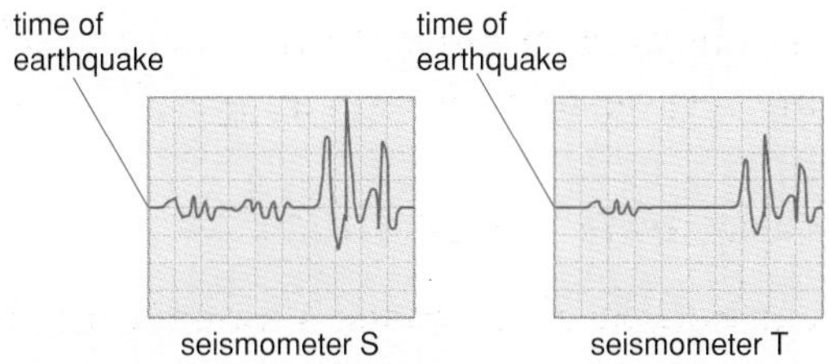

fig 40

a Make a sketch of the traces and label the traces produced by
  i L waves
  ii P waves
  iii S waves.

b Explain why the patterns from the two seismometers are different.

KEY WORDS

earthquake • epicentre • fault • focus • L waves • P waves • S waves • seismic wave • seismometer

4.7 The structure of the Earth

The core

The centre of the Earth consists of a solid inner **core** and molten outer core. Together they are 7000 km in diameter. Evidence for the structure of the core has come from earthquakes (see spread 4.6).

a Write a brief summary of how we know the inner core is solid and the outer core liquid.

The mantle

The major part of the Earth comprises the **mantle**. It is about 2800 km thick and is made up of rock containing compounds of magnesium, silicon and oxygen as well as iron. Its density is much greater than the density of most surface rocks because of the pressure from the rocks above. The rocks are also very hot and can sometimes melt to form **magma**. Sometimes molten rock comes to the surface in volcanoes. It can flow out as **lava** or be blasted out as **volcanic ash**.

b How do we know where an ancient volcano has been?

c Suggest why magma rises to the surface.

The lithosphere

The Earth's **crust** and the outermost part of the mantle form the **lithosphere**. The crust is much thicker under continents than it is under the oceans. The continental crust is between 25 km and 90 km thick whereas the oceanic crust has a thickness of only 5 km to 10 km. The lithosphere is typically 70 km to 125 km thick. Although these thicknesses sound quite large, compared to the diameter of the Earth (12 800 km) the lithosphere is really a very thin skin. Continental crust is comprised mainly of granite-like rock and oceanic crust of more dense rocks like basalt.

d The deepest mine in the world is a South African gold mine. It is 3582 m deep. Which layer(s) of the Earth does it enter?

e The deepest borehole in the world is in the Kola peninsular in Russia. It is 12 km deep. What fraction of the Earth's diameter does it pass through?

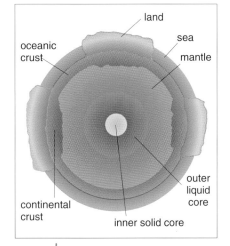

fig **41** | Structure of the Earth

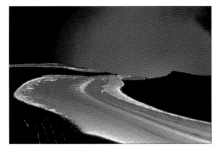

fig **42**

IDEAS AND EVIDENCE

Continental drift

As early as 1596 it was suggested that the continents had not always been in the positions we know them. The Dutch map maker Abraham Ortelius wrote in his work *Thesaurus Geographicus* that the Americas were 'torn away from Europe and Africa ... by earthquakes and floods'.

In 1912, a German meteorologist named Alfred Lothar Wegener published two articles that introduced the idea of **continental drift**. He suggested that originally there was only one land mass – a super-continent known as Pangaea. His theory was that this super-continent began to break up about 225–200 million years ago. Initially it split into two land masses, Laurasia and Gondwanaland, and eventually into the continents as we know them today.

Wegener's idea was partly based on similar coastal outlines. 'Doesn't the east coast of South America fit exactly against the west coast of Africa, as if they had once been joined?', 'This is an idea I'll have to pursue.' he wrote in December 1910.

There was also the evidence from fossils. Similar plant and animal fossils are found on the matching coastlines of South America and Africa. Wegener believed that it would have been impossible for these organisms to have swum or have been transported across the oceans. The presence of these identical fossil species along the coastal parts of Africa and South America was the most important piece of evidence for the two continents to have once been joined. The discovery of fossils of tropical plants in Antarctica led Wegener to conclude that this frozen land must once have been situated much closer to the equator where swampy vegetation could grow.

Permian 225 million years ago

Triassic 200 million years ago

Present day

fig 43 | Continental drift

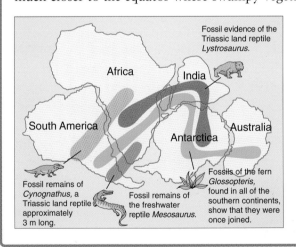

Fossil evidence of the Triassic land reptile *Lystrosaurus*.

Africa

India

South America

Antarctica

Australia

Fossil remains of *Cynognathus*, a Triassic land reptile approximately 3 m long.

Fossil remains of the freshwater reptile *Mesosaurus*.

Fossils of the fern *Glossopteris*, found in all of the southern continents, show that they were once joined.

As with many great scientists, the value of his work was not realised at the time and he was ridiculed. 'Utter, damned rot!' said the president of the American Philosophical Society. Anyone who 'valued his reputation for scientific sanity' would never dare support such a theory, said a British geologist.

It was not until the mid-1950s that scientists began to take these theories more seriously and despite differences in detail, Alfred Wegener was right in most of his major concepts.

fig 44 | The locations of fossil plants and animals on present-day continents form definite patterns (shown by bands of colour) if the continents are rejoined. The close similarity in coastline is also visible

Thinking further

■ **1** Give specific evidence which shows that

a South America may have been joined to Africa

b Antarctica may have been joined to India.

◆ **2** The average density of the Earth is 5.5 g/cm^3 and of surface rock 2.9 g/cm^3. What can we conclude about the density of the mantle and of the core?

┌─ **KEY WORDS** ─────────────────────────────────
continental drift • core • crust • lava • lithosphere • magma • mantle • volcanic ash
└───

4.8 Plate tectonics

- The lithosphere is made up of about fifteen tectonic plates which are constantly moving.
- Many earthquake zones are at plate boundaries.
- Where plates collide or separate, geological features such as mountains, island chains and rift valleys are formed.

The Earth's plates

The continental drift theory did not explain how the continents of solid rock could move. Today, we believe a theory based on the idea of **plates**.

With an estimated core temperature of 4000 °C, the mantle and crust act as insulators to reduce the cooling process. Convection currents can occur because of the high temperature of the core. Radioactive materials in the mantle break down and release energy, which heats the mantle causing it to flow like plasticene.

The lithosphere is broken into about fifteen large slabs of rock called plates. These plates move on a layer of flowing mantle known as the **asthenosphere**. They do not move very fast.

We use the theory of plate **tectonics** to explain the formation of mountains, volcanoes and earthquakes. The word tectonic comes from the Greek word 'to build', so plate tectonics is how the Earth is built of plates.

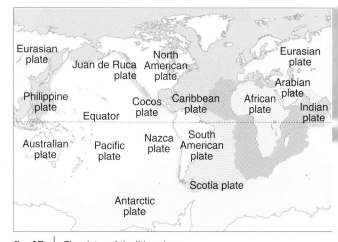

fig 45 | The plates of the lithosphere

a Compare the positions of the plate boundaries and the major earthquakes. What do you notice?

Colliding plates

Fig 46 shows what happens when a continental plate meets an oceanic plate. The continental plate moves up over the more dense oceanic plate. A **trench** forms. Over millions of years, the sediment is compressed, folded and may be pushed upwards to form a range of mountains or an island chain. The Andes were probably formed in this way when the oceanic Pacific Plate was pushed under the continental South American Plate.

The areas where the oceanic plate descends beneath the continental plate are known as **subduction zones**. At these zones, the increased temperature and pressure can cause **metamorphism** producing new rocks by recrystallization. During metamorphism, no melting occurs.

When two continental plates collide, neither descends as they have similar densities. As the continental plates are moved together, sediment that was deposited in the ocean between them becomes

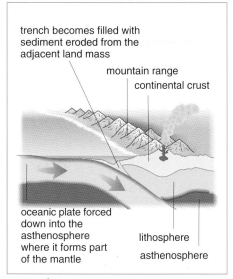

fig 46 | Colliding continental and oceanic plates

compressed, folded and heated to form large mountain ranges such as the Himalayas.

When two oceanic plates collide, for example where the fast-moving Pacific Plate converges against the slower moving Philippine Plate, one plate is usually subducted under the other.

The boundaries between colliding plates are **destructive boundaries** because lithosphere is being destroyed.

Separating plates

When two plates are moving apart, new crust is created by magma pushing up from the mantle to fill the cracks. New oceanic crust is formed in oceanic mountain ridges.

The submerged mountains of the Mid-Atlantic Ridge extend from the Arctic Ocean to beyond the southern tip of Africa. Although the rate of separation is measured as two to three centimetres each year, **sea-floor spreading** over the past 100 to 200 million years has caused the Atlantic Ocean to grow from a tiny strip of water between the continents of Europe, Africa, and the Americas into the vast ocean that exists today.

Sometimes, a continental plate will split and the continents move apart. A rift valley forms, which may become flooded to form a narrow sea. The Red Sea was probably formed like this. The boundaries between separating plates and splitting plates are **constructive boundaries** because new lithosphere is being formed.

Volcanoes

At oceanic ridges, about 20 cubic kilometres of magma is produced each year, which solidifies into new ocean floor. Most other areas of volcanic activity are at plate boundaries on the landward side of trenches where plates are destroyed. Therefore, most volcanoes and earthquakes are linked to plate movements.

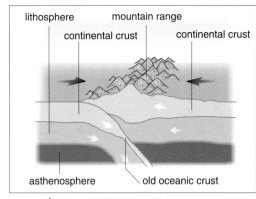

fig 47 | Colliding continental plates

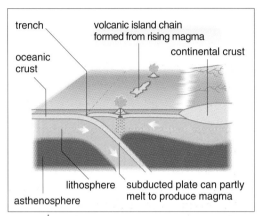

fig 48 | Colliding oceanic plates

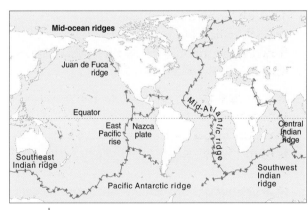

fig 49 | The best known example is the Mid-Atlantic Ridge

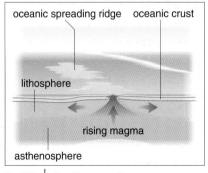

fig 50 | Sea-floor spreading

Thinking further

1 a When plates collide, heat is generated. What type of force generates this heat?

b When a subducting plate heats up, some of it melts. What happens to the molten rock?

2 The distance between Africa and South America is approximately 7000 km. Estimate the average speed at which they have drifted apart during the past 200 million years.

KEY WORDS

asthenosphere • constructive boundary • destructive boundary • metamorphism • plate • sea-floor spreading • subduction zones • tectonic • trench

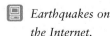 *Earthquakes on the Internet.*

Questions on using waves

● **1** Which of the following statements are true and which are false?

a Gamma radiation has a longer wavelength than infrared radiation.

b X-rays are more penetrating than radio waves.

c Ultraviolet radiation is used for the remote control of televisions and hi-fi systems.

d Radar is a series of high frequency sound pulses.

e Total internal reflection takes place at all angles greater than the critical angle. *(5)*

2 For each of the following situations, say which part of the electromagnetic spectrum is involved. Choose your answers from this list.

gamma · infrared · microwaves · radio · ultraviolet · visible · X-rays

● **a** causes a suntan

● **b** is used to detect broken bones in a horse

● **c** is used to sterilise surgical equipment

■ **d** is diffracted around hills

● **e** is used to preserve food

■ **f** is emitted by a warm object such as a human being

● **g** is used to transmit signals to satellites in space

■ **h** stimulates the cells of the retina in the human eye *(8)*

3 Fig 51 shows an infrared thermograph of a house. Most energy loss from an uninsulated house is from the roof.

fig 51 | The colour scale of the thermograph goes from green for low energy loss to yellow then red for high energy loss.

● **a** Does the house have good insulation in its roof?

■ **b** How does the thermograph provide your answer? *(3)*

● **4** List four properties common to all parts of the electromagnetic spectrum. *(4)*

● **5** Copy and complete the following sentences. Choose words from this list.

core · crust · lithosphere · magma · mantle · volcano

a The outer layer of the Earth is called the _____.

b The largest part of the Earth's structure is the _____.

c When rocks become hot and melt they form _____. *(3)*

■ **6** Fig 52 shows an analogue signal and a digital signal before, during and after transmission. Explain why it is better to transmit a digital signal instead of an analogue signal. *(4)*

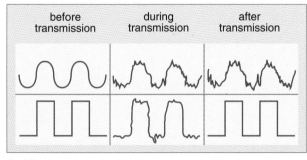

| before transmission | during transmission | after transmission |

fig 52

■ **7a** Fig 53 shows a 'Catseye' reflector from the centre of the road. Copy and complete the diagram to show how the light from the car headlamp reaches the driver's eye. *(4)*

b Suggest why the front of the catseye is curved. *(2)*

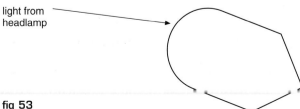

light from headlamp

fig 53

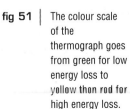

◆ **8** A seismograph trace of an earthquake shows a ten-minute interval between the arrival of the P wave and the S wave. P waves travel at 10 km/s and S waves at 6 km/s. How far away from the seismometer was the earthquake? *(5)*

IDEAS AND EVIDENCE

9 Read the following information. Then use it to help you answer the questions that follow.

Harry Hammond Hess, a professor of geology at Princeton University, was very influential in setting the stage for the emerging plate-tectonics theory in the early 1960s. He believed in many of the observations Wegener used in defending his theory of continental drift, but he had very different views about large-scale movements of the Earth.

Hess was interested in the geology of the ocean basins. Even during World War II, he was able to conduct echo-sounding surveys in the Pacific while cruising from one battle to the next. Hess' research resulted in a ground-breaking hypothesis that later would be called *sea-floor spreading*.

In 1962, his ideas were published in a paper titled 'History of Ocean Basins'. In this paper, Hess outlined the basics of how sea-floor spreading works: molten rock *(magma)* oozes up from the Earth's interior along the mid-oceanic ridges, creating new sea-floor that spreads away from the active ridge crest and, eventually, sinks into the deep oceanic trenches.

This explained several very puzzling geologic questions. If the oceans have existed for at least 4 billion years, why is there so little sediment deposited on the ocean floor? Hess reasoned that the sediment has been accumulating for 300 million years at most. This interval is approximately the time needed for the ocean floor to move from the ridge crest to the trenches, where oceanic crust descends into the trench and is destroyed. Meanwhile, magma is continually rising along the mid-oceanic ridges, where the 'recycling' process is completed by the creation of new oceanic crust. This recycling of the sea-floor also explained why the oldest fossils found on the sea-floor are no more than about 180 million years old. In contrast, marine fossils in rock strata on land can be considerably older. Most importantly

Hess' ideas also resolved a question that plagued Wegener's theory of continental drift: how do the continents move? Wegener had a vague notion that the continents must simply 'plough' through the ocean floor, which his critics rightly argued was physically impossible. With sea-floor spreading, the continents did not have to push through the ocean floor but were carried along as the ocean floor spread from the ridges.

The theory was strengthened further when dating studies showed that the sea-floor becomes older with distance away from the ridge crests. Finally, improved seismic data confirmed that oceanic crust was indeed sinking into the trenches.

As an example of the effect of sea-floor spreading on life, consider the lemurs of Madagascar. Lemurs are small, dog-faced, monkey-like animals. They do very well on Madagascar. Long ago, Madagascar separated from Gondwanaland. Water then separated the lemurs from the other monkey and ape-like animals. The lemurs did not have to compete with them for food. If Madagascar had remained connected to Gondwanaland, then the lemurs may never have survived the competition with the more intelligent and larger apes and monkeys.

a Explain how sea-floor spreading is responsible for continents moving apart. *(4)*

b What fossil evidence is there for sea-floor spreading? *(2)*

c What additional evidence helped to confirm Hess' theory of sea-floor spreading? *(2)*

d Sea-floor spreading is accompanied by volcanic activity. What effect does this have on deep water temperatures? *(1)*

e What is the name of a geological feature (about 70 000 km long) found on the ocean floor as a result of sea-floor spreading? *(1)*

f Which of the continents we know today made up the super-continent of Gondwanaland? *(5)*

Radioactivity

fig 1 | Marie Curie

When Antoine Becquerel discovered radioactivity in 1896 it was an accident. He found that some uranium compounds affected a photographic plate, even when it was protected from the light by being wrapped in black paper. Marie and Pierre Curie discovered radium and plutonium within the next fifteen years.

At that time, little was known of the dangers of being exposed to radioactivity and Marie died as a result of her work with radioactive materials.

In 1945, the first atomic bomb showed the tremendous power of the atom. Albert Einstein, who worked on the production of the bomb, was dismayed at its effect.

Today we know much more about radioactivity and how to harness the atom for the benefit of mankind.

fig 2 | An atomic blast

Check-up

Radioactivity is not a topic you have met at Key Stage 3, but have a go at the following questions. They remind you of what you may already know about the structure of atoms from your Sc3 (Chemistry) topic.

	mass	charge
electron		
neutron		
proton		

fig 4

a Copy and complete the table by writing in the mass and charge of the particles found in an atom.

b What is the name given to the central part of an atom?

c What **two** particles are found in this central part?

d Explain what is meant by the terms **isotope**, **atomic number**, **mass number**.

If you have difficulties, your teacher has a Summary sheet you can have.

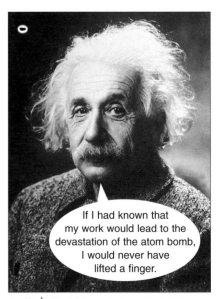

If I had known that my work would lead to the devastation of the atom bomb, I would never have lifted a finger.

fig 3 | Einstein

Contents of the Teaching block

This Teaching block is divided into six double page spreads.

5.1 What is radioactivity?

You already know about the particles in an atom. In this unit, we will examine how the nucleus behaves when it emits radiation.

5.2 Properties of radiations

There are three important types of radiation which are emitted by the nucleus. They behave very differently and it is this different behaviour which makes isotopes useful for particular jobs.

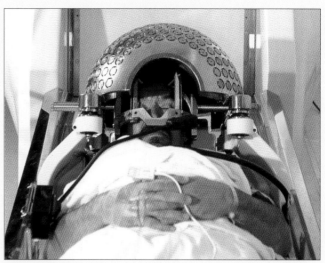

fig 5 | The gamma knife is a focused array of 201 intersecting beams of low-level gamma radiation

5.3 Radioactive decay

When a nucleus has emitted radiation it is said to have decayed. It has changed into a different nucleus, which may also be radioactive, but may not be. Different atoms decay at different rates and this too can make particular isotopes useful.

5.4 Using penetrative power of radioactivity

The uses of radioactivity today are numerous. Without it we would not have treatment for certain cancers.

5.5 Other uses

Without our understanding of radioactivity, we would not know as much about the age of the Earth. Sterilising surgical equipment would be more difficult and less effective without radioactivity.

5.6 Safety

The main problem with radioactivity is that we do not know it is there without using special detectors. When we do use radioactivity, we have to take special safety precautions to avoid our bodies being permanently damaged.

Links with other Teaching blocks

Chemistry 3.1 **Atomic structure**

4.3 **Using waves**

6.2–6.3 **The Earth and the Universe**

5.1 What is radioactivity?

Radioisotopes

Isotopes (sometimes called **nuclides**) of an atom have the same number of protons but a different number of neutrons. Hydrogen exists in three forms; hydrogen-1, hydrogen-2 and hydrogen-3. Hydrogen-1 is stable but the other two isotopes are unstable because of the additional neutrons and are radioactive. They are **radioisotopes**. We use symbols to represent isotopes. These include the chemical symbol, the atomic number (Z) and the mass number (A). The atomic number is the number of protons in the nucleus and the mass number is the number of protons plus neutrons (nucleons). Symbols are written $^{A}_{Z}X$, where X represents the chemical symbol of the element.

a What is the atomic number of $^{2}_{1}H$?

b What is the mass number of $^{3}_{1}H$?

c $^{226}_{88}Ra$ is an isotope of radium. How many protons are in the nucleus? How many neutrons are in the nucleus?

Types of radiation

Alpha

An **alpha particle** is the same as the nucleus of a helium atom. It has two protons and two neutrons. When a radioisotope emits alpha radiation, its **atomic number** decreases by two and its **mass number** decreases by four.

$$^{219}_{86}Rn \rightarrow ^{215}_{84}Po + ^{4}_{2}He$$

d Write equations to show how the following isotopes emit alpha radiation: $^{231}_{91}Pa$, $^{238}_{92}U$, $^{237}_{93}Np$.

e What is the charge on a helium nucleus?

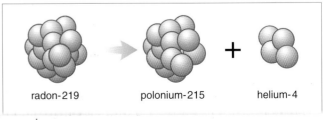

radon-219   polonium-215   helium-4

fig 6 | Alpha emission

Beta

A **beta particle** is the same as an electron, but it comes from the nucleus. In the nucleus, a neutron breaks down to form a proton, and an electron. (A small particle called an **antineutrino** is also produced.)

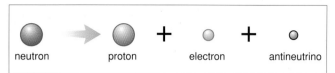

fig 7 | A neutron changes into a proton, electron and antineutrino

$$^{1}_{0}n \rightarrow {}^{1}_{1}p + {}^{0}_{-1}e$$

When a radioisotope emits beta radiation, its atomic number increases by one and its mass number stays the same.

$$^{14}_{6}C \rightarrow {}^{14}_{7}N + {}^{0}_{-1}e$$

f Write equations to show how the following isotopes emit beta radiation: $^{40}_{17}Cl$, $^{66}_{29}Cu$, $^{238}_{93}Np$.

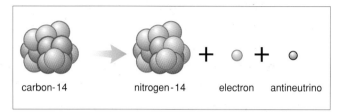

fig 8 | Beta emission

Gamma

Gamma radiation is a very short wavelength part of the electromagnetic spectrum. It is emitted when the nucleus loses energy. The mass number and atomic number do not change when gamma radiation is emitted.

Background radiation

Even if there are no radioactive sources nearby, radiation detectors will still show the presence of radiation. This **background radiation** comes mainly from natural sources such as the ground beneath our feet and cosmic rays from the Sun. Very little comes from atomic weapons or the nuclear power industry.

fig 9 | Granite rock is particularly radioactive

Thinking further

■ **1** Fig 10 shows how much background radiation we are exposed to from different sources.

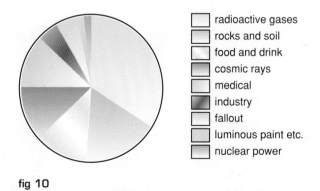

- radioactive gases
- rocks and soil
- food and drink
- cosmic rays
- medical
- industry
- fallout
- luminous paint etc.
- nuclear power

fig 10

a From what source do we receive most radiation?

b What fraction of our exposure to radiation comes from natural sources?

◆ **2** $^{232}_{90}$Th in a naturally occurring radioisotope. It emits an alpha particle to form $^{228}_{88}$Ra, which in turn emits a beta particle and the process continues until a stable isotope is formed.

Use the information in this decay chain to identify the stable isotope.

$^{232}_{90}$Th $\xrightarrow{\alpha}$ $^{228}_{88}$Ra $\xrightarrow{\beta}$ □ $\xrightarrow{\beta}$ □ $\xrightarrow{\alpha}$ □ $\xrightarrow{\alpha}$ □ $\xrightarrow{\alpha}$ □ $\xrightarrow{\alpha}$

□ $\xrightarrow{\beta}$ □ $\xrightarrow{\beta}$ □ $\xrightarrow{\alpha}$ stable

KEY WORDS

alpha particle • antineutrino • atomic number • background radiation • beta particle • gamma ray • isotope • mass number • nuclide • radioisotope

5.2 Properties of radiation

Ionisation

When **radiation** passes through a material it causes **ionisation**. This means that the atoms in the material have electrons removed leaving them as positively charged ions.

Alpha radiation causes the most ionisation; beta radiation is approximately ten times less ionising than alpha, and gamma radiation a further ten times less ionising.

a How many times more ionising is alpha radiation compared to gamma radiation?

Speed

Alpha radiation is relatively slow moving, travelling at one tenth the speed of light. Beta radiation is nine times faster than alpha radiation. Gamma radiation, being part of the electromagnetic spectrum, travels at the speed of light.

b What is the speed of beta radiation?

Range

Alpha radiation has a very short range. It travels only a few centimetres in air before being destroyed. Beta radiation has a range of a few metres, but the range of gamma radiation is, in theory, infinite. Gamma radiation obeys an inverse square law.

$$\text{radiation detected} \propto \frac{1}{\text{distance}^2}$$

c What happens to the amount of radiation detected if a gamma source is moved from 5 cm to 20 cm from the detector?

Penetration

Alpha radiation is absorbed by thin, not very dense materials such as paper or skin.

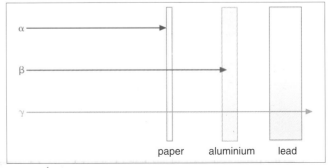

fig 11 | Penetrative properties of alpha, beta and gamma radiation

Beta radiation will pass through paper or skin but is absorbed by a few millimetres of aluminium. Gamma radiation has very high energy and can penetrate many centimetres of lead and even thicker amounts of concrete.

Detecting radiation

Geiger–Müller tube

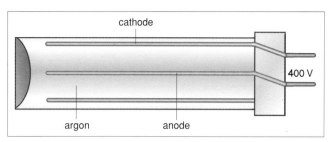

fig 12 | A Geiger–Müller tube

The **Geiger–Müller (G–M) tube** contains argon gas that ionises when ionising radiation passes through it. The positive ions move to the cathode and the negative electrons move to the anode. This produces a small electric current, which is either detected on a counter, or causes the characteristic 'click'.

Spark counter

A **spark counter** works in a similar way. There is a metal grid a few millimetres above a fine wire. The grid is earthed and the wire has a high voltage applied to it. Alpha radiation ionises the air and causes a spark.

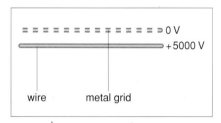

fig 14 | A spark counter

fig 13 | A Geiger–Müller counter

Film badge

Film badges are worn by people who are exposed to ionising radiation in their jobs. The plastic badge contains a special type of photographic film that records the amount of radiation received. The badge is lined with different thicknesses of different metal and plastic. The badge works because of the different penetrative properties of alpha, beta and gamma radiations.

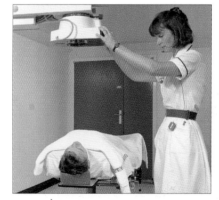

fig 15 | A radiographer wears a film badge

Thinking further

■ **1** A Geiger counter, near to a radioactive source, is counting at an average rate of 700 counts per minute. When a sheet of paper is placed in front of the G–M tube the count rate falls to 655 counts per minute. Explain what type of radiation is being emitted from the source.

◆ **2** A film badge has three areas; open to the air, aluminium foil, thin lead. After being exposed to radiation, the film under the open area is black, under the foil the film is slightly exposed, but the film under the lead is unexposed. Explain what type or types of radiation has reached the film in the badge.

KEY WORDS

film badge • Geiger–Müller tube • ionisation • radiation • spark counter

 Absorption of radioactivity.

5.3 Radioactive decay

Key points

- When a radioisotope emits radiation and changes into another isotope this is known as radioactive decay.
- Radioactive decay is random.
- The activity of an isotope is a measure of its rate of decay.
- The time it takes for radioisotopes to decay varies from isotope to isotope – even isotopes of the same element.
- We measure the radioactive decay time in a 'period' called half-life.
- Different half-lives allow us to use isotopes for particular jobs.

Decay

Radioactive **decay** is a random process. This means that it is impossible to predict exactly when a particular atom will emit radiation. However, even the smallest amount of radioactive material will contain millions of atoms. Although decay is random, the large number of atoms means that an average pattern of behaviour is obtained.

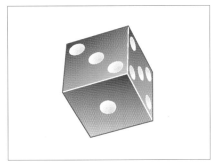

fig 16

Imagine throwing a die. Each time you throw there is a one in six chance of throwing a six. Each throw is random, but after a very large number of throws, one sixth of them will be a 'six'.
The same thing can be done using a computer to generate a sequence of random numbers. These numbers were produced in this way.6, 1, 6, 2, 1, 3, 5, 3, 4, 3, 5, 1, 5, 4, 4, 6, 5, 5, 3, 2, 5, 5, 4, 1, 1, 3, 4, 2, 1, 2.

With just 30 numbers, the pattern is quite varied. As many as seven 'fives' and as few as three 'sixes'.

a If the experiment with dice was repeated 1000 times, how many sixes would be thrown?

Measuring activity

The decaying nucleus is known as the **parent nuclide** and the nucleus formed from the decay is called the **daughter nuclide**. The **activity** of a radioactive sample is a measure of the rate of decay and is measured in units called **becquerels** (Bq).

$$\text{activity} = \frac{\text{number of nuclei which decay}}{\text{time taken in seconds}}$$

Half-life

The **half-life** of an isotope is the average time it takes for the number of undecayed nuclei in a radioactive sample to halve. If at the beginning of an experiment there are **N** undecayed nuclei, after one half-life there will be **N**/2. After a further half-life there will be **N**/4 and so on. Half-lives can vary from less than a microsecond to thousands of millions of years.

Fig 17 shows graphically the results from an experiment investigating how a sample of sodium-24 decayed.

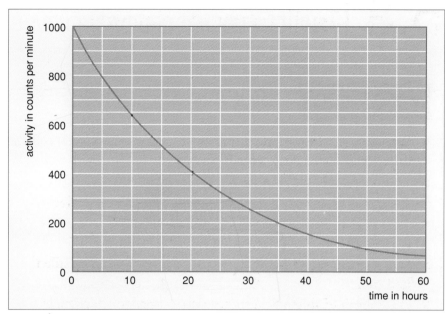

fig 17 | Decay curve for sodium-24

Use the graph for the decay of sodium-24 to answer these questions.

b What was the count rate after 10 hours?

c What is the half-life of sodium-24?

d After how many hours was the count rate 100 counts per minute?

e After how many hours would the count rate be 50 counts per minute?

Thinking further

■ **1** The decay of a radioactive source is measured for ten minutes. During that time 36 600 nuclei decay. Calculate the average activity of the source during that time.

◆ **2** A Geiger counter was used to measure the radiation from a source of chlorine-38 every fifteen minutes for $1\frac{1}{4}$ hours starting at 3 o'clock. The table shows how the count rate (in counts per minute) changed during the experiment.

time of day	3.00	3.15	3.30	3.45	4.00	4.15
count rate in counts per minute	780	591	440	340	255	194

fig 18

Plot a suitable graph and use it to find the half-life of chlorine-38.

KEY WORDS

activity • becquerel • daughter nuclide • decay • half-life • parent nuclide

Simulation of radioactive decay.

5.4 Using penetrative power of radioactivity

Key points

- Radioactivity has a large number of uses which rely on the differing penetrative power of radiation.
- These uses include thickness measurement, smoke alarms, treatment of cancer and tracer techniques.
- The isotope used is chosen because of both its penetrative properties and its half-life.

Thickness measurement

The amount of radiation which passes through a material depends on the nature of the radiation and the thickness of the material. Radioactive sources can be used to control thickness of paper and metal sheeting in rolling mills.

The radioactive source is placed on one side of the material to be measured with a detector on the other. If the material is too thick, less radiation is detected and a signal can be fed back to the rollers to increase the pressure and so produce thinner material.

fig 19 | Checking liquid levels in a bottling plant

Bottling and canning plants use a similar principle to find out if bottles and cans are filled to the correct level.

a Explain why gamma radiation is not suitable to use in a paper rolling mill.

b Why is gamma radiation used in a canning plant and not beta radiation?

Flaw detection

When metals are cast, or when pieces of metal are welded together, it is not possible to see the inside of the cast or weld. X-rays are not penetrating enough but gamma radiation can pass through the metal. If there is a flaw (for example an air bubble in a casting) more radiation will pass through than expected. This will be detected by a photographic film placed on the other side of the casting to the source of gamma radiation.

Smoke alarms

Smoke alarms rely on the ionisation properties of alpha radiation. A source of americium-241 ionises the air and allows a small current to pass in a circuit. Smoke absorbs the radiation so the circuit is incomplete and an alarm sounds.

c The half-life of americium-241 is 460 years. Why is it sensible to use a material with a long half-life in a smoke detector?

fig 20 | A smoke alarm

Treatment of cancer

Radiation kills living cells because it ionises the atoms and molecules within them. **Cancer** cells are destroyed by radiation. The gamma radiation from cobalt-60 is used to treat internal cancers because the gamma radiation is very penetrating. Skin cancers are treated with beta sources such as phosphorus-32 or strontium-90. Fig 5, page 83 shows a brain tumour being treated with a 'gamma knife'. This is not really a knife at all, but a non-invasive tool that replaces the scalpel with a focused array of 201 intersecting beams of low-level gamma radiation.

d Why is skin cancer treated with beta radiation and not gamma radiation?

Tracer techniques

A small quantity of radioisotope (**tracer**) injected into a liquid in a 'tube' can indicate how the liquid is moving along the tube. Tubes can vary in size from oil pipelines across deserts to capillaries in the human body. The passage of the radioisotope is monitored outside the tube with an appropriate detector. The radioactive source used would emit either beta or gamma radiation and usually have a relatively short half-life. Fig 21 shows how easily liquid flow in an underground pipeline can be monitored. Fig 22 shows the uptake of iodine in the thyroid gland.

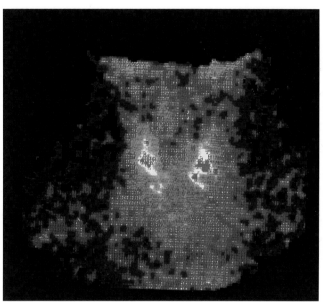

fig 22 | The thyroid gland is located in the front of your neck. The thyroid secretes a hormone, thyroxine, that controls your metabolic rate. Thyroxine contains iodine. Radioactive iodine is used as a tracer to detect whether the uptake of iodine in the thyroid gland is at its correct level. If, within 24 hours of the tracer being given, there is a larger than normal amount of radioactive iodine in the thyroid, it means that the thyroid has an abnormal 'hunger' for iodine. The red and yellow areas show the position of the thyroid gland in the neck. The different colours give an indication of the amount of radiation detected.

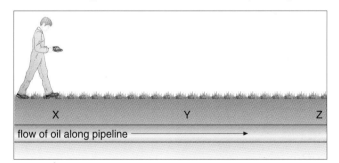

X   Y   Z

flow of oil along pipeline ⟶

fig 21 | Using a Geiger counter to monitor flow in a pipeline

Thinking further

1 Fig 21 shows a pipeline **XYZ** being monitored above ground with a Geiger counter. A source of beta radiation has been used as the tracer. Describe how the reading on the Geiger counter changes as the person walks from X to Z if there is a **leak** at **Y**.

2 How would the pipe be monitored to detect a **blockage** in the pipe at **Y**? What results would you expect as the person walks along the pipe?

3 Suggest why there are a large number of beams of low-level radiation in the gamma knife and not just one intense beam.

KEY WORDS
cancer • tracer

 Demonstrate smoke alarm.

5.5 Other uses of radioactivity

Key points

■ Radioactivity has a large number of other uses including sterilisation and dating of artefacts and rocks.

Sterilisation

Large amounts of gamma radiation will destroy bacteria. Many everyday items are **sterilised** by gamma irradiation. Food is preserved for longer if there are no **bacteria** to make it rot.
The ingredients in cosmetics, sterilised compost and the surgical instruments used by doctors and nurses are all routinely sterilised by high levels of gamma radiation.

a Suggest why it is better to sterilise plastic syringes by gamma radiation instead of by boiling in water.

fig 23

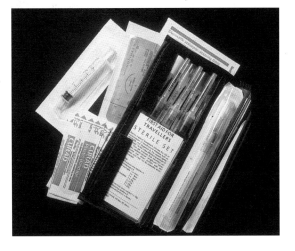

Dating artefacts

All living things take in carbon. Plants need carbon dioxide for photosynthesis. Most of the carbon in carbon dioxide is stable carbon-12 but a small portion is in the form of carbon-14, an unstable radioactive isotope, which decays to nitrogen.
When living things die, they stop taking in carbon and the carbon-14 already present continues to decay. Because it decays at a steady, known rate, scientists can measure the amount of carbon-14 remaining. They then compare the amount of carbon-14 with the amount of carbon-12. The lower the proportion of carbon-14, the older the sample.

As well as plants and animals being used as samples, materials made from plants such as, cotton, parchment, linen and coal can also be tested for their carbon-14 content.

On Thursday, 19 September, 1991, Helmut and Erika Simon were enjoying a walk high in the Alps. They saw a gully filled with ice and melting water. Suddenly a brown object caught Helmut's eye. At first they thought the object was a large doll which had been left in the mountains, but they soon realised that it was a human body frozen in the ice. The body's skin was stretched taut, making its bones and spine clearly visible. Erika Simon later said, 'We thought the accident probably happened ten or twenty years ago'. **Radiocarbon dating** showed the Iceman to be between 5300 and 5350 years old.

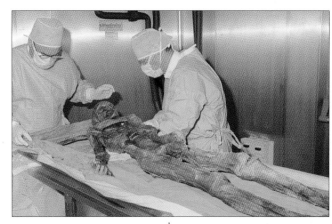

fig 24 | The Iceman

Other important artefacts to be dated with the aid of radioactive carbon have been the Turin Shroud (originally believed to be the cloth which was wrapped around Jesus in the tomb) dated at about 500–600 years old and the Dead Sea Scrolls (nearly 2000 years old).

b The carbon in living things comes from photosynthesis. How does the carbon find its way into animals?

Dating rocks

In a similar way to radiocarbon dating, the dating of rocks works by looking at the relative amounts of isotopes in the rocks. In rocks, uranium-238 slowly decays, via other elements with relatively short half-lives, to stable lead-206.

If the quantities of $^{238}_{92}$U and $^{206}_{82}$Pb are the same, then the rock is one half-life old (4.5×10^9 years). The more uranium-238 there is, the newer the rock.

fig 25 | The face on the Turin Shroud

This technique has been used to date rock from the Moon. The estimated age of the Moon rock is 4400 million years old.

c The Earth is estimated to be between twelve and eighteen billion years old. What does the dating of Moon rock tell us about the Moon?

Thinking further

■ **1** Suggest why the ingredients in cosmetics are sterilised before manufacture.

◆ **2** Why is it of benefit that the intermediate isotopes in the uranium-lead decay chain have relatively short half-lives?

◆ **3** Suggest why it is not possible to be precise when dating artefacts and rocks.

— **KEY WORDS** —————————
bacteria • radiocarbon dating • sterilised

 Research on Turin shroud, Iceman and radiocarbon dating from Internet.

5.6 Using radioactivity safely

Key points

- Exposure to radioactivity is dangerous.
- Radiation effects are cumulative.
- Radiation can cause burns, sickness, reduction in lymphocyte count, hair loss, as well as cancer.
- People who use radioactivity need to observe safety precautions based on the properties of the radiations.

Biological effects

Alpha, beta and gamma radiations are examples of ionising radiations. This means the radiation can change the nature of any other atom they collide with. This causes changes in the structure and behaviour of molecules in cells. If a large number of cells are damaged, it affects the processes going on in the body. The person exposed to a high dose of radioactivity feels very ill. This is called **radiation sickness**. The skin is also probably damaged by **radiation burns**. These are similar in appearance to heat burns but take much longer to heal.

High levels of radiation also cause a reduction in the **lymphocyte** count. This means that the person's ability to resist infection and fight disease is reduced. Hair loss is a common consequence of exposure to radiation. People who have radiotherapy as part of their medical treatment often suffer hair loss.

a Explain why a person receiving treatment for cancer might feel very sick afterwards.

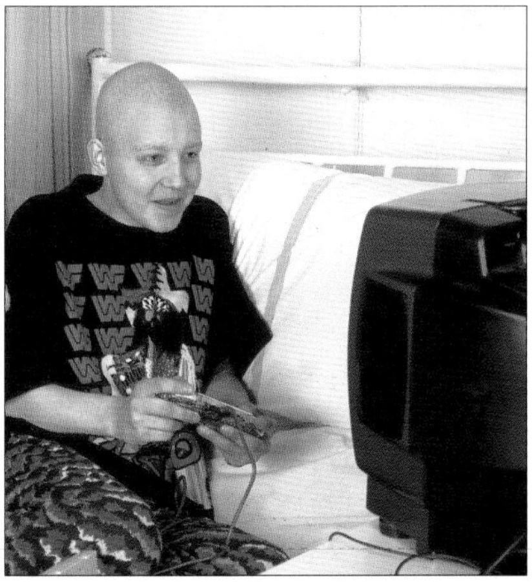

fig 26 | A patient having received radiotherapy suffers hair loss

Often, exposure to radioactivity does not have an immediate effect. It is **cumulative** and long lasting. People often develop leukaemia or cancer several years after being exposed to radiation.

An important chemical in cells is **DNA**. If the DNA is damaged, the cell may behave very differently from normal. This is called **mutation**. Exposure to radiation can cause mutation. Sometimes this is not harmful but sometimes it causes the cell to divide uncontrollably. Uncontrolled cell division may develop into cancer.

Protection

Distance

The further away you are from a radioactive source, the less radiation you receive. Even with gamma radiation, doubling the distance reduces the amount of radiation by a factor of four. In the laboratory, radioactive sources are handled with tongs, increasing the distance of the source from the user.

Shielding

The use of a shield between the user and the source reduces the amount of radiation. The type of shielding needed depends upon the nature of the radiation. Schools use 'sealed sources' which are housed in lead pots.

b What is the minimum shielding needed to protect a user from a source of beta radiation?

Time

Radioactive sources should be used for the shortest time possible before being returned to their storage. This reduces the cumulative effects of exposure to radiation.

Direction

Never point radioactive sources at the body, especially not at the eyes or reproductive organs. These parts of the body are ten times more easily damaged than the extremities – hands and feet.

Activity

Most experiments in school can be performed with sources that are not very radioactive. It is not necessary to use very radioactive sources in schools and all experiments should use the least radioactive source possible in order to do the experiment.

Transport

When radioactive material is transported, it is done so in flasks which have to withstand the worst possible accident.

In 1984, at a British Rail test track in Leicester a 140 tonne train, travelling at 100 miles an hour, was driven into a flask which had been placed on the track in its most vulnerable position. Although the train was destroyed, the flask in the train crash received only minor damage.

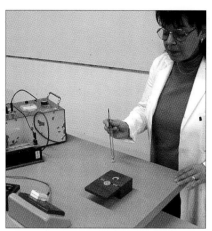

fig 27 | The teacher handles the sealed source with tongs and returns it to a lead pot as soon as she has used it

fig 28 | Collision between a train and a flask designed to hold radioactive material

Thinking further

■ **1** The law does not allow students under the age of sixteen to handle radioactive material. Suggest why this is so.

◆ **2** A Geiger counter gives a count rate of 770 counts per minute at a distance of 1 cm from a source. The teacher handles the source with tongs 10 cm long. How does this affect the amount of radiation he is exposed to?

KEY WORDS

cumulative • DNA • lymphocyte • mutation • radiation burns • radiation sickness

Questions on radioactivity

1 Finish the following sentences by choosing the **best** words from this list.

electrons • negative • neutrons • nucleus • positive • protons

Alpha radiation contains _____ and _____ which come from the _____ of the atom.

Beta radiation contains high speed _____ which come from the _____ of the atom.

The charge of alpha radiation is _____.
The charge of beta radiation is _____. *(7)*

2 Describe how gamma radiation is different from alpha and beta radiation. *(2)*

3 Americium-241 emits alpha radiation. It is the source used in smoke detectors. Suggest **two** reasons why a smoke detector uses alpha radiation. *(2)*

4 A radioisotope changes to another isotope with an atomic number higher than the original. Which of the following statements are true and which are false?

A The radioisotope has decayed by emitting **only** alpha radiation.

B The radioisotope has decayed by emitting beta radiation.

C The radioisotope could have emitted gamma radiation. *(3)*

5 $^{235}_{92}$U and $^{238}_{92}$U are two important isotopes of uranium. How are the atomic structures of the two isotopes similar and how are they different? *(3)*

6 Marie uses a Geiger counter and measures background radiation as 50 counts per minute. She then measures the count rate from a sample of radon gas. It records 1650 counts per minute. The half-life of the radon gas is 56 seconds. After how long will the count rate from the radon gas be similar to background radiation? *(3)*

7 a A source of gamma radiation and a source of alpha radiation are held 30 cm away from a person. Explain why the gamma radiation is more harmful. *(3)*

b A source of gamma radiation and a source of alpha radiation are swallowed by a person. Explain why the alpha radiation is more harmful. *(3)*

8 Uranium-235 has a half-life of 700 million years. It decays to form lead-207. Why is it not suitable to use to estimate the age of Earth rocks? *(1)*

9 A radioactive sample was tested with a Geiger counter every six hours. The average count rates in counts per minute were recorded.

time in hours	0	6	12	18	24
count rate in counts per minute	1113	1082	1054	1091	1090

fig **29**

a Explain why the count rates are different. *(1)*

b The average background count rate for the day was 32 counts per minute. Describe the sample in as much detail as possible. *(3)*

IDEAS AND EVIDENCE

10 Read the following report from *The Daily Telegraph* newspaper, 1 October 1999. Then answer the questions which follow.

Lessons of Chernobyl not been learned

Disaster fear after blast hits N-plant

The accident at the Tokaimura re-processing plant is the most serious peacetime nuclear disaster Japan has faced, but is nowhere near as serious as Chernobyl.

The Chernobyl accident had international repercussions because the explosion rocketed ▶

far into the atmosphere, where winds were able to scatter the radioactivity for thousands of miles.

At Tokaimura, there was a limited amount of fuel and fallout from the explosion was much more localized. Deaths are likely to be confined to the immediate vicinity of the plant, experts said last night. However, the accident has startled nuclear experts because it was a true nuclear explosion, rather than a more common problem such as a leak of coolant. Dr John Large, a nuclear engineer said: "The worst case scenario seems to be happening.". A true nuclear explosion happens when there is an excessive build-up of neutrons, which eventually attack the uranium fuel causing nuclear fission – the splitting of the atom. This fission releases even more neutrons, which attack more uranium producing an out-of-control chain reaction likely to continue until the uranium runs out. The dramatic evidence that this was a true nuclear explosion was the blue flash of neutron radiation – produced as molecules of air ionized, spewing out vast quantities of radiation. Last night, the reaction appeared to be continuing with such ferocity the authorities could not approach it. To try to bring it to a halt they would have to drench the area with the chemical boron to soak up the neutrons. The worst case scenario, is that pipes have been broken, providing a continuous flow of uranium into the reaction so that it continues for some time. The fall-out from such an incident could be up to a radius of 30 kilometres, he said. Being close to such an explosion means almost certain death from acute radiation sickness as the body endures the full force of the neutrons and gamma rays. Normally, workers are protected by metres of concrete from a critical explosion. How such a reaction could have occurred outside a purpose built reactor in a standard, small processing plant was puzzling experts last night. The work at the plant will have been devoted to taking enriched uranium, which has an excessive proportion of the splittable form, uranium-235, and converting it to uranium oxide. This puts the uranium in a convenient form for making fuel rods to supply a reactor. During the process it is dissolved in nitric acid. Usually, the plant uses 2.3 kg of uranium at a time for this

reaction but for some reason the engineers used nearly eight times the amount – 16 kg.

The excess uranium will have increased the amount of neutrons in the atmosphere, which should have been spotted by detectors. In this case warning appears not to have been given, and sufficient neutrons built up to set off nuclear fission.

The health effects will have been vastly more severe for those nearby who will instantly have developed acute radiation sickness. Dr Mike Clark, of the National Radiation Protection Board, said: "It is life threatening to anybody nearby so the workers that are ill are probably going to be lucky to escape with their lives." Further away, the environment will become laced with the breakdown products when uranium is split, such as radioactive iodine and caesium. At Chernobyl there has been a long-term increase in thyroid cancer as a result of children inhaling such iodine. But other predicted long-term health effects have not been seen, raising hopes that the long-term health effects in Japan will not be too serious.

a Why was the accident at Chernobyl more serious than the one at Tokaimura? *(1)*

b What is meant by the term **nuclear fission**? *(1)*

c When will an out-of-control chain reaction stop? *(1)*

d Write down the name of an element which absorbs neutrons. *(1)*

e What effect would there be on people living within 30 km of a nuclear explosion? *(2)*

f What normally protects workers from the effects of radiation? *(1)*

g What is **enriched uranium**? *(2)*

h Why should the process of dissolving the uranium in nitric acid only use a maximum of 2.3 kg of uranium? *(2)*

i What elements might be formed as a result of nuclear fission? *(2)*

j What effect do these products have on humans? *(2)*

The Earth and Universe

From the very beginning of civilisation people have been fascinated by what they have seen in the sky above them. The shapes made by the stars have been given names such as Orion, the Great Bear, and the Plough.

Early man thought that Earth was at the centre of everything and the Sun, the Moon and the stars in the heavens were in orbit around our planet. But early man could not see very far.

The first telescopes allowed man to see further into space. With today's technology of space telescopes, such as Hubble, and space exploration missions we can start to unravel the many mysteries of the Universe.

fig 1 | Star trails indicating relative motion

fig 2

fig 3 | Hubble Space telescope

Check-up

Have a go at the following questions. They will remind you what you should already know about the Earth and Universe.

a Write down the names of the nine planets in order from the Sun.

b What is the name of Earth's only natural satellite?

c What force keeps planets in orbit about the Sun?

d Some bodies in space are sources of light. Some reflect light. Which of the following are sources of light and which reflect light?

Earth • Mars • Moon • Star • Sun

e Artificial satellites have many uses. List five uses of artificial satellites.

If you have difficulties, your teacher has a Summary sheet you can have.

Contents of the Teaching block

This Teaching block is divided into three double page spreads.

6.1 Our Solar System

You already know the names and positions of the planets in our Solar System. We will now look at other bodies and explain how and why they behave as they do.

fig 4 | The Solar System

6.2 The life cycle of stars

Stars have not always been there. They are born and they die. Thanks to present-day technology, we are able to witness the changes.

fig 5 | The formation of stars captured by the Hubble Space telescope

6.3 The origin and evolution of the Universe

Scientists have various theories about how the Universe began billions of years ago, how it is changing now and how it will evolve in the future. We will examine some of these theories.

Links with other Teaching blocks

2.4 **Forces and energy**   5.1, 5.5 **Radioactivity**

6.1 Our Solar System

planet	diameter in km	average distance from Sun in millions of km	time to orbit Sun in Earth units
Mercury	4800	57	88 days
Venus	12 200	108	224 days
Earth	12 800	149	1 year
Mars	7000	228	1.9 years
Jupiter	143 000	780	11.9 years
Saturn	120 000	1425	29.5 years
Uranus	49 000	2900	84 years
Neptune	50 000	4500	165 years
Pluto	4000	5900	248 years

fig 6

Planets

Earth and the other eight **planets** orbit the Sun. They form part of our **Solar System**. There are also minor planets or **asteroids** and **comets**.

The planets are all different sizes. They take different times to orbit the Sun. Fig 6 gives some information about the planets.

a Which planet comes closest to the Earth?

b Two planets are much larger than the rest. Which are they?

c Pluto was not discovered until 1930, much later than other planets. Suggest two reasons for this.

fig 7 | The asteroid Gaspra

Asteroids

Most asteroids are in a 'belt' between two of the major planets.

d One of the asteroids in this 'belt' is called Gaspra. It takes 3.29 years to orbit the Sun. Between which two planets are most asteroids found?

Another asteroid, called Eros, is being studied. It is closer to the Sun than most asteroids. It has an orbit time of only 1.76 years, which means that it is quite close to Earth. Some scientists are worried that it might collide with Earth.

fig 8 | Comet Halley

Comets

Comets

- are made of lumps of ice, dust and gas
- orbit the Sun in elliptical orbits which pass very close to the Sun; many extend beyond Pluto.

When they pass close to the Sun, some of the ice melts forming a large cloud of dust and gas. The solar wind from the Sun blows

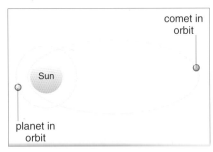

fig 9

this cloud into a tail which stretches for maybe hundreds of millions of kilometres.

Fig 9 shows a planet and a comet orbiting the Sun.

e How are the orbits of the planet and the comet different?

Gravitational forces

All bodies are attracted to all other bodies by gravitational forces. These forces are usually quite weak unless the mass of the bodies is very large. The Sun, the planets and the moons in our Solar System are massive, so the gravitational forces are large. With no atmosphere in space to provide friction, bodies would continue travelling in straight lines without the pull of **gravity**.

Consider a **satellite** orbiting Earth. (Remember, the Moon is a satellite as well.) The satellite travels at such a speed that it is falling to Earth at the same rate as Earth is falling away from it, so it stays the same distance away from Earth.

Imagine throwing a ball from the top of Mount Everest (fig 10). Ball A is not thrown very fast and soon falls to Earth. Ball B is thrown faster so goes further before falling to Earth and ball C is thrown faster still and 'falls' into orbit.

Artificial satellites orbit Earth at different heights depending on their job. The greater the height, the longer it takes to orbit Earth.

A weather satellite, 700 km above the Earth's surface, takes 100 minutes to orbit. A communication satellite, 36 000 km above the Earth's equator, takes 24 hours to orbit. We call this type of orbit **geo-stationary**.

f Suggest why a satellite orbiting at 36 000 km is said to be in geo-stationary orbit.

g Weather satellites are often in **polar orbit**. Suggest what is meant by polar orbit.

The greater the distance between the Sun and any other body in the Solar System, the weaker the gravitational attraction. The size of the force is inversely proportional to the square of the distance between them. $\text{force} \propto \dfrac{1}{(\text{distance})^2}$

The name given to this force, which keeps things moving in a circle, is a **centripetal force**. It is acting towards the centre of the circular orbit.

h The force of attraction between the Sun and Mercury is about sixteen times greater than the force of attraction between the Sun and Mars. Use the table on page 100 to explain this.

For any body in orbit, the greater the gravitational force, the faster the body moves.

i Copy the diagram showing the path of a comet around the Sun. Mark an X on the orbit to show where the speed of the comet is greatest.

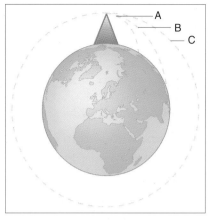

fig 10

Thinking further

1 Use the data from the table (fig 6) on page 100 to plot a graph of time to orbit the Sun against distance from the Sun. Use this graph to find out how far Gaspra is from the Sun.

2 The radius of Earth is 6400 km. Use the information about geo-stationary orbits to calculate the speed of a satellite in geo-stationary orbit.

3a Calculate the speed of each planet in millions of km per day.

b Plot a graph to show that the distance of a planet from the Sun is proportional to $\dfrac{1}{(\text{speed})^2}$.

┌─ **KEY WORDS** ─────────
asteroid • centripetal force • comet • geo-stationary orbit • gravity • planet • polar orbit • satellite • Solar System
└────────────────────────

🖳 *Internet research with NASA sites.*

6.2 The life cycle of stars (1)

The birth of a star

A star is formed when large clouds of gas and dust start to clump together. These clouds are called **nebulae**.

Gravity pulls the gas and dust closer together and it becomes a spinning ball of gas. The ball of gas is so tightly packed together that it starts to get hot and after some time it starts to glow. This **protostar** shines but cannot be seen because it is hidden by the cloud of gas and dust. As it gets smaller it gets even hotter. After millions of years the protostar's core is hot enough for hydrogen nuclei to join together to form helium. This is called nuclear fusion and is the same reaction as in a hydrogen bomb. In **nuclear fusion**, six hundred million tonnes of hydrogen are changed into helium every second. Some of this mass is lost as energy.

fig 11 | The Eagle nebula

a Deuterium and tritium are isotopes of hydrogen. What is meant by the term isotope?

The adult star

Once a star starts to produce energy, it does not change much for many millions of years. As long as there is a supply of hydrogen gas it will continue to shine.

The time it takes for the hydrogen to be used up depends on the size of the star. Surprisingly, smaller stars live longer than larger ones. Although they have more fuel to start with, the larger stars make more energy and so use up their hydrogen faster. Very large stars may only shine brilliantly for millions of years. Smaller stars start with less hydrogen gas, use it up more slowly and shine for billions of years. Our Sun's lifetime will be about 10 billion (10×10^9) years.

b Use the information about the expected lifetime of the Sun and the rate at which hydrogen is being converted to explain whether the following statement is true or false.

Our Sun contains nearly 2×10^{26} tonnes of hydrogen.

The death of a star

When a star has used up the hydrogen gas in its core and cannot make any more energy it starts to die. When an average sized star, like our Sun, stops making energy, its core starts to contract. But the outer part of the star expands, gets cooler and changes from yellow to red. It becomes a **red giant**. The Sun may expand to a hundred times its present size. It will swallow up Mercury and Venus. Its outer edge may even reach Earth.

All that is left of the original star is the hot core that has shrunk down until it is about the size of Earth. It is very hot and shines as a tiny white star called a **white dwarf**. It no longer makes energy, so very gradually it cools and fades. Its colour changes from white to yellow to red. It then stops shining. Eventually it becomes a **black dwarf.**

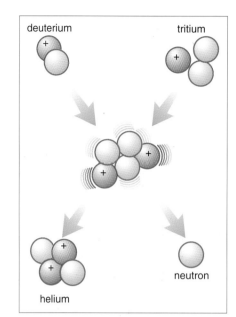

fig 12 | Hydrogen nuclei fuse to form helium and release energy

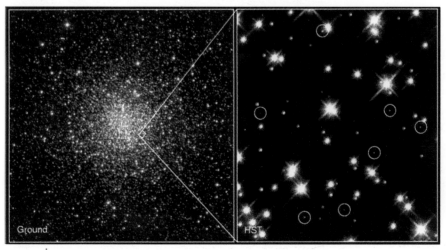

fig 13 | Seven white dwarfs (circled) photographed by the Hubble Space telescope

continued ▶

6.2 The Life cycle of stars (2)

Large stars, which contain at least eight times more material than the Sun, will end with a gigantic explosion. They only live for a few million years, shining brightly as **blue supergiants**, but when the hydrogen is used up they expand into **red supergiants**, similar to the red giants from smaller stars.

The core of such a large star shrinks and becomes very hot; hot enough for the atoms of gas to combine to make other new materials, including carbon, oxygen and iron. These materials form in layers, the densest on the inside. While this is happening the star is making energy and is still shining. It stops making energy when the core contains mainly iron. In a very short space of time, less than a second, the core collapses and there is a violent explosion. The whole star, except the core, is thrown outwards and destroyed. This explosion is called a **supernova** and the resulting core, containing mainly neutrons, is called a **neutron star**. A neutron star is very dense. Imagine adding a teaspoonful of sugar to a cup of tea. Just that one teaspoonful of a neutron star would have a mass of one hundred million tonnes.

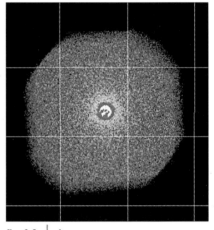

fig 14 | A supernova

The star may shine very brightly for a short time. It may even outshine the rest of its galaxy. The material thrown out by the explosion makes a shell of gas, which expands outwards bumping into the gas and dust in space. Astronomers can see these huge glowing clouds of gas, which are called **supernova remnants**.

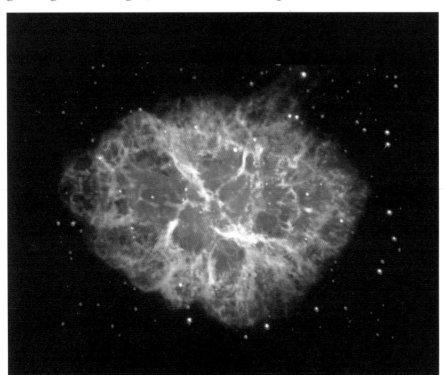

fig 15 | The Crab Nebula seen from Earth

One famous supernova remnant is called the Crab Nebula because of its strange shape. The explosion that threw out this glowing cloud was seen by Chinese astronomers nearly a thousand years ago in 1054. It was so bright that it could be seen in the daylight for three weeks.

Eventually, the supernova remnant will merge into the other gas and dust in space and the whole life cycle will start again. The Solar System is made of these recycled materials. Planets contain material that must have come from the inside of giant stars or from supernova explosions.

c Our Sun is sometimes called a 'second generation star'. Explain why.

Depending on the size of the star, the core could continue to collapse even more. When this happens, it becomes extremely dense.

The object at the centre of fig 16 weighs as much as three billion suns, but is concentrated into a space no larger than our solar system. Gravitational forces are so large that not even light can escape. This former star is called a **black hole.**

d Suggest why a **black** hole is given this name.

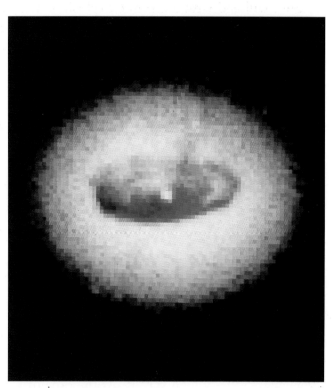

fig 16 | A black hole

Thinking further

■ **1** Fig 17 represents the life cycle of stars. Copy and complete the diagram by writing the correct words in the circles.

◆ **2** The Sun produces energy at a rate of 400×10^{24} joules each second.
Einstein's famous equation $E = mc^2$ relates the amount of energy produced (E) to the mass lost (m) and the speed of light (c). If the speed of light is 300×10^6 m/s, calculate the loss in mass of the Sun each second.

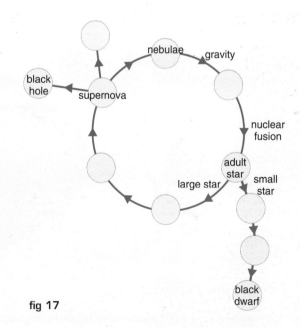

fig 17

KEY WORDS

black dwarf • black hole • blue supergiant • isotope • nebulae • neutron star • nuclear fusion • protostar • red giant • red supergiant • supernova • supernova remnants • white dwarf

6.3 The evolution of the Universe (1)

Key points

- The whole Universe is expanding.
- It might have started billions of years ago in one place with a huge explosion – the Big Bang.
- Theories for the origin of the Universe take into account that light from other galaxies is shifted to the red end of the spectrum *and* the further away galaxies are, the greater the red shift.
- One way of explaining this is that other galaxies are moving away from us very

quickly *and* galaxies furthest from us are moving fastest.
- There are possible futures for the Universe depending on the amount of mass in the Universe and the speed at which the galaxies are moving apart.
- Knowledge of the rate of expansion of the Universe enables its age to be estimated.
- Scientists are trying to find evidence for life on other planets in the Solar System and elsewhere in the Universe.

The Big Bang Theory

Scientists believe that the Universe was formed about fifteen billion years ago with an enormous explosion – the **Big Bang**. Following the explosion, all the matter in the Universe started to move apart at very high speeds. At the time of the Big Bang, there were no galaxies, stars or planets. The Universe was extremely hot, but as it expanded, it cooled down and galaxies formed. These galaxies continue to move away from each other whilst stars have formed within them.

Astronomers are able to measure the distance between galaxies and the speed at which they are moving. They can therefore predict where the galaxies started from. All their calculations indicate that all of the galaxies started in the same place. This supports the idea of a Big Bang.

a Which galaxy is our Solar System a part of?

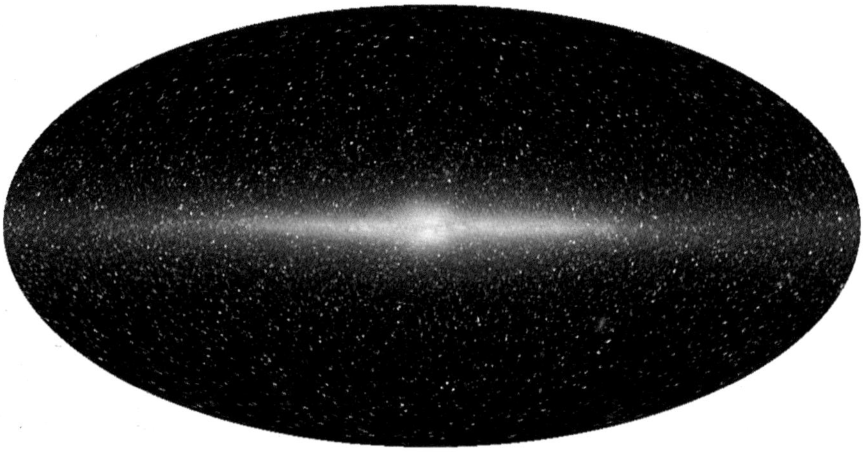

fig 18 | The Milky Way

The expanding Universe

It was not until the 1920s that Edwin Hubble made the discoveries which have shaped the way scientists think today. Hubble discovered that galaxies were not only far away, but also that with the exception of a few nearby ones, the others seem to be moving away from us. He also discovered that the more distant the galaxy, the faster it is moving away. Every galaxy is moving away from every other galaxy. This could only mean that the whole Universe is expanding.

Astronomers can tell that the Universe is expanding by looking at the light coming from the galaxies. If a galaxy is moving away from us, then the wavelength appears longer, and the light will be redder than usual. This is called **red shift**. The red shift is larger if the galaxy is moving away more quickly.

The Doppler effect

You have all probably experienced the **Doppler effect**. When a police car is coming towards you sounding its siren, the pitch (frequency) appears to increase. When it passes and moves away from you, the pitch suddenly decreases.

A stationary police car with its siren sounding sends out circular sound wavefronts. Fig 20 shows how these wavefronts spread out.

fig 19

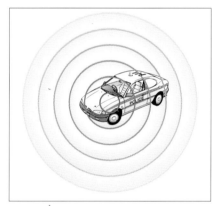

fig 20 | Sound wavefronts spread out from a stationary vehicle

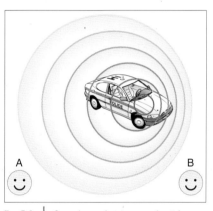

fig 21 | Sound wavefronts spread out from a moving vehicle

But if the police car is moving, it has changed its position between the time it produces one note and the next.

The car is moving away from the person at A. The wavelength appears longer so the pitch is lower. The reverse is true for the person at B. The wavelength appears shorter so the pitch is higher.

Exactly the same thing happens with light. The longer wavelength shifts colours to the red end of the spectrum.

b Fig 22 shows our nearest neighbouring galaxy, Andromeda. What is the main colour from the galaxy?

c Suggest a name for this effect.

d What does this tell us about the Andromeda galaxy?

fig 22 | The Andromeda galaxy

continued ▶

6.3 The evolution of the Universe (2)

The age of the Universe

The most distant objects visible are called **quasars**. They are thought to be the most luminous objects in the Universe. Light from them shows large amounts of red shift, suggesting that they are travelling at nearly the speed of light. Using Hubble's theories, it is estimated that they could be twelve billion light years away. Astronomers use information like this to estimate the age of the Universe.

The future of the Universe

Nobody knows whether the Universe will continue to expand or whether something will happen to stop it. The future of the Universe depends on the amount of matter contained within it.

- With our present knowledge, scientists believe that there is not enough matter in the Universe to stop the expansion. If this is true, the galaxies will get further and further away from each other. The gas and dust that have been making the stars in the galaxies will be used up. No more stars will be formed.

e Suggest what will happen to the brightness and temperature of the Universe if no more stars are formed.

- If there is more matter than we know about, then gravitational forces will slow the rate of expansion and the Universe could become of a stable finite size.

- With the possibility of even more matter, then not only would the Universe stop expanding but it would start collapsing instead. The galaxies would start moving towards each other and everything would be squashed together again as it was at the time of the Big Bang. This is sometimes known as the **Big Crunch.** What might happen then? The cycle could start again with another Big Bang or the enormous density might result in the formation of a very large black hole.

Life elsewhere?

The early science fiction writers wrote about man landing on the Moon. For many years they have told stories of aliens in space and the search for life on other planets. Today, science fiction is becoming science fact. Man first walked on the Moon more than 30 years ago.

Inhabited space stations orbit Earth. There have been suggestions that the conditions on Mars are such that life could have existed there.

fig 23

fig 24 | Exploring the Martian landscape

Attempts are being made to contact other life forms if they do exist. In 1974 a coded radio signal was sent in the direction of another galaxy. Because of the large distances involved, the signal will take 25 000 years to reach any planet in the galaxy and another 25 000 years before any reply is received.

Spaceships containing plaques showing pictures of a man and a woman, together with a diagram of our Solar System are on journeys out of our Solar System. Voyager space probes carry records containing sounds of Earth and greetings in many languages.

The conquest of space is only just beginning. It will still be many years before man visits another planet and a very long time before another galaxy is visited.

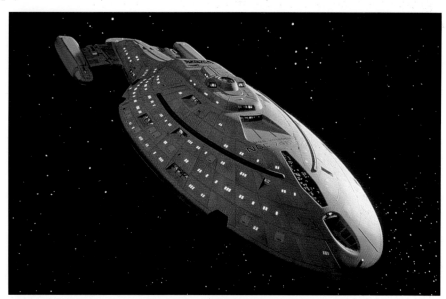

fig 25 | Is today's science fiction tomorrow's science fact?

Thinking further

■ **1** The age of the Universe is estimated to be between twelve and eighteen billion years. What evidence is there to support this?

◆ **2** Mars is one of our nearest neighbours. What conditions will need to exist on Mars before mankind could live there? How could we establish a colony on Mars?

┌─ **KEY WORDS** ─────────────────────────────
Big Bang • Big Crunch • Doppler effect • quasar • red shift
└──

Questions on the Earth and Universe

● **1** Which of the following statements are true and which are false?

A The Moon is a planet in the Solar System.
B Earth is part of the Andromeda galaxy.
C A galaxy showing blue shift is moving towards us.
D Some galaxies are moving at speeds faster than the speed of light.
E A light year is a measure of distance.
F The Universe is less than five billion years old.
G Nuclear fusion is the breaking up of heavy nuclei to release energy.
H Satellites orbit above the equator and above the poles. *(8)*

■ **2** A distant galaxy is moving in a spiral as it moves away from our own. When light from the galaxy reaches us, one side of it appears to be red and the other side blue. Suggest a reason for this. *(2)*

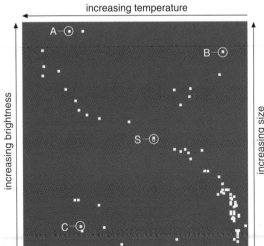

fig 26

■ **3** Fig 27 shows a Hertsprung–Russell diagram.

fig 27

It shows how the brightness, size and temperature of stars are related.

S is our Sun. What do the other labelled stars represent? Choose your answers from this list.

black dwarf • black hole
blue dwarf • blue giant
red dwarf • red giant
supernova • white dwarf *(3)*

◆ **4** On 18 May 1991, Helen Sharman became the first British astronaut.

fig 28

She worked on the Mir Space Station. Mir orbited the Earth at a height of 350 km at a speed of 7.85 km/s. The radius of Earth is 6400 km.

a Calculate the distance travelled by Mir as it orbited Earth once. *(3)*

b Calculate, to the nearest minute, how long it took for Mir to orbit Earth. *(3)*

5 Read the following report from *The Guardian* newspaper, 8 August 1996. Then answer the questions which follow.

Maybe we're all Martians, now

THEIR awe tinged with scientific caution, a panel of American scientists formally declared their belief yesterday that they had found 'evidence of past life on Mars', and immediately invited colleagues around the world to prove them wrong.

The US scientists' conclusions are based on $2^1/_2$ years of research on a meteorite, found in 1984 in Antarctica, which they believe was catapulted off Mars 16 million years ago. Research teams at Manchester University and the Open University at Milton Keynes are also studying fragments of the rock.

By coincidence, two NASA probes are about to leave for Mars in the **launch window** that comes every two years, when Earth and the red planet are aligned. The Mars Global Surveyor, to be launched in November, will map the planet. In December, the Mars Pathfinder will be launched as part of the Mars Environmental Survey and will take photographs and conduct chemical tests.

For one of the most profound moments in history, this first real evidence that we may not be alone in the universe was a curiously low-key event, as scientists gave detailed accounts of molecular chemistry and laser-induced ion maps.

'We conclude that, taken together, this is evidence for early life on Mars,' said David McKay, of the Johnson Space Centre. 'We have no confirming evidence. We don't have the chemistry. We don't know if they have cell walls or not. We have lines of evidence – none of them conclusive.'

Scientists came to Washington from US universities and government and private laboratories for the announcement. At the heart of it all was a potato-sized chunk of rock, sliced on one side where the scientists had taken samples.

At least 3.5 billion years old, it had been hewn from the surface of Mars by a meteorite strike, then tumbled through space for 16 million years before finally landing in Antarctica about 16 000 years ago.

The rock was found just in time for the latest in mass spectrometers and electron microscopes to discern fossils of bacteria. For the scientists, it was a moment of wonder. 'Who is to say that we are not all Martians, that Mars was where life first started?' said Professor Richard Zare of Stanford University, who devised the new instruments.

Mr McKay said: 'Wherever we look on Earth where we find chemicals and we find water, we find life. Why wouldn't it have evolved also in other places in the solar system?'

This latest discovery was expressed in the most prosaic terms. 'We believe the samples of magnetite we have found were produced by bacteria, based on their distinctive shape, on their chemistry, and on their environment,' said Kathy Thomas-Keprta, of Lockheed. Yesterday's panel included a sceptic, Professor Bill Schopf of UCLA, who insisted that 'extraordinary discoveries require extraordinary proof, and I think more work needs to be done'.

a What material have scientists been researching? *(1)*

b How old is the evidence they are using? *(1)*

c When did the evidence leave Mars? *(1)*

d When did the evidence arrive on Earth? *(1)*

e What has happened to the evidence in the meantime? *(1)*

f When was the evidence found? *(1)*

g Suggest what is meant by the term **launch window**. *(1)*

h 'There is definitely proof that life has existed on Mars.' Discuss whether or not this is true. *(5)*

Using electricity

The development of electricity has probably had a greater effect on people's lives than any other scientific idea in the last century. Indeed, very little progress would have been possible without the ready availability of electricity; from electric lamps to the complexities of modern computers. Just think how many electrical appliances are used every day, at home, at school and in the workplace.

This wonderful resource needs treating with respect. As well as improving our lifestyle it has the potential to maim and kill. We need to understand it and to learn how to use it safely.

This Teaching block considers some of the ways in which electricity is used, as well as some of the problems it causes. In particular we will look at electricity in our homes and the measures taken to ensure our safety.

fig 1

Check-up

Have a go at the following questions. They will remind you what you should already know about using electricity.

a List five electrical appliances that you use at home.

b List five items that use electricity outside the home.

c What is the difference between an electrical conductor and an electrical insulator? Give two examples of each.

d What do you understand by an 'electric current'? Give its unit.

e What do you understand by 'voltage'? Give its unit.

f What causes electrical resistance? Give the unit of resistance.

g Write down the formula linking current, voltage and resistance.

fig 2

h The current in the element of an electric kettle is 10 A. The voltage is 230 V. Calculate the resistance of the element.

i In what form is energy dissipated in a kettle element?

j The current in a television is less than 1 A. Suggest why the current needs to be much bigger in an electric kettle.

If you have difficulties, your teacher has a Summary sheet you could have.

Contents of the Teaching block

This Teaching block is divided into six double page spreads.

7.1 Electrostatic phenomena

We look at static electricity. Electric charges can collect on insulating materials where there is no conducting path for them to move away. This build up of charge can occur due to friction, or by a process called induction.

7.2 Uses and problems of electrostatics

Electrostatics has been put to good use, for instance in photocopiers and paint sprayers. Electrostatics also causes many problems and can be highly dangerous when near large quantities of fuel.

fig 3

7.3 Electrostatics and current

We link static and current electricity and show that they are fundamentally the same. Static charges build up on insulators, whereas an electric current requires a conducting path.

7.4 Electricity in the home

We consider how electricity is supplied to our homes as an alternating current. Electrical power can be calculated from current and voltage values.

7.5 Electrical safety

Electricity is supplied to our homes at a voltage of 230 V; this is potentially lethal. We look at the measures that are taken to ensure that we can use electricity safely.

7.6 Paying for electricity

How much does it cost to watch television all evening with an electric fire on? We see how to work this out.

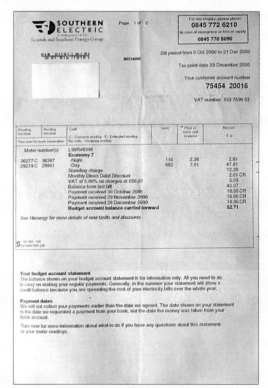

fig 4

Links with other Teaching blocks

1.1–1.3 **Electric circuits**	Chemistry 2.3–2.4	**Metals – electrolysis**
8.2, 8.6–8.7 **Electromagnetism**	Chemistry 3.1–3.4	**Atomic structure and the Periodic Table**

7.1 Electrostatic phenomena

> ### Key points
>
> - Electrical insulators can become charged by friction or by direct contact. Charging involves the movement of electrons.
> - Law of electric charge – like charges repel, unlike charges attract.
> - Objects can also become charged by induction.

Charging by friction

If you take your sweater off quickly you may hear a crackling sound and, if you are in the dark, you may see sparks! You sometimes feel an electric shock after walking across a nylon carpet.

In these examples you have become **charged** by **friction** (rubbing). There is a transfer of **electrons** between you and your sweater, or you and the carpet.

- If you *gain* electrons you become *negatively* charged.
- If you *lose* electrons you become *positively* charged.

If a polythene rod is rubbed with a duster it becomes *negatively* charged, but if an acetate or perspex ruler, is rubbed with a similar duster, it becomes *positively* charged.

Note: These materials are all **insulators**, so electrons cannot move along them. Electrons move along **conductors**, so a conducting path, such as a finger, discharges an object.

Why does this happen?

In an atom, negatively charged electrons orbit a very small but massive **nucleus** containing positively charged **protons** and uncharged **neutrons**. The size of the charge on an electron is the same as the size of the charge on a proton. There are equal numbers of protons and electrons, so an atom is uncharged.

When a polythene rod is rubbed with a duster, electrons rub off the duster more easily than they rub off the polythene. The polythene therefore gains electrons and becomes negatively charged. The duster loses electrons and becomes positively charged. Remember – only electrons can move.

a Explain, in terms of electron movement, how a perspex ruler becomes positively charged when rubbed with a duster.

fig 5 | Van de Graaff generator

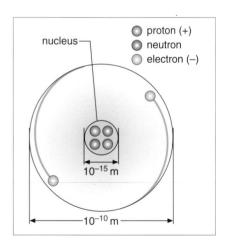

fig 6

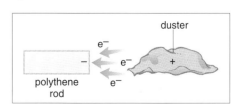

fig 7 | Electrons move *from* the duster *to* the polythene rod

Charging by contact

If you rub a balloon on your sweater it becomes negatively charged – it has gained *extra* electrons. When an uncharged object is placed in contact with the charged balloon, electrons move from one to the other so that they both become negatively charged.

Forces between charges

If two negatively charged balloons are brought together a **force** moves them apart. This suggests that two like charges **repel** each other.

This can be confirmed by balancing a charged polythene rod on an inverted watch glass and bringing up another charged polythene rod and then a charged acetate (or perspex) rod.

fig 8 | Like charges on the balloons repel

Like charges repel, unlike charges attract.

b If you have fine hair the strands sometimes separate when you comb it. Use your ideas about electric charge to explain this.

The effect is much more noticeable if you place your hands on a **Van de Graaff generator**; this stores a lot of electric charge. The metal dome and person are insulated so charge cannot escape.

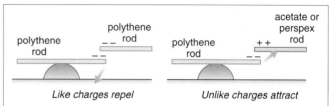

fig 9

Charging by induction

If a balloon is charged by friction it will 'stick' to the wall. The negatively charged balloon repels the electrons in the wall, leaving the surface of the wall with a positive charge. Opposite charges attract so the balloon sticks to the wall. The wall becomes charged by **induction**. We call the separated charges in the wall 'induced' charges.

c A charged comb can pick up tiny pieces of paper by inducing charges in the paper. Explain this with the aid of a diagram.

fig 10

Thinking further

■ **1** When 'cling film' is pulled off a roll it often sticks to itself. Why?

■ **2** Two charged balls are hung side by side. They settle as shown. What can you say about the charges on the balls?

fig 11

◆ **3 a** Jaina is combing her hair. The comb becomes positively charged. Explain carefully how this happens.

b How does this affect Jaina's hair?

◆ **4 a** Alex rubs a perspex ruler on his sleeve. He holds it *near* water flowing from a tap. The water moves towards the ruler. Explain.

b What difference would it make if the ruler were made of polythene?

KEY WORDS

charge • conductor • electron • force • friction • induction • insulator • neutron • nucleus • proton • repel • Van de Graaff generator

 Demonstrations with a Van de Graaff generator.

7.2 Uses and problems of electrostatics

> ### Key points
>
> - Electrostatics can be put to good use in a variety of ways.
> - Some problems caused by static electricity include the risk of explosion when re-fuelling aircraft.

Uses of electrostatics

Electrostatic precipitators

To remove dust and ash from chimneys at coal-burning power stations and factories **electrostatic precipitators** are used. There are negatively charged wires in the chimney. The wires attract dust particles and give them a negative charge. The charged particles are then repelled from the wires and attracted to positively charged plates nearby. The dust sticks to the plates so that the smoke coming from the chimney is clean. Every few minutes the plates are hit and the ash falls down into trays. It is used to make building bricks.

a Would this work if the wires were positively charged and the plates negatively charged? Explain.

Photocopiers

An image of the document to be copied by a **photocopier** is projected onto a special plate that becomes positively charged in the dark. The dark parts of the plate are now positively charged and attract the negatively charged **toner** (a dark powder). Next a piece of positively charged paper is placed on the plate and the toner is attracted to it. The paper is then heated so that the toner melts and gives a copy of the document. This sounds very complicated but it all happens in a few seconds!

Ink-jet printers for computers work in a similar way.

Paint spraying

The paint becomes charged due to friction as it is forced out of the nozzle of the spray gun. If the object to be painted is given the opposite charge the paint will stick to it well.

Farmers use a similar technique when crop-spraying.

b The paint spreads out as it emerges from the spray gun. Why? What is the advantage of this?

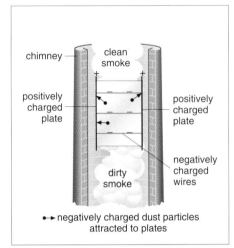

fig 12 | Action of a smoke precipitator

fig 13 | Using a photocopier

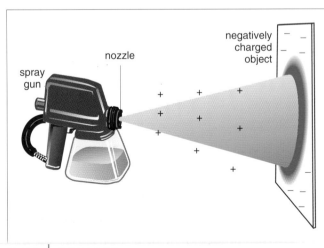

fig 14 | Paint spraying

Some problems caused by static electricity

A television screen becomes charged because its inner surface is hit by millions of electrons. The kinetic energy of these electrons is converted into light energy by a special material on the screen; this produces the picture. But the electrons cannot be left to accumulate on the screen. They are removed by a conducting coating on the inside of the *cathode ray tube*. You can get a slight shock if you touch the TV screen.

fig 15

c Why does the television screen need dusting more frequently than other things in a room?

Lightning occurs when clouds become highly charged. Air is normally an insulator, but if there is a very large voltage difference between two objects the air can become conducting and a spark may be seen.

Aircraft require large quantities of aviation fuel for each flight. In the re-fuelling process, the fuel may become charged by friction when flowing through the fuel pipe from the tanker. This could create a spark and cause the fuel to ignite, with disastrous results. The aircraft and re-fuelling tanker are always connected together by a copper wire. This ensures that they have the same voltage so no charge can flow between them.

fig 16

In a similar way there is a risk of explosion when cleaning the tanks on oil tankers using high-speed water-jets. The tanks are filled with an **inert** gas such as nitrogen before cleaning starts.

d How does the inert gas make the process safer?

fig 17

Thinking further

■ **1** Spare petrol for cars must always be carried in a metal can. Why is a plastic can dangerous?

■ **2** Why do you sometimes get an electric shock on closing the car door after a journey?

■ **3** Why should you never shelter under a tree during a thunderstorm?

◆ **4** Aircraft tyres are made from a type of rubber that conducts electricity. Why?

◆ **5** Fingerprints on paper can be seen by a method similar to that used in electrostatic precipitators. The paper is placed near a charged wire and a fine black powder is used instead of smoke. Suggest how it works.

┌─ **KEY WORDS** ─────────────────────────────
electrostatic precipitator • inert • lightning • photocopier • toner
└──

More uses and hazards of electrostatics.

7.3 Charge and current

> ## Key points
>
> - Electric current is a flow of charge.
> - Current in a metal is due to electrons.
> - Current in an electrolytic solution is due to ions.
> - Charge and current are linked by the equation
>   charge = current × time
> - Voltage is the energy transferred by unit charge.
>   1 volt = 1 joule/coulomb

More about electric currents

We read in spread 1.2 that an **electric current** is a flow of charge.
We can show this by setting up the apparatus shown in fig 18.
The uncharged ball moves first to one plate and becomes charged
by contact. Like charges repel so the ball moves to the other plate,
where it acquires the same charge as that plate and is again
repelled. Therefore the conducting ball moves to and fro, carrying
charge from one plate to the other. A sensitive ammeter would
indicate a current – a flow of charge.

a What do you think would happen if the plates were moved
closer together?

If a Van de Graaff generator is connected directly to a sensitive
ammeter via a copper wire, a current is indicated, showing that
charge has flowed from the dome to the ammeter along the wire.
This is an electric current.

Current in metals

Look at the circuit (fig 20) for a cell being used to light a lamp.
Electrons are negatively charged so they will be attracted to the
positive terminal of the cell and repelled from the negative terminal.
This is in the *opposite* direction to that normally considered for a
current. We say that the **conventional current** direction is from the
positive terminal of a cell to the negative terminal. (The reason for
this confusion is that the conventional current direction was
decided before electric currents were fully understood.)

Current in an electrolytic solution

An electrolytic solution contains both positively and negatively
charged particles called **ions**. The *positive* ions move towards the
negative terminal of the battery and the *negative* ions move
towards the *positive* terminal.

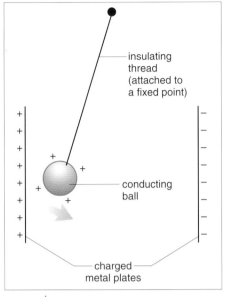

fig 18 | Flow of charge = current

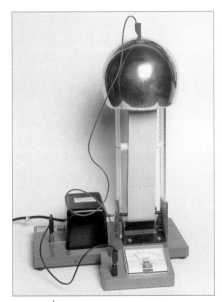

fig 19 | A Van de Graaff generator connected
to a sensitive ammeter

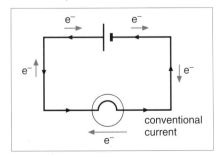

fig 20 | Electrons move in the opposite
direction to a conventional current

$Q = It$

current = rate of flow of charge, or

$$\text{current } (I) = \frac{\text{charge } (Q)}{\text{time } (t)}$$

$$Q = It$$

- I is measured in amperes (A)
- Q is measured in **coulombs** (C)
- t is measured in seconds (s)

b A current of 2 A passes through a resistor for one minute. How much charge passes through the resistor?

The charge on one electron is *very* tiny – only 1.6×10^{-19} C – so the answer to **b** represents a large number of electrons.

c How many electrons make up 1 coulomb of charge?

Your answer is the number of electrons passing any point in a circuit *every second* when the current is 1 A.

Voltage extra

In spread 1.3 we saw that voltage is the work done, or energy transferred to other forms, when there is a current in a resistor.

The voltage, in volts, between two points in a circuit, is the number of joules of energy transferred for each coulomb of charge that passes between the two points.

This means that 1 V = 1 J/C

d How much energy does a 12 V battery give each coulomb of charge that passes through it?

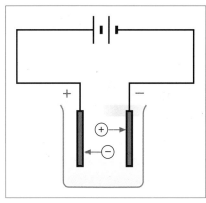

fig 21 | Movement of ions in solution

Thinking further

■ **1** Draw a circuit diagram to show how you would connect a model motor to a battery. Mark the current direction. Now add arrows to show the direction in which the electrons move.

■ **2** The current in a wire is due to electron flow. Give two changes, in terms of electrons, which would increase the current.

◆ **3** The current in a 12 V lamp is 2 A. It is switched on for 30 s. Calculate

a the total charge flowing in this time

b the total energy transferred to the lamp

c the light energy produced if the lamp has an efficiency of 10%.

◆ **4** Look at fig 18.

a Why must the ball have a metallic surface for this to work?

b The ball is said to act like a 'charge carrier'. Explain what is meant by this.

KEY WORDS

conventional current • **electric current** • **ion** • **coulomb**

Use of Van de Graaff generator to link charge and current.

7.4 Electricity in the home

$P = VI$

$$\text{power} = \frac{\text{energy transferred}}{\text{time}}$$

Consider a 12 V lamp with a current of 2 A. A charge of 2 C flows through the lamp every second.

A voltage difference across the lamp of 12 V means that each coulomb of charge transfers 12 J of **energy** to heat and light. So 2 C of charge transfers 12 × 2 = 24 J of energy in 1 s. Therefore the power of the lamp is 24 J/s, or 24 W.

This means power = voltage × current or $P = VI$

Power is measured in **watts** (W) or **kilowatts** (kW). (1 kW = 1000 W).

• A higher voltage gives more power because each electron has more energy.
• A higher current gives more power because there are more electrons to transfer energy.

a Sam's hairdryer is connected to the 230 V mains and has a power rating of 1150 W. Calculate the current in the hairdryer when working normally.

Alternating current

Cells and batteries deliver **direct current (d.c.)**. The electrons keep moving in the *same* direction.

The electricity supplied to our homes (mains electricity) is an **alternating current (a.c.)**. This means that the electrons keep changing direction – they oscillate. Every domestic appliance has a label on it; the one on Sam's hairdryer is shown on the right.

As well as telling Sam the operating voltage and **power rating** of her hairdryer, the wavy line indicates that the supply must be a.c. with a **frequency** of 50 Hz. This means that the electrons move back and forth 50 times every second.

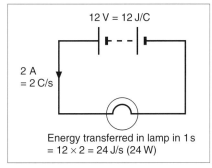

fig 22

fig 23

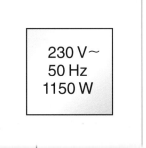

fig 24 | Labelling on a hairdryer

Household wiring

The mains electricity supply comes into your house through the **live** (red) and **neutral** (black) wires. The neutral wire provides the return path for the electric current. It is connected to the ground – earthed – at the power station. The live wire is very dangerous – it is at a high voltage.

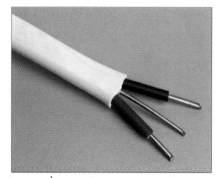

fig 25 | Mains cable with bare earth wire

A **fuse** is a length of wire that melts if the current becomes too large. This prevents the appliance overheating and causing a fire.

b Why are switches and fuses always connected on the *live* side of an appliance?

A mains cable usually has a third wire in addition to the live and neutral wires. This is the **earth** wire. We shall see how it works later.

Each wire in the cable connecting appliances is coated in a plastic sheath; these are colour-coded:
- brown for the live wire (L)
- blue for the neutral wire (N)
- green/yellow for the earth wire (E).

It is essential to insulate the live wire from the neutral and earth wires as its voltage is high.

c Look at the simplified diagram of household wiring (fig 26). Why are the power and lighting circuits connected in parallel?

Power points connected in a **ring main** take a maximum current of 13 A. Appliances such as cookers and immersion heaters require more than 13 A, so have separate circuits each with a 30 A fuse.

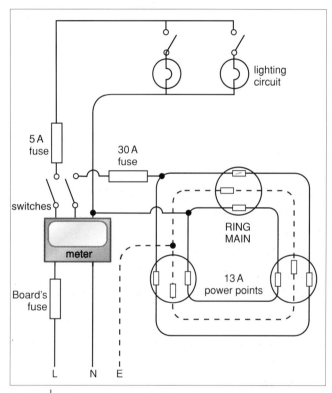

fig 26 | Lighting and power circuits in a house

Thinking further

■ **1** Copy and complete the table.

appliance	voltage in V	current in A	power in W
toaster	230	3.5	
kettle	230		2645
computer	230	0.4	

fig 27

■ **2 a** Electric cookers are connected permanently to the mains via a separate circuit. Why is this necessary?

◆ **b** Calculate the power used when the cooker takes 30 A at 230 V.

◆ **3** Why is a ring-main circuit usually used for power sockets?

◆ **4** The maximum current in a lighting circuit is 5 A. How many 60 W lamps can be switched on at the same time without melting the fuse?

Find the power rating of various appliances.

7.5 Electrical safety

Fuses and circuit breakers

The plugs attached to household appliances include a cartridge fuse connected to the live terminal. The cartridge contains a length of resistance wire specially chosen to melt, breaking the circuit, if the current exceeds a certain value. This could happen if the insulation was broken. The live and neutral wires could touch, shorting out the appliance and causing a fire.

a Explain why a **short circuit** may cause a fire.

The correct value fuse to use depends on the current taken by the appliance when working normally. The fuse chosen should be rated *just* higher than the normal current.

The normal current can be calculated using $P = VI$.

b A toaster has a power of 920 W. It is connected to the 230 V mains. 3 A, 5 A and 13 A fuses are available. Which one should be used?

If the fuse in the plug fails to melt for any reason, the main fuse box in the house also has a fuse for each circuit. Nowadays the house fuses are likely to have been replaced by **circuit breakers.** If the current becomes too large an electromagnet becomes strong enough to separate a pair of contacts, breaking the circuit. This can be reset when the fault has been corrected, instead of having to replace a melted fuse.

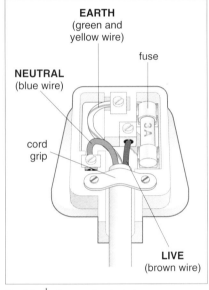

fig 28 | A correctly wired plug

Earth wire

The earth wire is so called because it is connected to the ground. In normal use no current passes through the earth wire. It is connected to the metal case of an appliance

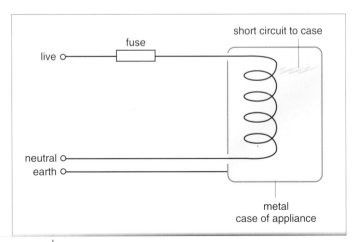

fig 29 | An earth connection

so that if a fault occurs and a live wire touches the case it provides a lower resistance path to the ground than the user who might touch the case. This causes a large current in the live and earth wires and so the fuse melts (or circuit breaker trips). This breaks the circuit and the user cannot get an **electric shock**.

c Describe in detail what would happen if a fault developed in an electric fire with a metal case and no earth connection.

Double insulation

Some appliances, such as Sam's hairdryer in spread 7.4, do *not* have an earth connection. This is because there are no electrical connections to the case. The appliance is said to be **double-insulated** and is marked with the symbol shown.

Residual current device (RCD)

A **residual current device (RCD)** responds more rapidly than a fuse or a circuit breaker if a fault occurs. It can detect a very small change in the current in the live and neutral wires and breaks the circuit immediately. A current difference of as little as 30 mA can be detected, so the circuit is broken before a person could receive a fatal electric shock.

RCDs are used with power tools such as electric lawn mowers or hedge trimmers, where there is a chance of accidentally cutting the cable. They do not detect a short circuit or excess current in an appliance so are used *in addition* to fuses and circuit breakers.

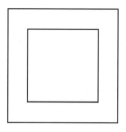

fig 30 | Symbol for double insulation

fig 31 | Using a residual current device (RCD)

Thinking further

■ **1** Why is it dangerous to touch an electrical supply with wet hands? What extra safety measures are needed in bathrooms?

■ **2** Copy and complete the table below. 3 A, 5 A and 13 A fuses are available. The mains voltage is 230 V.

appliance	power in W	current in A	fuse
TV	115		
fan heater	1150		
video recorder	46		
washing machine	2760		

fig 32

◆ **3** The power ratings vary greatly for the appliances in question 2. Suggest a common factor for high-powered appliances.

◆ **4** The diagram shows a thermal circuit breaker. Brass expands more than iron when heated equally. Explain how it works.

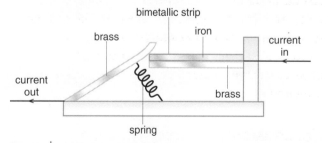

fig 33 | Thermal circuit breaker

KEY WORDS

— **KEY WORDS** —
circuit breaker • double insulation • electric shock • residual current device (RCD) • short circuit

7.6 Paying for electricity

fig 34

Calculation of energy transfer

energy = power × time

We can use this equation to find the energy transferred in joules. Power must be measured in W and time in s.

a Find the energy transferred if a 60 W lamp is left on for 2 hours.

If we need to calculate the power we can use the equation $P = VI$ (from spread 7.4) where voltage (V) is in V and current (I) is in A.

b A kettle connected to the 230 V mains has a current of 10 A. It takes 6 minutes to boil some water. How much energy is transferred?

fig 35

The electricity boards calculate the energy transferred in a different unit – the **kilowatt-hour (kWh)**.

A kilowatt-hour is the energy transferred by a 1 kW appliance in 1 hour.

energy in kWh = power in kW × time in hours

c Find the energy transferred, in kWh, by the lamp in question **a** and the kettle in question **b**.

d How many joules of energy is equivalent to 1 kilowatt-hour?

Domestic electricity meters

A domestic electricity meter is calibrated in kWh. This means that it measures the energy transferred in kilowatt-hours instead of the usual energy unit, the joule.

fig 36

Electricity bills

When you pay your electricity bill you are paying for the energy dissipated into other forms by your electrical equipment.
The unit that the electricity boards use is the kilowatt-hour.
The cost of one unit varies but is typically about 10p.

total cost = number of units (kWh) × cost per unit

This can be used to work out your quarterly electricity bill. The number of units used is the difference between the meter readings at the start and the end of the quarter. A fixed standing charge is also paid and VAT is added to the total bill.

e Sanjay used 1500 units in a quarter. Find the cost of these units if 1 unit costs 10p.

The equation above can also be used to find the cost of running a particular appliance.

f Debbie uses her 1 kW iron for 4 hours each week. Find the weekly cost at 7p per unit.

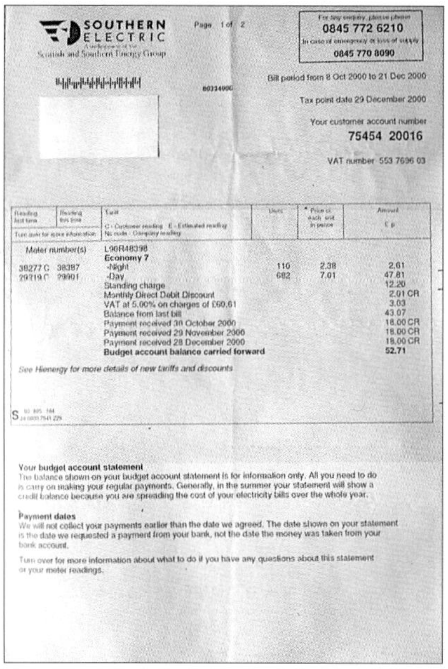
SOUTHERN ELECTRIC
Scottish and Southern Energy Group
Page 1 of 2
For any enquiry, please phone 0845 772 6210
In case of emergency or loss of supply 0845 770 8090
Bill period from 8 Oct 2000 to 21 Dec 2000
Tax point date 29 December 2000
Your customer account number 75454 20016
VAT number 553 7696 03

Reading last time	Reading this time	Tariff (C - Customer reading, E - Estimated reading, No code - Company reading)	Units	Price of each unit in pence	Amount £ p
Meter number(s)		L90R48398			
		Economy 7			
38277 C	38387	-Night	110	2.38	2.61
29219 C	29901	-Day	682	7.01	47.81
		Standing charge			12.20
		Monthly Direct Debit Discount			2.01 CR
		VAT at 5.00% on charges of £60.61			3.03
		Balance from last bill			43.07
		Payment received 30 October 2000			18.00 CR
		Payment received 29 November 2000			18.00 CR
		Payment received 28 December 2000			18.00 CR
		Budget account balance carried forward			**52.71**

See Hienergy for more details of new tariffs and discounts

Your budget account statement
The balance shown on your budget account statement is for information only. All you need to do is carry on making your regular payments. Generally, in the summer your statement will show a credit balance because you are spreading the cost of your electricity bills over the whole year.

Payment dates
We will not collect your payments earlier than the date we agreed. The date shown on your statement is the date we requested a payment from your bank, not the date the money was taken from your bank account.

Turn over for more information about what to do if you have any questions about this statement or your meter readings.

fig 37

Thinking further

■ **1** Copy the table and use it to calculate the cost of using each appliance for the time indicated. The cost per unit is 10p.

appliance	power in W	time in h	energy in kWh	cost
drill	900	0.5		
shower	8000	2		
fire	2000	20		
vacuum cleaner	500	1.5		
CD player	60	20		

fig 38

■ **2** Calculate the energy transferred by each of the appliances in question 1 in joules.

■ **3** Alex fell asleep leaving a 100 W lamp switched on for 7 h. How much money did he waste, if he pays 8p a unit for his electricity?

◆ **4** A 3 kW heater is fitted with a 30 W indicator lamp and a 20 W fan. Calculate the cost of using it for 5 hours if the electricity board charges 8p a unit.

◆ **5** Write down five electrical appliances used in your house. Estimate the power rating of each appliance. (The power ratings of many appliances are given in this Teaching block.) Estimate how many hours the appliance is used for each week. Taking the cost per unit (kWh) as 10p, estimate the total cost of using these five appliances each week.

KEY WORDS
kilowatt-hour (kWh)

Use of spreadsheet to compare cost of using various appliances.

Discuss ways of reducing your household electricity bill.

Questions on using electricity

● **1** Copy and complete the following sentences. Use words from the list. You can use them more than once.

attract(s) • **duster** • **electrons** • **insulators** • **like** • **negatively** • **opposite** • **positively** • **protons** • **repel** • **rod**

A polythene rod is rubbed with a duster. _____ leave the _____ and move to the _____. The polythene becomes _____ charged and the duster _____ charged.

Conductors allow _____ to travel through them; _____ do not.

A positively charged object attracts tiny pieces of paper to it. It _____ electrons in the paper. This leaves the surface of the paper _____ charged.

They stick together because _____ charges _____.   *(11)*

● **2 a** Dilip walked across a nylon carpet in his room and got an electric shock when he touched the metal door handle. Why?   *(3)*

b Emma rubbed a plastic set square with a duster. It became positively charged. Explain why this happened.   *(3)*

● **3** The readings on an electricity meter for the month of March are shown.

kWh	1 7 3 1 3		kWh	1 8 0 2 2

1 March   31 March

a How many kWh were used?   *(1)*

b How much did this cost at 8p per unit?   *(2)*

4 Pat's family has bought a microwave oven. The instruction manual includes three statements that Pat is asked to explain to his family.

● **a** 'This appliance must be earthed'.
  i How would the appliance be earthed?   *(1)*
  ii Why does earthing make the appliance safe?   *(2)*

■ **b** 'The power of the oven is 500 W'. What does this mean?   *(2)*

■ **c** 'The plug should be fitted with a 3 A fuse'.
  i What is the purpose of the fuse?   *(2)*
  ii Do a calculation to show that 3 A is the correct value for the fuse.   *(3)*

■ **5** Select the power rating from the list that is likely to be nearest to the power rating of each of the appliances listed below. (Use each one once.)

60 W • **120 W** • **250 W** • **750 W** • **1000 W** • **3000 W**

vacuum cleaner • **electric blanket** • **lamp** • **kettle** • **one-bar electric fire** • **CD player**   *(6)*

■ **6** The Shah family uses electricity at home for heating and lighting only. They have three heaters rated at 1 kW, 1.5 kW and 2 kW. They have six lights, one 150 W, three 100 W, one 60 W and one 40 W. On average, the heaters are used for 4 hours and the lights for 6 hours each day.

  a How many kWh does the family use each day?   *(3)*

  b One unit (kWh) of electricity costs 8p. Estimate the cost per quarter (90 days). *(2)*

7 An electric fire is rated 230 V 3 kW. It is switched on for 2 hours.

■ **a** How many joules of energy are transformed
  i in 1 second
  ii in 2 hours?   *(3)*

■ **b** How many units of electricity (kWh) must be paid for when the fire is used for 2 hours? *(1)*

◆ **c** How many joules are there in 1 kWh?   *(2)*

■ **8** A car is being painted using a spray gun in a factory. The paint coming out of the nozzle is positively charged.

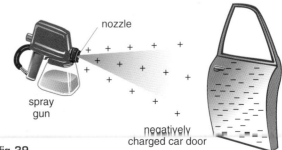

fig 39

a **i** How does the paint become charged? *(1)*

   ii What effect does this have on the paint
     as it travels towards the car? Explain. *(2)*

   iii Why is this useful? *(1)*

The car body is given a negative charge.

b Why do you think this is done? *(2)*

9 Charlie is using an electric lawnmower.
The lawnmower cuts the cable insulation
and the outer casing of the
lawnmower becomes live.
The current could pass
to earth through Charlie
or through the
lawnmower.

fig 40

Look at some of the effects of electric current
on people.

current in mA	effect on person
1	maximum safe current
2–5	tingling effect
10	muscle spasm, could be fatal
100	probably fatal

fig 41

■ **a** Why doesn't the 13 A fuse in the lawnmower
    protect Charlie from electric shock? *(2)*

■ **b** What *does* the fuse protect against? *(1)*

Charlie *should* be using a residual current
device (RCD). This switches off the supply if a
very small current passes to earth for a very
short time. One version does so after a current
of 30 mA has passed for 0.02 s.

◆ **c** **i** Use the table to decide how effective
       you think this would be. *(2)*

   ii If the RCD switches off the supply when
       Charlie receives the maximum safe
       current, what is the current in the
       lawnmower? *(1)*

   iii What does this tell you about the
       resistance of the lawnmower? *(1)*

◆ **d** What sort of footwear should Charlie wear
    to give himself the maximum protection
    against electric shock? Explain your choice.
    (2)

IDEAS AND EVIDENCE

10 Read the following passage adapted from an
article in *The Times*, 29 July 2000 and then
answer the questions which follow.

Former world motor racing champion Nigel
Mansell, who lives in Jersey, is no doubt raising
one of his distinctive
eyebrows at the latest
motoring addition to
his Channel Island
home; the British Isles'
first electric hire cars.

fig 42

With no gears and a surprisingly high top speed
of 80 mph, four electric cars are now on offer to
tourists on the nine by five mile-wide island. On a
single battery charge they have a range of 125
miles – enough for about four days' use for most
sightseeing visitors.

When batteries run low, drivers can top them up
at one of six hotels, which have introduced
recharging stations. There is also a recharging point
in the middle of St. Helier, the capital, and car
rental employees will visit holiday-makers staying
at accommodation without charge-up facilities for
overnight top-ups. Recharging takes seven hours.

So far the omens are good. As the top speed in
Jersey is 40 mph, the cars are having no trouble
keeping up with the traffic and have shaken off
the old 'milkfloat' gibes.

The electric cars, which are appropriately coloured
green, have almost no engine sound, so drivers are
advised to use horns regularly.

a Petrol fuelled cars are based on the internal
    combustion engine. What replaces petrol in an
    electric car? *(1)*

b What is meant by *milkfloat gibes*? *(2)*

c **i** Justify the statement that one battery charge
       lasts the average sightseer about four days. *(2)*
   ii Why isn't this a problem for visitors? *(1)*

d Do the cars use an a.c. or d.c. supply? *(1)*

e Discuss the environmental advantages of
    electric cars compared to traditional petrol
    fuelled cars. *(2)*

f What are the disadvantages of these electric
    cars? *(2)*

Electromagnetism

When a conductor with a current in it is placed in a magnetic field, there is a force on the conductor. If the conductor is a coil of wire it will rotate. This led to the development of the motor. Think how many things you have at home that have a motor in them – washing machines, food processors, electric shavers, and many, many more.

Michael Faraday discovered the principle of generating electricity in 1831, an effect called electromagnetic induction. He found that when a magnet is pushed in and out of a coil of wire a voltage is produced. This simple experiment has resulted in the network of power stations linked by the National Grid, a system of cables that brings us electricity in our homes at the flick of a switch. If you have ever had a power cut at home you will know the problems that arise without electricity and appreciate the genius of Faraday and other scientists whose discoveries have such a huge impact on all our lives.

fig 1 | Michael Faraday

fig 2

Check-up

Have a go at the following questions. They will remind you what you should already know about magnetism and electromagnets.

a What is a magnetic material? Give two examples.

b Look at the magnets in fig 3. What happens in each case?

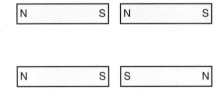
fig 3

c What is the difference between hard and soft magnetic materials? Give an example of each.

d What is a magnetic field?

e What is magnetic induction? How could you demonstrate it?

f A current is passed through

i a long straight wire, ii a solenoid, as shown in fig 4.

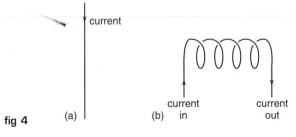
fig 4 (a) (b)

Copy the diagrams and add the magnetic field pattern around each conductor.

g The current direction shown in fig 4 is reversed. What happens to the field pattern in each case?

Check-up (continued)

h The solenoid in fig 4 behaves like a bar magnet. Mark its polarity on your diagram.

i An iron rod is placed in the solenoid. What happens to it when the current is

i switched on, ii switched off?

How would your answers change if the rod were made of steel?

j Give one use of an electromagnet. Explain why the core needs to be made from iron.

If you have difficulties your teacher has a Summary sheet you can have.

Contents of the Teaching block

This Teaching block is divided into seven double page spreads.

8.1 Force on a wire in a magnetic field

When the magnetic field due to a current in a wire is combined with the field due to a permanent magnet, there is a force on the wire.

8.2 Electric motors

The principle of the force on a wire in a magnetic field is extended to a coil of wire, producing a turning effect. We see how this is adapted to produce continuous rotation in an electric motor.

8.3 Electromagnetic induction

We see that a voltage is produced when a conductor moves in a magnetic field or when a conductor is placed in a changing magnetic field.

8.4 Generators and mutual induction

This idea is extended to generators. These are used to produce electricity for the lights on your bicycle as well as on a large scale in power stations.

8.5 Transformers

Transformers are used to increase (step up) and decrease (step down) alternating voltages. They are an essential part of many appliances used in the home.

8.6 Generating electricity

We see how electricity is generated at power stations. We also consider some of the environmental and social problems that arise with various methods of power generation.

8.7 Power transmission

This unit looks at how electricity is transferred from power stations to our homes and the important part played by transformers in this process.

Links with other Teaching blocks

8.1 Force on a wire in a magnetic field

Key points

- If a wire carrying a current is placed at right angles to a magnetic field there is a force on the wire that may make it move.
- A bigger current or a bigger magnetic field will increase the size of the force on the wire.

- Reversing the current *or* the magnetic field will reverse the direction of the force. Fleming's left-hand rule tells you the direction of this force.
- A loudspeaker makes use of this effect.

The force on a wire in a magnetic field

A straight wire connected to a power supply is placed between the poles of a powerful magnet as shown in fig 5. When the power supply is switched on the wire moves sharply – 'kicks' – in a direction at right angles to both the current and the **magnetic field**. This means that there is an unbalanced force on the wire.

Why does this happen?

The magnetic fields due to the current in the wire and the permanent magnet interact. Look at the diagrams in fig 6.

On one side of the wire the two magnetic fields act in the same direction, giving an extra strong field. On the other side of the wire the magnetic fields act in opposite directions, so that they partially cancel, giving a weak field. This means that there is an unbalanced force on the wire, so it moves sharply out of the magnetic field in the direction shown.

a This is sometimes referred to as a 'catapult' effect. Suggest a reason for this.

Making the force bigger

The size of the force can be increased by
- increasing the current in the wire
- using a more powerful magnet.

Changing the direction of the force

The direction of the force can be reversed by
- reversing the current direction in the wire
- reversing the poles of the permanent magnet.

b What would happen if the current and poles of the magnet were *both* reversed?

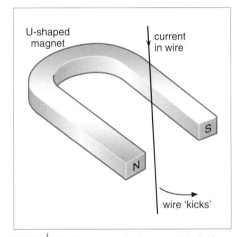

fig 5 | The force on a wire in a magnetic field

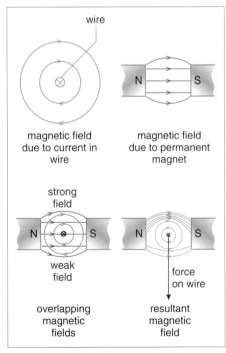

fig C | Two magnetic fields combine to produce a force on the wire

Fleming's left-hand rule

Fleming's left-hand rule tells us the direction of the force on the wire. Hold the thumb and first two fingers of your *left* hand so that they are at right angles to each other. If

- the **f**irst finger points in the direction of the magnetic **f**ield
- the se**c**ond finger points in the direction of the **c**urrent, then
- the **th**umb points in the direction of the **th**rust (force).

c Use Fleming's left-hand rule to check the direction of the force in figs 5 and 6.

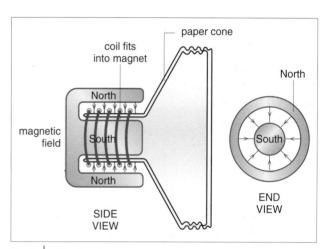

fig 7 | Fleming's left-hand rule

first finger
magnetic
field

second
finger
current

thumb
thrust

If the wire were not at right angles to the magnetic field, the size of the force would be reduced. It would be zero if the wire were parallel to the magnetic field.

Loudspeaker

- The input current to a **loudspeaker** is an alternating current of the same frequency as the original sound wave.
- The size of the current depends on the loudness of the original sound.
- The permanent magnets are circular so that the coil lies in the uniform magnetic field between the N and S poles.
- When there is a current in the coil, there is a force on the coil.
- As the current direction alternates, the direction of this force alternates.
- This makes the coil, and in turn the paper cone and surrounding air, vibrate at the same frequency as the original sound wave.

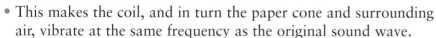

fig 8 | A loudspeaker

paper cone

coil fits
into magnet

North

magnetic
field

South

North

North

South

END
VIEW

SIDE
VIEW

d How does the loudspeaker produce a louder sound?

Thinking further

■ **1** Copy fig 9 and add an arrow to show the direction of the force on the wire. How could the force be **i** increased, **ii** reversed?

■ **2** What would happen to the force on the wire in question 1 if

   a four cells were used instead of two

   b a weaker magnet were used

   c the cells were replaced by an a.c. supply?

◆ **3** Look at fig 5. Suggest how the force on the

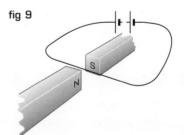

fig 9

wire would change if the wire were inclined to the vertical so that it cut the magnetic field at an angle.

◆ **4** The musical note called middle C is heard from a loudspeaker. How does the current in the coil of the loudspeaker change when a higher pitched note of the same intensity is heard?

KEY WORDS

catapult (effect) • Fleming's left-hand rule • loudspeaker • magnetic field

 Demonstration of 'kicking' wire experiment.

8.2 Electric motors

Key points

- When a coil of wire is placed in a magnetic field, equal and opposite forces act on the sides of it, making it spin.
- A split-ring commutator is needed to produce continuous rotation.
- Motors can be made more powerful by increasing the current in the coil, the number of turns on the coil or the strength of the magnetic field.

Forces on a coil in a magnetic field

A coil carrying a current is placed between the poles of a magnet. There is a force on each side of the coil, but in opposite directions, so the coil turns.

a Use Fleming's left-hand rule to check that the forces are marked correctly in the diagram on the right.

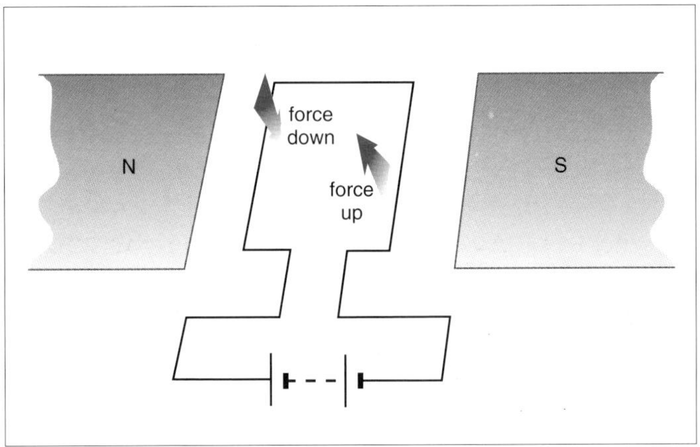

As shown, the coil can only rotate through 90 degrees. A **motor** needs to rotate through a full circle.

b Why can the coil only rotate through 90 degrees?

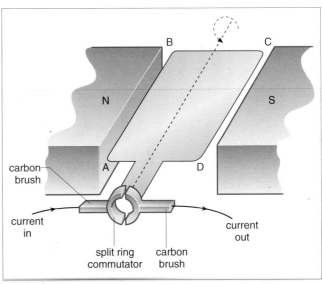

fig 10 | Forces on a coil in a magnetic field

The split-ring commutator

The **split-ring commutator** reverses the current in the coil each time the coil passes the vertical. This keeps the forces on the coil in the same direction so that it keeps turning.

The commutator and coil rotate between the fixed **carbon brushes**. These bring the current to and from the coil. The turning effect varies from a maximum when the plane of the coil is in the magnetic field direction, to zero when it is at right angles to the magnetic field. The momentum of the coil keeps it moving in this position.

Look at the plan views of the coil and brushes in fig 12. Note that the current in the coil changes direction as the coil passes the vertical.

fig 11 | Construction of a simple motor

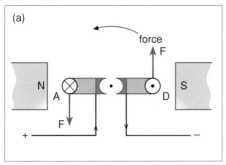

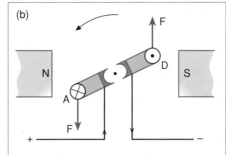

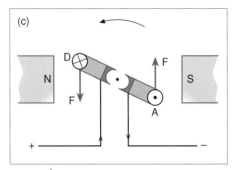

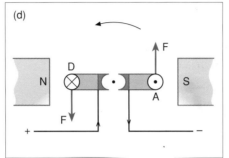

fig 12 | The action of a commutator through a complete rotation of the coil

Motors in practice

Motors that are used to start a car or to run a washing machine need to be very powerful. The power can be increased in many ways.

* Increase the current in the coil.
* Increase the number of turns on the coil.
* Use more powerful magnets.
* Wind the coil on an **iron core** to increase the magnetic field strength.
* Have several coils around the iron core, each with corresponding splits in the commutator. This increases the *total* force as the force on each coil is added.
* Use curved pole pieces so that the coil is always at right angles to the magnetic field – a **radial field**. This gives the maximum force and keeps it constant as the coil turns.

c Why is the core made of iron?

fig 13 | A radial magnetic field

fig 14

Thinking further

■ **1** Name three machines (apart from those mentioned already) that contain electric motors.

■ **2** Look at the diagram of an electric motor (fig 11). What would happen if

a the battery was reversed

b the battery voltage was increased?

◆ **3** Do you think it possible to replace the permanent magnet in a motor with an electromagnet? Explain.

◆ **4** Which of the ways of increasing the power of a motor should also make it run more smoothly? Explain.

— **KEY WORDS** —
carbon brushes • iron core • motor • radial field • split-ring commutator

How fast does the motor go?

8.3 Electromagnetic induction

> **Key points**
>
> - A voltage is generated when a conductor cuts magnetic field lines. The conductor or the magnet (or both) must move.
> - Faraday's Law tells us that the size of the induced voltage depends on the rate of cutting magnetic field lines.
> - Lenz's Law tells us that the direction of the induced voltage (or current) always tries to oppose the motion or change producing it. This is the law of conservation of energy.

Moving a wire in a magnetic field

When the wire moves down between the poles of the magnet the sensitive ammeter indicates a current – an **induced current.**

Electrons in the wire are given a push by the magnetic field. When the wire is moved up there is a current in the opposite direction.

a What does this tell you about the force on the electrons in the wire now?

To get an **induced voltage** (or current) the wire must cut the magnetic field lines. There is *no* induced voltage (or current) when the wire is moved *along* the field lines.

The size of the induced current can be increased by:
- using a more powerful magnet
- moving the wire faster.

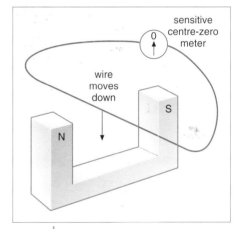

fig 15 | Electromagnetic induction

Faraday's Law

Faraday's Law states that the greater the rate of cutting the magnetic field lines, the greater the voltage (and current) induced.

Fleming's right-hand rule

Fleming's right-hand rule gives the direction of the induced current. It is very similar to his *left*-hand rule, but you must not confuse them.

Hold the thumb and first two fingers of your *right* hand so that they are at right angles to each other. If
- the first finger points in the direction of the magnetic field
- the thumb points in the direction of movement of the wire,
- the second finger points in the direction of the induced current.

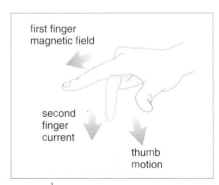

fig 16 | Fleming's right-hand rule

Moving a magnet in a coil

As the bar magnet enters the coil the meter registers a current. When the magnet is at rest in the coil there is no current. Because there is no movement, no magnetic field lines are being cut.

As the bar magnet is removed from the coil the meter registers a current in the opposite direction.

The size of the induced current can be increased by:

* using a more powerful magnet
* moving the wire faster
* increasing the number of turns on the coil.

b What do you think would happen if
  i the S pole of the bar magnet were pushed into the coil?
  ii the N pole of the magnet were pushed in the other end of the coil?
  iii the magnet were pushed in and out repeatedly?

Lenz's Law

Lenz's Law states that the direction of the induced current always opposes the movement or change producing it.

As the magnet enters the coil the induced current direction makes that end of the coil behave like a N pole so that it repels the magnet. This means that work has to be done to push the magnet into the coil. If the end of the coil were a S pole, the magnet would be attracted and no work would be required. This would contravene the law of **conservation of energy**.

As the magnet is removed, the current reverses because the polarity of the coil must reverse to try to stop the magnet leaving the coil.

c How can you tell the polarity of the coil from the current direction?

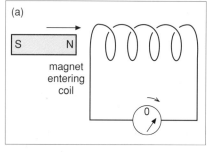
(a) magnet entering coil

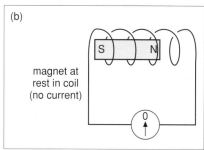
(b) magnet at rest in coil (no current)

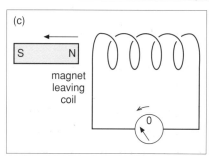
(c) magnet leaving coil

fig 17 | Direction of induced current

Thinking further

1 In fig 15, what would be the effect of moving the wire

  a up   **b** more slowly   **c** towards the N pole?

2 The coil in fig 17 is held vertically and a bar magnet dropped through it. Describe how the meter reading changes.

3 A toy car with a bar magnet on its roof runs at a steady speed through a tunnel made from a coil of wire (fig 18). Sketch a graph to show how the induced current varies as the car moves through the tunnel. Add another graph to show how the induced current would change if the speed of the car were doubled.

fig 18

KEY WORDS

conservation of energy • Faraday's Law • Fleming's right-hand rule • induced current • induced voltage • Lenz's Law

 Using a data logger to investigate electromagnetic induction further.   *Demonstration of electromagnetic induction.*

 How does voltage depend on speed?

8.4 Generators and mutual induction

An a.c. generator (alternator)

An a.c. **generator** (or **alternator**) looks similar to the motor studied in spread 8.2 except that there are **slip rings** instead of the split-ring commutator so that the contacts do not swap over every half turn. This means that the output is alternating, as can be seen from the graph.

As the coil rotates it cuts the magnetic field lines and a current is induced. Current direction is given by Fleming's right-hand rule.

a Use Fleming's right-hand rule to see if you agree with the current direction shown in fig 19.

The induced current is *greatest* when the coil is *horizontal*; this is when the coil cuts the magnetic field lines most rapidly. The induced current is *zero* when the coil is *vertical* as the coil is not cutting any field lines.

If the speed of rotation is increased:

- the size of the induced current increases since the magnetic field lines are cut more rapidly
- the frequency of the induced current increases as there are more rotations of the coil every second.

b Suggest two more ways in which the size of the induced current could be increased.

The magnetic field can be provided by an electromagnet. If the coil of a motor is rotated by hand, a d.c. current is induced.

Generators with moving magnets

Large generators, such as the ones used at power stations to provide electricity for our homes, have a fixed coil and rotating magnets. In large generators of this type rotating electromagnets are used.

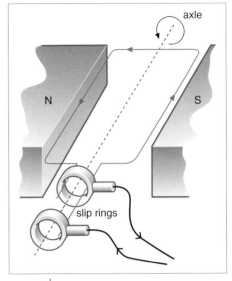

fig 19 | Structure of an a.c. generator

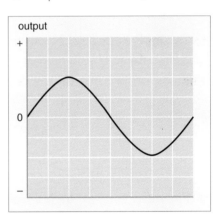

fig 20 | Graph of the output from an a.c. generator

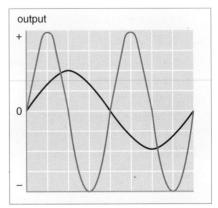

fig 21 | The red line shows the output of a generator when the speed of rotation is doubled

In a bicycle **dynamo,** as you pedal, a magnet rotates near a coil of wire so that it cuts the magnetic field lines.

Mutual induction

Mutual induction occurs when a changing magnetic field in one coil of wire induces a voltage in a nearby coil. This can be shown using the apparatus in fig 23.

As the switch is closed the ammeter moves to the right and returns quickly to zero. As the switch is opened the ammeter moves to the left and returns quickly to zero.

c Why are the induced currents in opposite directions?

d Why is there no induced current after the switch has been closed for a short time?

e If the d.c. supply is replaced with an a.c. one, a continuous alternating current is induced. Explain why.

The size of the induced current can be increased by:

• having more turns on the coil

• winding the coil on an iron core

• increasing the frequency of the applied a.c.

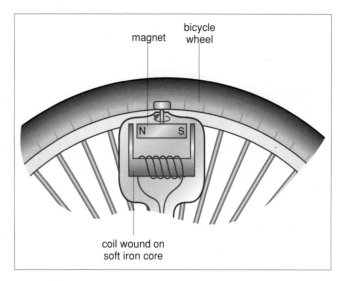

fig 22 | A bicycle dynamo

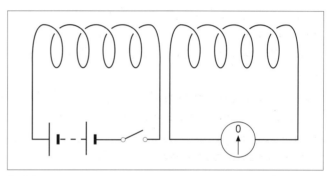

fig 23

Thinking further

■ **1** Mark rides a bicycle. He pedals very fast. How does this affect the output from his dynamo?

■ **2** What would be the effect on the output of a generator of doubling the number of turns on the coil?

◆ **3** The graph in fig 20 shows the output from a generator. Copy it and add graphs to show what would happen if

a the magnetic field strength is increased (label it M),

b the coil is rotated at half the speed (label it S).

◆ **4** When a dynamo is giving current it tends to slow down. Suggest a reason for this.

KEY WORDS

alternator • dynamo • generator • mutual induction • slip rings

 Electromagnetism induction.

 Demonstrating mutual induction.

8.5 Transformers

Construction of a transformer

A **transformer** consists of two coils of wire wound on an iron core. The **primary** coil is connected to an alternating supply. The iron core becomes magnetised, but because the current in the coil is changing all the time, the magnetic field is changing as well. The **secondary** coil is in this changing magnetic field and so a voltage is induced in it.

If there are more turns on the secondary than the primary, the secondary voltage V_S is greater than the primary voltage V_P (as shown in fig 25); this is a **step-up** transformer.

If there are more turns on the primary than the secondary, the secondary voltage is less than the primary; this is a **step-down** transformer.

fig 24 | A transformer

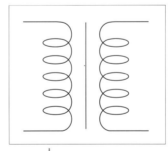

fig 25 | A step-up transformer

fig 26 | Circuit symbol for a transformer

Transformer formulae

If V_P = primary voltage, V_S = secondary voltage, N_P = number of turns on primary coil, N_S = number of turns on secondary coil,

$$\frac{V_P}{V_S} = \frac{N_P}{N_S} \quad \textbf{Turns ratio} = N_P : N_S$$

a A step-down transformer reduces the voltage from 230 V to 10 V. There are 9200 turns on the primary coil. How many turns are on the secondary coil?

Efficiency

The input power to the transformer, $P_{in} = V_P I_P$, where I_P is the current in the primary coil. The output power, $P_{out} = V_S I_S$, where I_S is the current in the secondary coil.

If the transformer is 100% efficient, $P_{in} = P_{out}$ so

$$V_P I_P = V_S I_S$$

In practice, transformers are *very* efficient (typically 95% or more) so this equation is a good approximation to the truth.

b In question **a**, what is the current in the primary coil if the current in the secondary coil is 5 A? (Assume the transformer is 100% efficient.)

Energy losses in transformers (though small) are due to:
- heat in the coils due to resistance (= I^2R)
- heat in the core due to currents induced in the core (**eddy currents**).

c For a given current, how can heat loss in the coils be reduced?

The iron core is **laminated** to reduce eddy currents. It is made from many thin sheets of iron rather than one large piece.

d How does a laminated core reduce eddy currents?

fig 27 | Laminated core of a transformer

Uses of transformers

In the home

Many pieces of equipment would be damaged by the 230 V mains voltage, so a step-down transformer is used. But a cathode ray tube (in a TV for instance) requires a very high voltage, so a step-up transformer is used.

Step-down transformers would be used for example in a computer, door bell, radio, CD player, and model train/car set.

In industry

Step-down transformers are used to produce very high currents (small V, large I). Such currents can be used to weld two pieces of metal together – resistance welding – or to melt metals or boil water very quickly – induction heating.

Thinking further

1 A transformer is supplied so that a 12 V model train can be operated from the 230 V mains. What can you say about this transformer?

2 Why doesn't a transformer work from a d.c. supply?

3 Copy and complete the table.

V_P in V	N_P	V_S in V	N_S
230	920	20	?
200	6000	?	300
132 000	?	11 000	1000

fig 28

4 A 9 V radio takes a current of 2 A. It is connected to a 230 V supply via a transformer.

a What is the turns ratio ($N_P : N_S$) for the transformer?

b What is the power of the radio?

c What is the primary current? What assumption have you made?

KEY WORDS

primary • **secondary** • **step-down** • **step-up** • **transformer** • eddy current • laminated • turns ratio

 Transporting the voltage.

 Demonstrating resistance heating and/or induction heating.

139

8.6 Generating electricity

Key points

- Electricity is generated on a large scale by rotating electromagnets within coils of wire, as seen in section 8.4.
- Conventional power stations burn fossil fuels to: heat water, produce steam, turn the turbines, rotate the electromagnets, generate electricity.
- Our supply of fossil fuels is decreasing rapidly, so alternative energy sources must be found.
- Different generation methods raise different social and environmental issues.

fig 29 | Steam train delivering coal to a power station in the 1950s

Coal-burning power station

Each generator at a power station has several large electromagnets rotating inside several sets of stationary coils.

In a **coal-burning power station:**

- coal is burned to boil water at high pressure in the boiler
- this water produces **superheated steam** (at about 700 °C)
- the kinetic energy of the high-pressure steam turns a turbine
- the turbine rotates the magnets in the generator
- this induces a voltage in the stationary coils of about 25 000 V.

fig 30 | Generator in a power station

The turbine also turns a d.c. generator, called the **exciter**, which provides current for the rotating electromagnets. The steam is cooled, condensed and returned to the boiler.

a Why is the exciter a d.c. generator?

b Why are power stations often built near the coast?

Oil-fired, **gas-fired** and **nuclear power** stations work in the same way; the only difference is in the **fuel** used to heat the water.

Hydroelectric power stations use the kinetic energy of falling water to turn the turbines to produce electricity.

> Energy flow through a coal-burning power station
>
> Chemical energy of coal
> ↓
> thermal energy of water/steam
> ↓
> kinetic energy of steam/turbine

Alternative energy

Our supply of **fossil fuels** is likely to run out before the end of this century. Alternative energy sources, such as wind, wave, tidal, solar and geothermal energy, are being developed but they pose social and environmental questions as well as technical problems.

fig 31 | Wave energy

Environmental and social issues

Pollution

The burning of fossil fuels produces the gases carbon dioxide and sulphur dioxide. These gases cause **pollution**. Sulphur dioxide dissolves in water to produce sulphurous acid; this is the cause of **acid rain**. Acid rain damages the stonework in buildings and kills trees. Damage can be widespread as the gases are carried by the wind.

fig 32 | An array of solar collectors

Global warming

Producing electricity always wastes energy as heat. This warms the Earth in two ways:

- extra heat from power stations, factories, homes etc.
- **greenhouse effect** – the extra carbon dioxide in the air traps heat.

A small increase in average temperature of 1 or 2 °C would melt a large amount of the polar ice caps, causing serious problems.

c What problems does **global warming** cause?

Nuclear power stations do not cause acid rain but they do produce dangerous, long-lasting waste. There is also the risk of a major nuclear accident, such as happened at Chernobyl in 1986.

d Do hydroelectric power stations cause pollution? Explain.

Renewable sources of energy can cause visual pollution, particularly as wind farms, dams and tidal barrages are often built in areas of natural beauty. They can occupy large areas of land and alter the habitat for wildlife and for humans. The Three Gorges Dam in the Hubei Province of China will flood vast areas of land, creating a lake 550 km in length and displacing an estimated 2 million people as well as destroying the habitat for local wildlife.

fig 33 | Geyser

Thinking further

■ **1** Why is steam *superheated* in a conventional power station?

■ **2** Select two renewable energy resources and describe their environmental impact.

◆ **3** Contrast the impact of building a wind farm in this country with building one in a third world country.

◆ **4** Imagine you are a scientist employed to advise the government on future energy supplies for the United Kingdom. What advice would you give so that we have the energy we require and protect the environment as far as possible?

KEY WORDS

acid rain • coal-burning power station • exciter • fossil (fuels) • fuel • gas-fired (power station) • global warming • greenhouse effect • hydroelectric (power), nuclear power, oil-fired (power station) • pollution • renewable source • superheated steam

---

Using the Internet to research global energy resources   *Videos etc. available from the electricity companies.*

Considering the advantages and disadvantages of a wide range of energy sources.

8.7 Power transmission

Key points

- A considerable amount of power can be wasted as heat when electricity is transferred over large distances.
- Power is transmitted at high voltages so that less power is lost.
- Transformers are used to step up the voltage at the power station and step it down at its destination.
- Transformers only work with alternating current. This is why mains electricity is a.c.
- Less power is lost at a high voltage because, for a given amount of power, the current, and hence heat loss ($= I^2R$), are low.

Power losses in transmission

The **National Grid** carries electric power around the country. It does so at voltages as high as 400 000 V. Such a high voltage is very dangerous but necessary to avoid large **power losses**.

In spread 1.3 we saw that a wire gets hot if there is a current in it. The bigger the current, the hotter it gets.

Power = voltage × current, so to keep the current (and so heat losses) small the voltage must be high.

fig 34

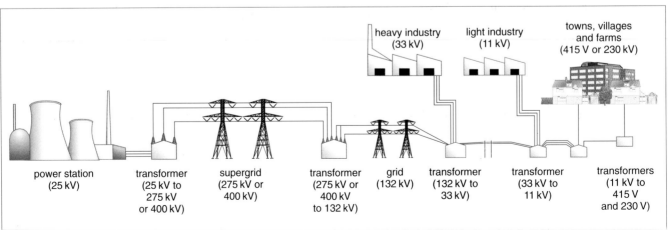

| power station (25 kV) | transformer (25 kV to 275 kV or 400 kV) | supergrid (275 kV or 400 kV) | transformer (275 kV or 400 kV to 132 kV) | grid (132 kV) | transformer (132 kV to 33 kV) | transformer (33 kV to 11 kV) | transformers (11 kV to 415 V and 230 V) |

heavy industry (33 kV)   light industry (11 kV)   towns, villages and farms (415 V or 230 kV)

fig 35 | Power transmission from power station to user

Use of transformers

Step-up transformers are used at the power station to increase the voltage to 400 kV before sending the power to the National Grid for **transmission** across the country. *Step-down* transformers are used at area **substations** to reduce the voltage to 11 000 V for factories and hospitals. Local substations then reduce the voltage to 230 V for domestic use.

Transformers only work with an alternating voltage as they require a *changing* magnetic field to induce a voltage in the secondary coil. This is why our mains electricity is a.c. (d.c. voltages can be changed but it is expensive and difficult.)

Calculating power loss

Suppose a power station generates 20 MW of power. This is to be transmitted to a place 300 km away along a cable of total resistance 15 ohms.

If it is transmitted at the generating voltage of 25 000 V, the current (I) in the cable is 20 000 000 / 25 000 = 800 A.

power lost = voltage drop along cable × current
= $IR \times I$
= I^2R
= $(800)^2 \times 15 = 9\,600\,000$ W or 9.6 MW

This means that nearly half of the power generated is wasted.

If the voltage is stepped up to 250 000 V, the current is 80 A.

power lost now = $(80)^2 \times 15 = 96\,000$ W or 0.096 MW

This is *much* less, because the power wasted is proportional to the *square* of the current.

a 25 MW of power is to be transmitted via 200 km of cable of resistance 10 ohms. Calculate the power wasted at
i 25 000 V **ii** 250 000 V

Thinking further

1 Birds often perch on the 400 kV power lines.
a Why do they like to perch on the power lines?
b Why don't they get an electric shock?

fig 36

2 Why is a high voltage used for power transmission despite the dangers?

3 Why is our electricity supplied as an alternating voltage?

4 In question **a**, the cable has a resistance of 10 Ω. Discuss whether it would be a good idea to reduce the resistance to 1 Ω.

5 230 000 W of power is to be delivered to the National Grid. This can be transmitted at 230 V or 230 000 V.
a Why would 230 000 V be used?
b 230 V is required for domestic use. How is this obtained?

KEY WORDS
National Grid • power loss • substation • transmission

 Demonstration of low voltage model power line.

Questions on electromagnetism

● **1** Use words from this list to match each description.

alternating voltage • alternators • brushes • commutator • loudspeakers • magnetic field • resistance • rotates • transformer

a This changes the current direction in the coil of an electric motor.

b This is what the coil of an electric motor does.

c If this is increased a motor is more powerful.

d This is used to increase or decrease voltages.

e These can be made of carbon.

f Generators produce this.   *(6)*

● **2**

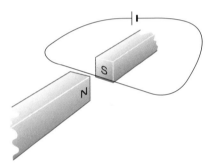

fig 37

Copy the diagram and add to it the following:

a the direction of the current   *(1)*

b the permanent magnetic field and its direction   *(2)*

c the direction in which the wire will move.   *(1)*

◆ **3** The output of a generator in a power station is connected to the National Grid. Explain why there is a transformer between the generator and the Grid.   *(3)*

■ **4** Nick turned the coil of a model generator. He used a data logger to measure the current induced every 0.2 s for 2.4 s. Here are his results.

a What are the missing values?   *(3)*

b Draw a graph of current against time.   *(4)*

c Is the current a.c. or d.c.? How do you know?   *(2)*

◆ **d** On the same axes draw graphs to show what would happen if
   i stronger magnets were used, (label it S) *(2)*
   ii the coil was rotated at *twice* the speed, (label it T).   *(2)*

● **5** The diagram shows a loudspeaker.

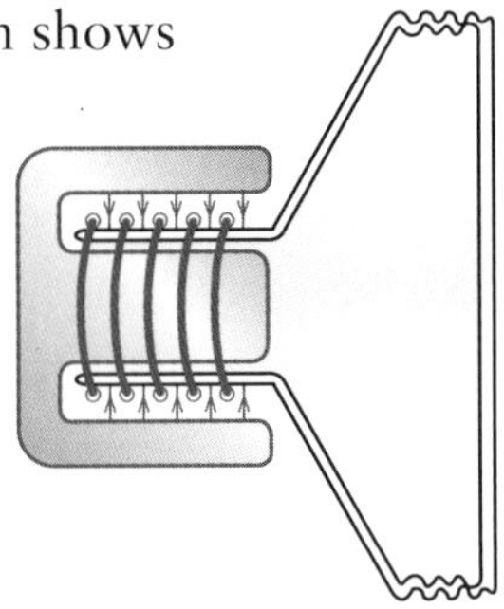

fig 39

a When there is a current in the coil the paper cone moves to the right.
● **i** Which way will it move when the current is reversed?   *(1)*
■ **ii** Explain why the paper cone moves when there is a current in the coil.   *(2)*

● **b** **i** What happens to the paper cone when there is an alternating current in the coil?   *(1)*
■ **ii** Explain why this happens.   *(2)*

c The current is increased. How does this affect
■ **i** the paper cone
■ **ii** the sound heard?   *(2)*

◆ **6** A power station generates 25 MW of power. The power is transmitted at 400 kV.

a What is the current in the power lines? *(3)*

b Explain why electricity is transmitted at such a high voltage.   *(3)*

c Why is mains electricity an alternating voltage?   *(2)*

time in s	0.0	0.2	0.4	0.6	0.8	1.0	1.2	1.4	1.6	1.8	2.0	2.2	2.4
current in A	0.0	1.5	2.6	3.0	2.6	?	0.0	−1.5	?	−3.0	−2.6	?	0.0

fig 38

7 The diagram shows a model electric motor.

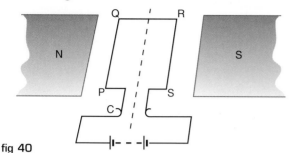

fig 40

■ **a** Will the coil PQRS rotate in a clockwise or an anticlockwise direction? Explain carefully how you decided. *(4)*

◆ **b** C is the commutator. Explain what it does. *(3)*

◆ **c** Give three ways in which the speed of the motor could be increased. *(3)*

◆ **d** The motor in an electric drill needs to be much more powerful than the model one. Give three ways in which the motor in the drill differs from the model one. *(3)*

A sensitive ammeter replaces the power supply in the model motor. The coil is now rotated by hand.

◆ **e** **i** What would you notice? *(2)*

  ii The coil is connected to a cathode ray oscilloscope (CRO). Sketch what you would expect to see on the screen of the CRO when the coil is rotated once, starting with the coil in a horizontal position. *(3)*

  iii Explain the shape of your sketch. *(3)*

IDEAS AND EVIDENCE

8 Read the following passage about wind energy and then answer the questions that follow.

Wind is created by the difference in densities of warm and cool air. Cold air near the North and South poles is denser than the warm air near the equator. The cold air moves towards the equator, pushing under the warm air. The cold air at the equator gets heated and the whole process begins again. The constant movement of air is called wind.

The most common way we use the wind today is to produce electricity. Machines that produce electricity from wind work in almost the exact opposite way to a portable fan. Wind blowing at the turbines causes them to move so that the wind can pass. As more wind tries to pass, the turbines begin to speed up. The turning of these wind turbines makes a small generator turn, producing electricity. Such a wind turbine could probably produce from 80 kW to 450 kW depending on its size. The reasons for these good electrical outputs come from new lightweight materials used in the wind turbines and better electrical generating products.

fig 41

The amount of wind energy used in future will depend on how committed we are to finding a better source of electricity than fossil fuels. Every kilowatt-hour of wind, solar or water based electricity we use offsets almost 1 kg of carbon dioxide released by fossil fuels.

a Name the process involved in creating wind. *(1)*

b How do wind turbines and portable fans work in opposite ways? *(2)*

c How does an increase in wind speed produce more electricity? *(2)*

d What locations are suitable for wind generators? *(2)*

e Give two reasons for the improved efficiency of modern wind generators. *(2)*

f Outline the way in which electricity is produced from the wind. *(4)*

g The kinetic energy of the wind increases by a factor of eight if the wind speed doubles. Explain the reason for this. *(4)*

h Explain why we need to develop alternative energy sources to fossil fuels. *(2)*

i Name three other alternative methods of producing electricity. *(3)*

j Give two advantages of using wind energy to generate electricity. *(2)*

k Give two disadvantages of using wind energy to generate electricity. *(2)*

A1 Electronics and control

fig 1

Links to Double Award

1 Electric circuits
8 Electromagnetism

Introduction

Electronics is a relatively new field of study; the electron was only discovered in 1897. An electronic circuit originally used thermionic valves. A valve is an evacuated glass tube containing electrodes, one so hot that electrons are emitted; these travel through the tube in various ways. The only such tube still in common use is the cathode ray tube found in televisions and computer monitors.

The development of semiconductor devices such as junction diodes and transistors first revolutionised electronics.

More recently the use of integrated circuits (chips) has made possible the wide range of electronic equipment we are familiar with today. Chips are cheap to build and run, robust and very small. The circuit of the chip is etched in silicon. One tiny chip is capable of storing over a million bits of information.

fig 2

 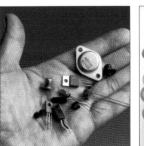
fig 3   fig 4

Check-up

Have a go at the following questions. They will remind you what you should already know about electronics and control.

a A lamp operated by a 230 V supply takes a current of 0.5 A.
   Find the resistance of the lamp.

b A current of 250 mA passes through a 500 Ω resistor.
   i What is the voltage across the resistor?
   ii What charge passes through the resistor in 1 minute?

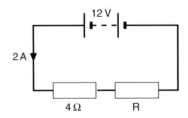
fig 6

c For the circuit shown in fig 6 find
   i   the voltage across the 4 Ω resistor
   ii the voltage across R
   iii the resistance of R.

d What is i a light dependent resistor, ii a thermistor?

fig 5

▶ Check-up (continued)

e In fig 7, how will
   i   the brightness of the lamp and
   ii the ammeter reading change when the switch is closed? Explain.

f What value fuse, 3 A, 5 A or 13 A, should be fitted to the plug attached to
   i   a 250 W computer
   ii a 2000 W fan heater?
   (Mains voltage = 230 V)

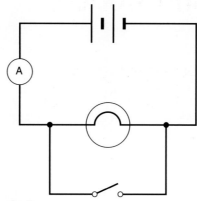

fig 7

g Why is iron used for the core of an electromagnet?

Contents of the Teaching block

This Teaching block is divided into seven double page spreads.

A1.1 Logic gates

Logic gates are electronic switches. The output voltage at any time depends on the voltage levels at the inputs. Truth tables summarise the behaviour of each logic gate.

A1.2 Inputs and outputs

Various components can be used to provide inputs to logic gates, depending on the purpose of the circuit. Relays are used to switch on large currents to operate motors, heaters etc.

A1.3 Electronic systems

An electronic system is a group of complex switches that performs a particular task. It consists of input, processor and output devices. It usually uses a chip with many gates on it.

A1.4 More truth tables

Logic gates can be combined to produce various outputs. We see how to work out truth tables for combinations of logic gates.

A1.5 The bistable and latch

Bistable and latch circuits store information. A bistable has two stable states. Bistables are widely used in computers. When only one output of a bistable is used it is known as a latch. The truth tables help us to explain how these circuits work.

A1.6 Potential divider

A potential divider uses two resistors to split a voltage in the ratio of the resistances. Light dependent resistors (LDRs) and thermistors can be used as sensors to provide a variable voltage to turn a light or a bell on or off. We see how to calculate the output voltage.

A1.7 Thermistors and LDRs

A thermistor or a light dependent resistor can be used as part of a potential divider to provide a signal for a logic gate. If they are used with a variable resistor the input signal has an adjustable threshold.

A1.1 Logic gates

Key points

- Simple logic circuits use mechanical switches.
- A truth table summarises the way in which the output of a logic circuit varies depending on the state of the inputs.
- Logic gates use electronic switches with electrical signals for inputs and outputs. At any time, the voltage level at the output depends on the voltage levels at the inputs.

- The input signal for a logic gate is either a high voltage (about 5 V) or a low voltage (about 0 V).
- The output voltage of a logic gate is high or low depending on its input signals.
- AND, OR and NOT are different logic gates.
- A truth table summarises the way in which the output of a logic gate varies depending on the state of the inputs. Truth tables use '1' for 'high' and '0' for 'low'.

Simple logic circuits

In fig 8 the lamp lights only if switches A *AND* B are closed. This is called an **AND** circuit.

We can describe the way this circuit works in a **truth table**.

a Check that you agree with the truth table in fig 9.

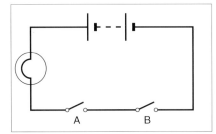

fig 8 | An AND circuit

inputs		outputs
switch A	switch B	lamp
open	open	off
open	closed	off
closed	open	off
closed	closed	on

fig 9 | Truth table for AND circuit

This kind of logic is used in a washing machine. For safety it must only work if the main switch is on AND the door is closed.

In fig 10 the lamp lights only if switch A *OR* switch B is closed. This is called an **OR** circuit.

The truth table for this circuit is shown in fig 11.

b Check that you agree with this truth table.

An OR circuit is used in a car so that the internal light comes on if either the driver's door OR the passenger's door is opened.

Logic gates

A **gate** has one or two input signals and produces a single output. **Logic gates** are 'decision making' circuits that use electronic switches. They perform complex switching operations, often controlled by **sensors**. Sensors detect changes in, for example, moisture, temperature or light intensity.

Logic gates make decisions depending on whether their inputs are 'high' (usually 5 V) or 'low' (0 V). These two states are sometimes referred to as 'on' and 'off' or 1 and 0.

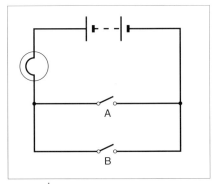

fig 10 | An OR circuit

inputs		outputs
switch A	switch B	lamp
open	open	off
open	closed	off
closed	open	on
closed	closed	on

fig 11 | Truth table for OR circuit

AND gate

The circuit symbol for an AND gate is shown in fig 12. There is an output only when *both* inputs are high.

The truth table (fig 13) is the same as that for the AND circuit in fig 8.

fig 12 | Symbol for an AND gate

inputs		outputs
A	B	
0	0	0
0	1	0
1	0	0
1	1	1

fig 13 | AND truth table

OR gate

The circuit symbol for an OR gate is shown in fig 14. There is an output when *either* of the inputs is high.

The truth table (fig 15) is the same as that for the OR circuit in fig 10.

fig 14 | Symbol for an OR gate

inputs		outputs
A	B	
0	0	0
0	1	1
1	0	1
1	1	1

fig 15 | OR truth table

NOT gate

A **NOT** gate is an **inverter**; the output is always the opposite of the input. The circuit symbol and truth table for a NOT gate are shown in figs 16 and 17.

Using logic gates

Sue wants an alarm to sound if it rains during the day so that she can bring in the washing before it gets wet. She needs to use sensors that detect moisture and light and a logic gate that gives an output (goes high) if it rains *and* it is light. This means she must use an AND gate.

c The motor in a cassette player must come on when 'play' is pressed and also when 'auto record' is pressed. What kind of logic gate must be used?

fig 16 | Symbol for a NOT gate

inputs	outputs
0	1
1	0

fig 17 | NOT truth table

Thinking further

■ **1** Some children are playing a game. They have two bags, one contains red and blue balls and the other contains red and blue cubes. They take one item from each bag. To win a child must pick two blue items. Draw up a truth table to show the possible outcomes. What sort of logic is shown?

■ **2** What sort of logic gate is needed to turn off the music at a disco if the noise level becomes too high?

◆ **3** What sort of logic gate is needed to switch on a fan in a greenhouse if it becomes too hot during the day?

◆ **4** Dan has a device that rings a bell when it gets dark. He wants to adapt it to wake him up when it gets light each morning. What sort of logic gate should he add to the device? How can he arrange it so that he only wakes up if it is a dry morning?

┌─ **KEY WORDS** ─────────────
AND • gate • inverter • logic gates • NOT • OR • sensor • truth table

 Logic Circuits using AND, OR and NOT gates.

 Think of more practical situations involving simple logic and logic gates and compile truth tables to describe them.

A1.2 Inputs and outputs

Inputs for logic gates

The input sensors chosen depend on the use to be made of the gate. As seen in spread A1.1, a switch directly affects an input, making it 'high' (logic 1) when closed or 'low' (logic 0) when open.

A light dependent resistor (LDR) can be used to vary the input with light intensity. The resistance of an LDR is low in the light giving a high input, but in the dark its resistance is high giving a low input.

A thermistor can be used to vary the input with temperature. The resistance of a thermistor is low when hot giving a high input, but high when cold giving a low input.

A **moisture sensor** (fig 18) can be made using two bare wires close together, but not touching, in a circuit. Water conducts electricity so any moisture present completes the circuit and gives a high input.

A resistor is placed in series with the sensor to make sure that the 'high' input voltage is at the correct level (5 V) so the logic gate is not damaged.

a What sensors would you use for the input of a logic gate designed to make sure that a new-born baby does not become overheated or need a clean nappy?

b What type of logic gate would you use?

Output for a logic gate

The output voltage of a logic gate is not sufficient to operate some components, such as a heater, motor, lamp or lock, directly. A **relay**, controlled by the logic gate, is used to switch on the larger current required.

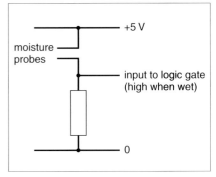

fig 18

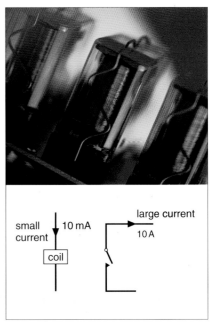

fig 19 | A relay

A relay is an electromagnetic switch. It uses a small current to magnetise the iron core of an electromagnet. This closes a switch in another circuit, switching on a large current to operate a heater, motor (or other component).

If the current to be switched on is not too large a **reed relay** can be used.

c Explain how the reed relay works.

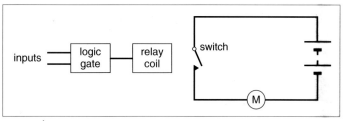

fig 20 | A relay can be used to switch on a motor

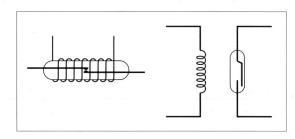

fig 21 | Construction of a reed relay

More about outputs

A light emitting diode (LED) is often used as an indicator to show whether the output of a logic gate is 'high' or 'low'.

d Why is a resistor connected in series with the LED?

e The voltage drop across the LED, when lit, is 2 V. The maximum current through it is 20 mA. Calculate the value of the series resistor R.

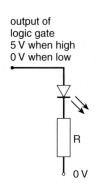

output of logic gate
5 V when high
0 V when low

R

0 V

fig 22 | The use of a LED and resistor as an indicator

If a logic gate is required to **switch** a current in a mains circuit a relay *must* be **used** because:
- a logic gate output cannot **supply** much power
- the relay isolates the low **voltage** logic gate from the high voltage **mains**.

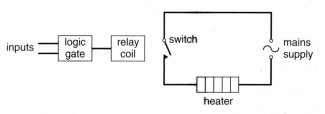

fig 23 | The use of a relay to switch on **mains** supply

Thinking further

■ **1** What input sensors are required for a logic gate designed to warn if the air in a greenhouse becomes too hot and too moist?

■ **2** Polly plans to connect the output of a logic gate to a 12 V lamp.
  a Why isn't this a good idea?
  b What should she do?

◆ **3** Imran wants to use a logic gate to turn on the central heating if it is cold when it gets dark.

a What input sensors should he use?

b Why does he need to include a relay to switch on the heating?

◆ **4** A LED is used as a logic indicator as shown in fig 22 above.

a Calculate the maximum current through the LED if the resistor has a resistance of 175 ohms and the maximum voltage across the LED is 1.5 V.

b What is the resistance of the LED then?

— **KEY WORDS** —————
moisture sensor • reed relay • relay

A1.3 Electronic systems

Electronic systems

In general a **system** is a group of parts working together to do something useful. In electrical circuits, a system is a group of switches that allows a job to be done.

In electronic systems complex electronic switches – logic gates – are used. All the components are mounted on a tiny piece of silicon called a **chip**. Most chips have many gates on them. Only the ones required for a particular system are connected. Chips are very cheap to produce so it does not matter if not all the components are used.

fig 24 | Components and chips

Parts of an electronic system

An electronic system has an input, a processor and an output.
- The **input** is anything that goes into a system.
- The **processor** changes the input in a specific way.
- The **output** is anything that comes out of a system.

A logic gate acts as the processor. It receives signals from the input sensors (high or low) and the chip processes this information, according to the type of gate connected, to produce an output signal (high or low). The output signal is then used to operate components such as lamps, heaters and motors.

fig 25 | Electronic systems allow the doors to open and close automatically

Inputs

Inputs are:
- switches, including pressure pads
- light dependent resistors (LDRs)
- thermistors
- moisture detectors

Processors

Processors are:
- electric circuits
- logic gates.

Outputs

Outputs are:
- lamps
- light emitting diodes (LEDs)
- buzzers and bells
- motors.

a What input device would you use for a fire alarm?

b What output device would you use?

Designing a system

To design a system you need to:

- decide exactly what you want the system to do
- decide which tasks are 'input', 'processing' and 'output'
- select circuits which do each of these tasks
- link the circuits together.

Dan works for a washing-machine manufacturer. He is designing a new model. The water pump must only come on when the main door and the powder drawer are both closed.

Dan decides to use switches attached to the main door and to the powder drawer. These switches will close when the door or drawer is shut.

The switches are input devices, the water pump is the output device and the circuit is the processor. Dan draws up a table (fig 28) to show what must happen when the switches are on or off.

fig 26 | Electronic systems help to prevent fires

fig 27 | Diagram of an electronic system

main door	powder drawer	water pump
open	open	off
open	closed	off
closed	open	off
closed	closed	on

fig 28

main door	powder drawer	water pump
0	0	0
0	1	0
1	0	0
1	1	1

fig 29

He then produces a truth table (fig 29). This shows Dan that he needs to use an AND circuit as the processor.

fig 30

Thinking further

■ **1** Name

   a an input device which detects changes in temperature

   b an output device which produces a sound

   c a processing device which gives an output when one input is high.

■ **2** Draw up the truth table for a heating system that will switch on the hot water pump if the living room or bedroom thermostat switches on. Identify the input, processor and output devices.

◆ **3** A lorry is fitted with an alarm system which warns if either door is open. Draw up a truth table for the system and decide on the type of processor required.

◆ **4** Design a system to warn if a car seat belt is unfastened when the seat is occupied.
(You must select the input and output devices, compile a truth table and decide on the type of processor required.)

KEY WORDS

chip • input • output • processor • system

A1.4 More truth tables

NAND and NOR gates

The output of a logic gate can be fed to the input of another logic gate. If the output of an AND gate is used as the input of a NOT gate, the output of the AND gate is reversed.

The truth table for an AND gate and a NOT gate (fig 31) is given. This is called a **NAND** (not and) gate.

a Check that you agree with the truth tables (figs 31 and 32).

If the output of an OR gate is fed into the input of a NOT gate, the output of the OR gate is reversed.

The truth table for an OR gate and a NOT gate (fig 34) is given. This is called a **NOR** (not or) gate.

b Check that you agree with the truth tables, (figs 34 and 35).

inputs A	B	C	out
0	0	0	1
0	1	0	1
1	0	0	1
1	1	1	0

fig 31 | AND + NOT

A	B	out
0	0	1
0	1	1
1	0	1
1	1	0

fig 32 | NAND

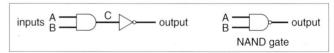

fig 33 | AND and NOT gates combine to make a NAND gate

inputs A	B	C	out
0	0	0	1
0	1	1	0
1	0	1	0
1	1	1	0

fig 34 | OR + NOT

A	B	out
0	0	1
0	1	0
1	0	0
1	1	0

fig 35 | NOR

fig 36 | OR and NOR gates combine to make a NOR gate

Combining other logic gates

Logic gates can be combined in various ways to produce the required output. Fig 37 shows how sensors and logic gates can be used to control a security light outside a house. The light is designed to come on if someone approaches the house at night.

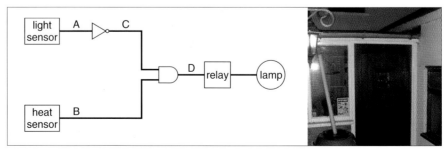

fig 37

c Copy and complete the truth table, fig 38, for the system and check that it performs as required.

d Why is a heat sensor included?

e Why is a NOT gate included?

f Why is a relay necessary?

inputs			
A	**B**	**C**	**D**
0	0		
0	1		
1	0		
1	1		

fig 38

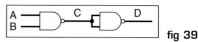

fig 39

NAND and NOR gates can be combined to produce all the other logic gates. For example, fig 39 shows how two NAND gates can be combined to produce an AND gate.

g Copy and complete the truth table, fig 40, to verify this.

inputs			
A	**B**	**C**	**D**
0	0		
0	1		
1	0		
1	1		

fig 40

Designing circuits to fit truth tables

Suppose we want to design a circuit to ring a bell when it is dark and cold. We can draw up a truth table to show the behaviour of the output device – the bell; it is shown on the right, fig 41.

light/dark	hot/cold	bell on/off
dark	cold	on
dark	hot	off
light	cold	off
light	hot	off

fig 41

The input sensors are:

• P light dependent resistor   low input when dark

• Q thermistor   low input when cold

The truth table can be rewritten using 0s and 1s (fig 42). This is the truth table for a NOR gate.

h Draw a diagram of the system required.

P	Q	bell
0	0	1
0	1	0
1	0	0
1	1	0

fig 42

Thinking further

◆ **1** What logic gate is equivalent to that shown in fig 43?

fig 43

◆ **2** Draw a truth table for the system shown in fig 44.

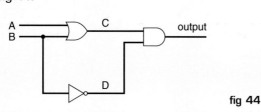

fig 44

◆ **3** A burglar alarm system is required with pressure pad sensors at two doors and a light sensor. Design a system that will trigger the alarm if any of the sensors is activated.

◆ **4** A circuit for a combination lock is shown in fig 45.

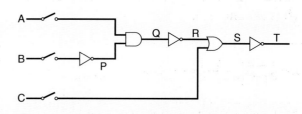

fig 45

What is the combination (at A, B and C) that opens the lock?

KEY WORDS

NAND (gate) • NOR (gate)

A1.5 The bistable and latch

The bistable

If two NOR gates are arranged so that the output of each is fed back to one of the inputs of the other, the circuit has two stable states; it is a **bistable** circuit.

Figs 46 and 47 show how two NOR gates are arranged to make a bistable. Notice how the outputs change.

Remember:

- the output (P or Q) of a NOR gate is only 1 if both inputs are 0
- if either input (or both) is 1 the output is 0
- input S sets the bistable, input R clears it, or **resets** it.

a Draw diagrams similar to figs 46 and 47 to show how two NAND gates can be used to make a bistable.

Computers

Bistables are used in computers. A bistable has two stable states, so it is a **digital** device. Data can be stored in **binary code** as a series of 1s and 0s. A computer contains millions of these bistables in its **Random Access Memory (RAM)**. Millions of bistables fit onto a few small silicon chips. Each bistable stores one **bit** (short for binary digit) of information.

The latch

When only one output of a bistable is used, as in fig 49, it is called a **latch**. The circuit flips between one stable state and the other. It is sometimes called a **flip flop**. The circuit remembers, or 'latches' the last thing that happened to it.

b Design a latch using two NAND gates.

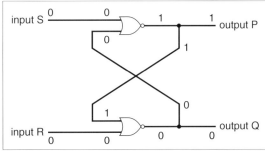

fig 46

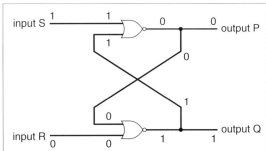

fig 47

fig 48

If input S is briefly made 'high' it sets the latch to state A.

If input R is briefly made 'high' it sets the latch to state B; this returns it to its original state so R is called the reset connection.

c Write down the truth table for a NOR gate. Use it to check the logic of the bistable for each setting in figs 46 and 47.

d Use the truth table for a NOR gate to check the logic of the latch for each stable state.

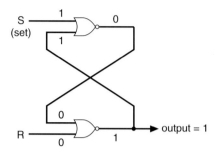

fig 49 | The action of a latch, stable state A

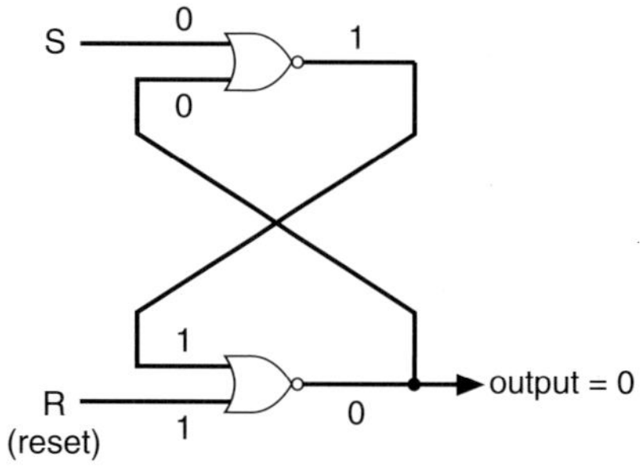

fig 50 | The action of a latch, stable state B

- S sets the latch – changes the output from 'low' to 'high'.
- R resets the latch – changes the output from 'high' to 'low'.
- a low signal at both inputs leaves the output signal unchanged.

Burglar alarm

We have seen (spread A1.3) how to use logic gates to make a burglar alarm. The alarm only sounds while the sensor is activated. It would be better if the alarm continued to sound when the burglar had moved past the sensor. A latch makes this possible.

Suppose a sensor (such as a pressure pad) is connected to input S in fig 49. If a burglar steps on the pressure pad, S goes 'high' and the output is latched on 'high'. A bell connected to the output sounds and continues to do so until the latch is reset.

e How is the latch reset?

Thinking further

■ **1** In a bistable circuit (see fig 46) what must happen to make it revert to its original state following an input signal?

◆ **2** Fig 51 shows a bistable circuit made from two NAND gates. The unconnected inputs R and S are 'high'. The output is also 'high'. Copy the diagram and mark on it the voltage levels of all the inputs to the two gates. What happens when input R is connected briefly to the low voltage level?

◆ **3** Steve is deaf. Design a circuit so that he can tell if the doorbell has rung since he last looked.

◆ **4** Draw a diagram to help you to explain how a motor can be turned on and off using a latch. (This is how the touch buttons used to start and stop a video recorder work.)

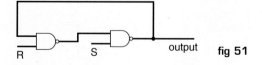

fig 51

KEY WORDS

binary code • bistable • bit • digital • flip flop • latch • Random Access Memory (RAM) • reset

A1.6 Potential divider

Dividing a voltage

A **potential divider** uses two resistors to split a voltage (also known as a potential difference) into two parts. Look at fig 52. The voltage across each resistor is proportional to its resistance because they both have the same current ($V = IR$). If $R_1 = R_2$ the voltage across each resistor will be 6 V.

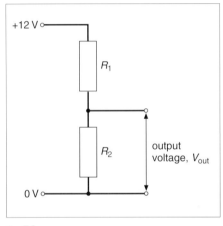

fig 52

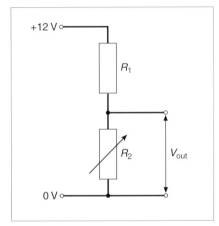

fig 53

a What is the output voltage if $R_1 = 2R_2$?

The arrangement of resistors allows you to obtain a smaller voltage than the one supplied.

Varying the output voltage

If one of the resistors is a variable resistor the output voltage can be varied as in fig 53.

As the resistance of R_2 increases the voltage across R_2 increases – the output voltage (V_{out}) increases.

b What happens to the voltage across R_1 as the resistance of R_2 increases?

c How would the output voltage change if R_1 was a variable resistor and R_2 had a fixed value?

Using a light dependent resistor (LDR)

The resistance of a LDR is low in the light and high in the dark. V_{out} therefore increases when it gets dark. This high output voltage can be used to switch on an outside light as night falls.

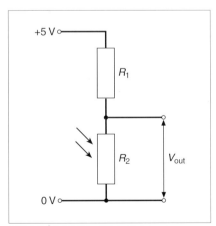

fig 54 | A potential divider using a LDR

d Suggest another use for this circuit.

e How would the circuit work if R_1 and R_2 were reversed?

The circuit can be adjusted to switch on a light when it is not quite dark by reducing the resistance of R_1.

Using a thermistor

The resistance of a thermistor is low when hot and high when cold. V_{out} will increase as the temperature falls.

This circuit could be used to control temperature by using the output voltage to switch on a heater when the temperature fell to a certain level.

f How could the circuit be adapted for use as a fire alarm?

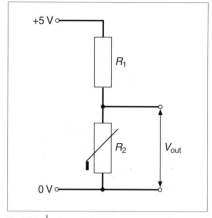

fig 55 | A potential divider with a thermistor

Calculating output voltage

Look at fig 56.

$V_1 = IR_1$ and $V_2 = IR_2$ $\dfrac{V_1}{V_2} = \dfrac{R_1}{R_2}$

Also $V = I(R_1 + R_2)$ so

$$\frac{V_1}{V} = \frac{R_1}{(R_1 + R_2)} \qquad \frac{V_2}{V} = \frac{R_2}{(R_1 + R_2)}$$

g Calculate the output voltage in fig 57.

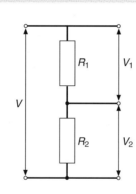

fig 56

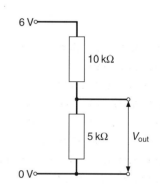

fig 57

Thinking further

■ **1** A potential divider is made from a fixed resistor and a LDR. The LDR is placed outside, away from any lights. How would the voltage across the fixed resistor change during a 24-hour period?

■ **2** A variable resistor is connected as shown in fig 58. It acts as a potential divider. Explain how the output voltage will change when the sliding contact is moved from A to B.

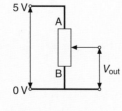

fig 58

◆ **3** Draw a circuit diagram to show how 15 Ω and 45 Ω resistors can be used to obtain an output of 3 V from a 12 V supply.

◆ **4** At school Rachel connected the circuit shown in fig 59. The voltmeter has a high resistance and can be connected across different parts of the circuit.

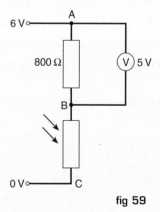

fig 59

a What was the voltmeter reading when connected across BC?

b What was then the resistance of the LDR?

c What will happen to the voltmeter readings across AB and BC when it gets dark?

KEY WORDS

potential divider

A1.7 Thermistors and LDRs

Key points

- A light dependent resistor (LDR) can be used with a fixed resistor to provide a signal for a logic gate that varies with light intensity.

- A thermistor can be used with a fixed resistor to provide a signal for a logic gate that is temperature dependent.

- A LDR or a thermistor can be used with a variable resistor to provide a signal with an adjustable threshold for a logic gate.

Using a light dependent resistor (LDR)

As seen in spread A1.6 the resistance of a LDR is low in the light and high in the dark. In fig 60(a)

$$V_{out} = \frac{R_{LDR}}{(R + R_{LDR})} \, V_{in}$$

V_{out} therefore increases when it gets dark so it can be used as an input for a logic gate that goes 'high' when it becomes dark.

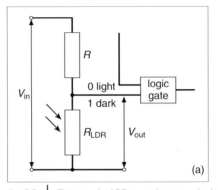
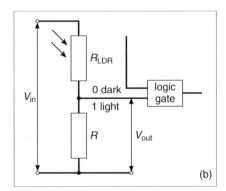

fig 60 | The use of a LDR as an input to a logic gate

If the LDR and resistor are interchanged the logic is reversed. The input to a logic gate would go 'high' if a light were shone on the LDR as in fig 60(b).

a Write down an expression for V_{out} in fig 60(b).

Using a thermistor

Spread A1.6 showed us that the resistance of a thermistor is low when hot and high when cold.

$$V_{out} = \frac{R_{thermistor}}{(R + R_{thermistor})} \, V_{in}$$

V_{out} therefore increases as the temperature falls.

This high output voltage could be used to give a 'high' input to a logic gate when the temperature falls.

b How could the circuit be adapted for use as a fire alarm?

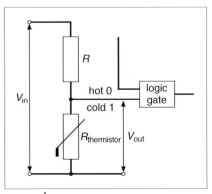

fig 61 | The use of a thermistor as an input to a logic gate

Combining input sensors

Fig 62 shows a LDR and a thermistor being used to make a system that warns if the temperature falls *and* it becomes dark.

c Draw a diagram to show how this system could be adapted to warn if the temperature rises *or* it becomes dark.

Varying the threshold signal

The LDR circuit in fig 60 can be adjusted to switch on a light when it is not quite dark by reducing the resistance of R. If R is replaced by a variable resistor, the light intensity which makes the input to the logic gate change from 'low' to 'high' can be adjusted; the variable resistor acts as a **sensitivity control**.

d Explain how the resistance of the variable resistor must change if the input is to go 'high' in a dim light.

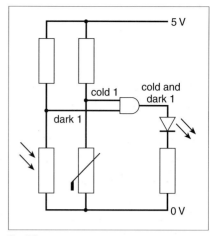

fig 62

Thinking further

◆ 1 Fig 63 includes an unidentified logic gate, G.

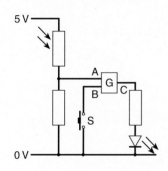

fig 63

The LED glows during the day but goes out if S is pressed. At night the LED does not glow whether S is pressed or not.

a Draw a truth table to show the states of A, B and C. (B is 'high' unless S is pressed.)

b What sort of logic gate is G?

c The LDR and fixed resistor are changed around. How will the circuit behave now?

◆ 2 Fig 64 shows a circuit used in the wrapping section of a chocolate factory to reject bars that are too long. (If the bars are too long the machinery becomes jammed.)

a Why is a relay needed?

b Copy and complete the truth table, fig 65. Use it to explain how the circuit works.

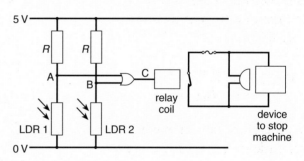

fig 64

LDR 1	LDR 2	voltage states			buzzer
		A	B	C	
light	light				
light	dark				
dark	light				
dark	dark				

fig 65

If the bars were too short the consumers would not be happy and the manufacturer could be prosecuted for selling under-weight goods.

c How could the manufacturer alter the circuit to detect chocolate bars that are too short?

Questions on electronics and control

1 Copy and complete the following sentences using 'high' or 'low'.

a If one of the inputs of an AND gate is 'low' the output is _____

b An OR circuit is so called because if the output is 'high' one, or both, of the inputs is _____

c To get a 'low' output with an OR gate both inputs must be _____ *(3)*

2 In the circuit below, X is a logic gate. The buzzer sounds only when the switches A and B are positioned as shown.

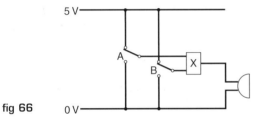

fig 66

a Draw up a truth table for X. *(2)*

b What kind of logic gate is X? *(1)*

c State one use that could be made of circuit X. *(1)*

3 a Design a circuit using a 5 V supply, LDR, resistor and voltmeter to act as a light meter. *(3)*

b Explain how your circuit works. *(3)*

c How would you calibrate the voltmeter to read light intensity? *(2)*

4 A cassette player will only start to record if the 'record' and 'play' buttons are pushed together. Draw a diagram, including a logic gate, to show how this can be done. *(4)*

5 Copy and complete the truth table (fig 68) for the logic system shown in fig 67, using the inputs given. *(4)*

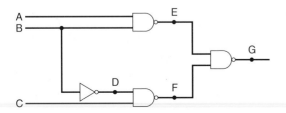

fig 67

A	B	C	D	E	F	G
0	0	0				
0	1	0				
1	0	1				
1	1	1				
0	0	1				
0	1	1				
1	0	0				
1	1	0				

fig 68

6 A photographer sets up a circuit, fig 69, to warn people not to enter his dark room while he is developing films. The resistance of the LDR is $200\,\Omega$ in the light but $2\,M\Omega$ in the dark.

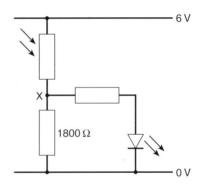

fig 69

a Where should the photographer put
  i the LDR   **ii** the LED? *(2)*

b What is the voltage level at X when the darkroom light is on? *(3)*

c Is the LED on? Explain. *(2)*

d The darkroom light is switched off. Find the new voltage at X and explain what happens to the LED now. *(4)*

e The photographer decides to replace the LED with a mains lamp.
  i Why is this not a good idea? *(1)*
  ii Show how he could modify his circuit so that he could use a mains lamp successfully. *(3)*

7 The block diagram below shows a burglar alarm. The alarm bell sounds when the alarm system is set and someone steps on the pressure pad sensor placed under a doormat.

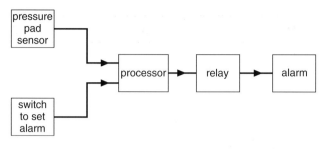

fig 70

■ **a** What logic gate should be used for the processor? *(1)*

■ **b** Why is a relay necessary? *(2)*

■ **c** What happens when a burglar steps off the doormat? Explain. *(2)*

d The alarm system could be improved by connecting a latch between the pressure sensor and the processor.

■   **i** What is a latch? *(2)*

■   **ii** How would this improve the alarm system? *(2)*

◆   **iii** Draw a diagram of a latch and explain how it works. *(6)*

IDEAS AND EVIDENCE

8 Read the following passage and answer the questions that follow.

The light emitting diode (LED) was developed in the 1970s, originally as a light source for use with optical fibres. Its power is low and it emits light of a single colour, originally red.

LEDs are frequently used instead of filament lamps to indicate that an appliance is on 'stand by' – connected to the mains but not functioning. Red is the usual colour for LEDs used as indicators, but LEDs emitting green, yellow, orange and even blue light are now available.

A series resistor is needed to protect the LED. Typically a red LED needs a forward voltage of 1.7 V with a maximum current of 20 mA. A diode does not conduct if it is reverse biased, so care must be taken to connect it the right way round. If the reverse voltage exceeds 5 V the LED may be damaged. When using a LED with alternating current it must be protected from the large reverse voltages which could damage it by connecting a diode in parallel with the LED.

fig 71

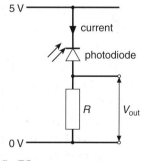

fig 72

A photodiode is connected in reverse bias so that it does not normally conduct. It has a small window so that light can fall on it. This produces a very small reverse current that is proportional to the light intensity. This current ranges from 10^{-9} A to 10^{-4} A, but it can be used to produce a measurable output voltage if the resistance, R, is large (about 1 MΩ). Photodiodes are used to detect signals passed down optical fibres and in infrared TV and video remote control systems.

a Why is a LED particularly suitable for use with optical fibres? *(2)*

b Why are LEDs preferred to filament lamps for 'stand by' indicators? *(2)*

c **i** Why is a protective resistor necessary when using a LED? *(2)*

  ii The voltage across a red LED and its protective resistor is 5 V. Estimate the value of resistor required. *(3)*

d **i** Why is an alternating current more likely to damage a LED than the same value direct current? *(2)*

  ii Draw a circuit diagram to show how a LED can be protected from such damage. Explain how your circuit works. *(4)*

e **i** Compare the action of a LED and a photodiode. How do their circuit symbols illustrate this? *(3)*

  ii Sketch a graph of the current produced in a photodiode against the light intensity falling on it. *(2)*

  iii If the current recorded were 0.10 mA, would the photodiode be in the dark or the light? Explain. *(3)*

  iv Use the data given to estimate the smallest output voltage that must be capable of being measured. *(3)*

A2 Processing waves

Links to Double Award

3 Wave properties
4 Using waves

When light passes from one transparent material into another, it changes direction. The change in direction is due to a change in speed. This is known as refraction.

Waves are caused by vibrations which may be either longitudinal or transverse. Among the properties of a wave are its wavelength, frequency, amplitude and speed.

Check-up

Have a go at the following questions. They will remind you what you should already know about waves.

a Sketch a transverse wave and show clearly on the diagram what is meant by wavelength and amplitude.

b Copy and complete the following sentences by choosing the best words from this list.

less than • equal to • greater than

When a ray of light enters a more dense material along the normal the angle of refraction is _____ the angle of incidence.

When a ray of light enters a more dense material at an angle of 10° the angle of refraction is _____ the angle of incidence.

When a ray of light enters a less dense material at an angle of 10° the angle of refraction is _____ the angle of incidence.

c Fig 1 shows the path of a ray of light as it passes through three different materials **A**, **B** and **C**. One material is air, one glass and the other water. (Glass is optically denser than water.) Identify the three materials and explain your answer.

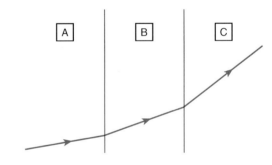

fig 1

d A string is vibrated five times each second. A transverse wave is produced with a wavelength of 30 cm.

  i What is the frequency of the wave?
  ii Calculate the speed of the wave.

Contents of the Teaching block

This Teaching block is divided into eight double page spreads.

A2.1 Refractive index

When light is refracted, the amount of refraction depends on the materials through which the light is travelling. Refractive index is a measure of how much refraction takes place.

A2.2 How convex lenses work

The curved surface of a lens means that the light refracts differently at each point on the surface. This allows light to be focused.

A2.3 Uses of convex lenses

The ability of a lens to focus light makes it a useful optical device. We examine how the camera, magnifying glass and projector work.

A2.4 Resonance

Everything has its own natural frequency at which it vibrates with a larger amplitude than any other.

A2.5 Resonance in strings

Stringed instruments work because their strings are forced to vibrate at a particular frequency, which produces a distinctive note.

A2.6 Resonance in pipes

Wind instruments work because the air is forced to vibrate at a particular frequency, which produces a distinctive note.

A2.7 Interference

When two waves meet, they interfere. This can sometimes help but at other times the interference is a nuisance.

A2.8 The nature of light

Light sometimes behaves as if it is a particle and sometimes as if it is a wave. We examine the evidence for both sorts of behaviour.

A2.1 Refractive index

Changing direction

The **refractive index** of a material is defined as the ratio of the speed of light in a vacuum to the speed of light in the material.

$$\text{refractive index} = \frac{\text{speed of light in vacuum}}{\text{speed of light in material}}$$

In practice, the speed of light in air and in a vacuum are very similar.

a The speed of light in air is 300 000 km/s. When light enters glass, it slows down to 200 000 km/s. Calculate the refractive index of glass.

In the school laboratory, it is not possible to measure the speed of light, but we can find out the refractive index of a material.

Fig 2 shows the relationship between the angle of refraction (r) and the angle of incidence (i) for light passing from air into glass.

Plotting sine of angle of incidence against sine of angle of refraction produces a straight line graph passing through the origin. This means that the two quantities are **proportional**.

b Measure the slope of the straight line graph. How does it compare with the value for the refractive index of glass found in question **a**?

By examining the graph we see that,

$$\text{refractive index} = \frac{\text{sine of angle of incidence}}{\text{sine of angle of refraction}}$$

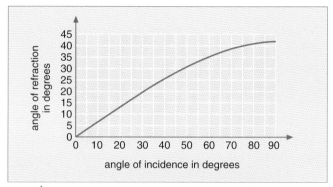

fig 2 | Graph of angle of refraction against angle of incidence

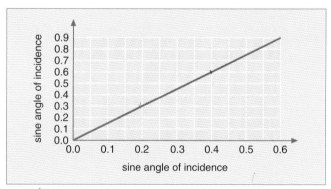

fig 3 | Graph of sine of angle of incidence against sine of angle of refraction

Dispersion

Different colours have different refractive indices. This means that for a particular angle of incidence, each colour has a different angle of refraction. If the incident light is white, the result is the formation of the visible spectrum. The spreading out of the colours in this way is called **dispersion**.

The table, fig 4, shows the refractive indices of four colours of the spectrum for glass.

colour	refractive index
red	1.520
orange	1.523
green	1.529
violet	1.538

fig 4

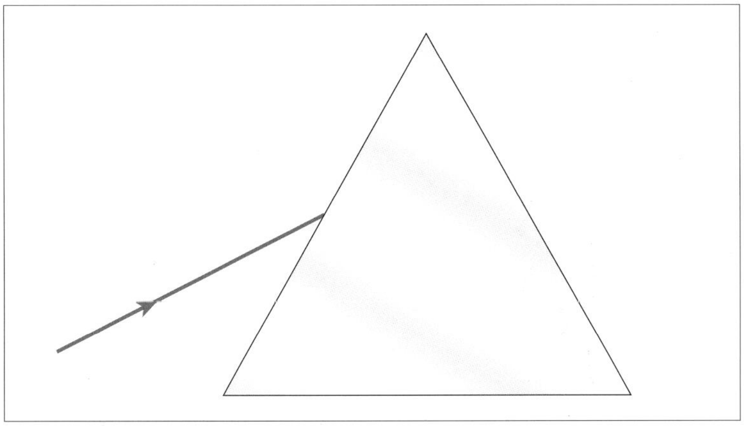

fig 5

c A ray of white light enters an equilateral glass prism as shown in fig 5. Copy and complete the diagram to show the path of the ray through and out of the prism. Clearly indicate any colours.

Thinking further

◆ **1** Nadia obtained these results when measuring angles of incidence and refraction at an air/water boundary.

angle of incidence, i, in degrees	10	20	30	40	50	60	70
angle of refraction, r, in degrees	7	15	22	29	35	38	45

fig 6

◆ **2** The refractive index of glass is 1.5, and of water is 1.3. Calculate the critical angle for glass and for water.

a Plot a graph of sine i against sine r.

b Draw the best straight line through the points.

c Nadia appears to have misread one of the angles of refraction. Which angle has she misread? What should the angle have been?

d Use the graph to work out the refractive index of water.

e Calculate the speed of light in water.

KEY WORDS
dispersion • proportional • refractive index

🖥 *Use a spread sheet to investigate the relationship between* i *and* r.

A2.2 How convex lenses work

Properties of convex lenses

There are three different types of convex lens, depending on the curvature of each surface, fig 7.

The centre of the lens is known as the **optical centre**. The line through the optical centre at right angles to the lens is the **principal axis**.

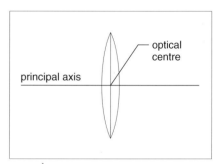

fig 7 | Types of lenses

bi-convex plano-convex convex meniscus

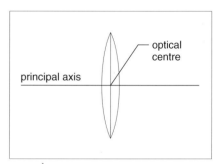

fig 8 | Optical centre and principal axis

optical centre
principal axis

Light passing through a convex lens is refracted at both surfaces and should be drawn as such. However, lenses are usually quite thin and the amount of refraction is small. In this case, an approximation can be made by just showing refraction taking place at the centre of the lens. When we do this, we draw a line down the centre of the lens.

The **focal point** (sometimes called principal focus) of a convex lens is the point through which all rays parallel and near to the principal axis pass after refraction at the lens.

The distance from the optical centre to the focal point is called the **focal length**. We can estimate the focal length of a convex lens quite simply by focusing light from a distant object onto a screen.

a Suggest why it is a *distant* object, not a near object, which needs to be focused to find the focal length.

To measure focal length more accurately in the laboratory, we can set up the apparatus shown in fig 12. We adjust the distance between the object and the lens until a clearly focused image appears next to the object.

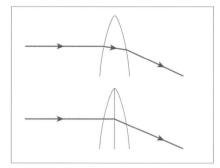

fig 9

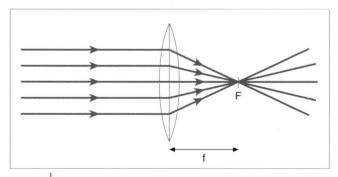

fig 10 | Focal point of a convex lens

f

fig 11

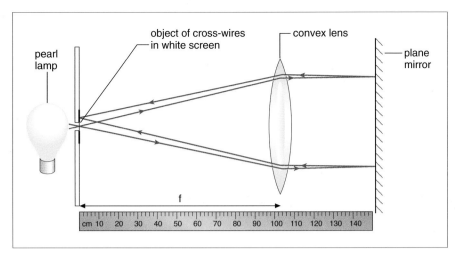

fig 12

Ray tracing through a convex lens

We use three standard ray paths to help us work out how a convex lens behaves.

- Rays passing through the optical centre of a thin convex lens are undeviated.
- Rays parallel and near to the principal axis are refracted through the focal point.
- Rays passing through the focal point are refracted parallel to the principal axis.

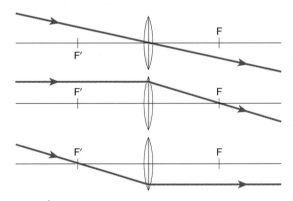

fig 13 | Ray path through a convex lens

To find the position of the image of an object, we draw ray diagrams using the standard ray paths.

Example Consider an object more than twice the focal length away from the lens.

The image is:

- between the focal length and twice the focal length from the lens
- **inverted**
- **diminished**
- **real.**

If the diagrams are drawn to scale, the actual sizes and positions of the image can be found.

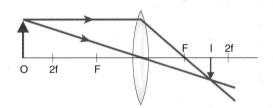

fig 14

Thinking further

■ **1** When Sonia used the apparatus shown in fig 12 to measure the focal length of a lens, she found the distance from the lens to the cross-wires was 75 mm and from the lens to the mirror was 120 mm.

  a What is the focal length of the lens?

  b What happens to the image if Sonia moves the mirror closer to the lens?

◆ **2** Draw accurate ray diagrams to find the position and properties of the image when the object is

  a at twice the focal length (2f)

  b between the focal point and twice the focal length, from a convex lens.

--- KEY WORDS ---
diminished • **focal length** • **focal point** • inverted • **optical centre** • **principal axis** • **real**

A2.3 Uses of convex lenses

Key points

- How a convex lens is used depends on where the object is placed relative to the focal point.
- A camera has the object at a relatively large distance from the focal point.

- A projector has the object between the focal point and a distance twice the focal length from the lens.
- A magnifying glass has the object between the focal point and the lens.

Camera

The camera uses a convex lens to focus a large distant object onto a photographic film. The image on the film is real, diminished and inverted.

Fig 14 shows the ray construction diagram for the camera.

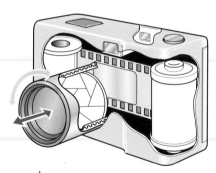

fig 15 | Image formation in a camera

To produce a clearly focused image over a wide range of object distances, the photographer adjusts the camera by changing the distance between the lens and the film.

a Draw ray diagrams to find out how the photographer must change the lens-to-film distance between taking a distant scene and a close-up head and shoulders portrait.

b Some cameras have automatic focusing which uses either an infrared beam or ultrasound. How can these be used to measure distance?

fig 16 | Turning the lens assembly causes it to move in or out

Projector

The projector works by placing the object (film or slide) between the focal point and a distance of twice the focal length from the lens.

The image is:
- further from the lens than twice the focal length
- inverted
- **magnified**
- real.

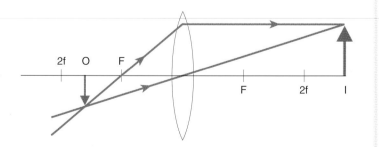

fig 17 | Image formation in a projector

c Why is the slide put in the projector upside down?

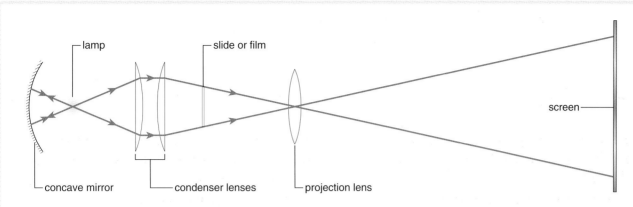

lamp · slide or film · concave mirror · condenser lenses · projection lens · screen

fig 18 | Construction of a projector

Projectors contain more than one lens. The light from the bulb is reflected from a concave mirror, then passes through a **condenser** before reaching the film and projection lens.

As with a camera, the projection lens can be moved backwards and forwards depending on the distance to the projection screen.

d Suggest why there is a concave mirror behind the bulb.

e What is the distance between the centre of the bulb and the first condenser lens? Explain your answer.

Magnifying glass

fig 19

The magnifying glass works by producing an image on the same side of the lens as the object. The user looks through the lens at the object.

The object is placed between the lens and the focal point.

The image is:
- beyond the object
- magnified
- erect
- virtual.

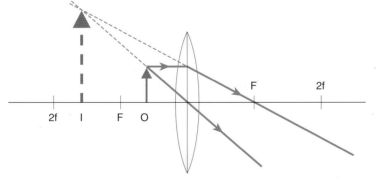

2f · I · F · O · F · 2f

fig 20

KEY WORDS
condenser • erect • magnified

Thinking further

◆ **1** The distance between the film and projection lens in a slide projector is 20 cm. The focal length of the lens is 18 cm.

a Draw a ray diagram to scale and find the distance of the screen from the lens if the image is clearly focused.

b What must happen to the film to projection lens distance if the screen is moved further away?

c What happens to the size of the image if the screen is moved further away?

◆ **2** Some cameras have a fixed lens which cannot be moved.

a Explain why these cameras are suitable for taking pictures of any object further than a few metres away.

b What happens to the image on the film if the object is very close to the camera?

A2.4 Resonance

Natural vibrations

All objects have their own **natural frequency** of vibration. A child on a swing will swing backwards and forwards with a certain frequency as will the pendulum of a clock.

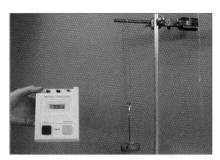

fig 21 | A mass on a vibrating spring

A given vibrating spring will bounce up and down with a frequency which depends on the mass hanging on the spring.

a When Kate investigated the vibration of a spring with different masses hanging on it, these were her results.

mass on spring in g	100	200	300	400	500
time for ten vibrations in s	4.49	6.17	7.40	8.47	9.32

fig 22

   i Calculate the frequency of vibration for each mass.
   ii Plot a graph of frequency against mass.
   iii How does mass affect the natural frequency of a vibrating object?

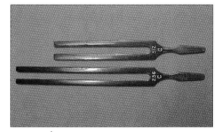

fig 23 | Tuning forks

Tuning forks have their own natural frequency. The larger the fork the lower the frequency produced.

Forced vibrations

A tuning fork does not make a very loud sound because it does not cause much air to vibrate. If the stem is placed on a table, the whole table vibrates. The **forced vibration** of the table is not very big but the larger amount of air in contact with the table vibrates so the sound is much louder.

If the metal sphere is pushed and starts to swing, so do all of the weighted paper cones. Most of them have very small swings which seem to stop and start.

One of the cones swings with the same frequency as the metal sphere and gradually builds up the amplitude of its swing.

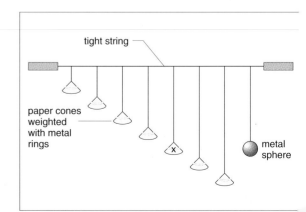

tight string

paper cones weighted with metal rings

metal sphere

fig 24

The cone X is on a string of the same length as the metal sphere. It is being forced to vibrate at its own natural frequency. This is known as **resonance**.

Resonance

fig 25

If you have ever jumped up and down on a small footbridge, you will know that the bridge starts to vibrate. If you time your jumps to be in time with the vibrating bridge then the vibrations get bigger. Similarly, when pushing a child on a swing, the person pushing the swing does so in time with the natural swing. If they do not do so, the amplitude of the swing will not build up.

Some opera singers can sing such high notes that wine glasses, for example, start to resonate and then shatter.

In 1940, a new suspension bridge over the Tacoma Narrows in the United States started to vibrate in the wind and eventually collapsed. One theory is that the movement of the wind matched the natural frequency of the bridge which started to resonate. Today, designers of bridges and tall structures take resonance into account.

fig 26

fig 27 | The collapse of the Tacoma Bridge

Thinking further

◆ 1 Factory chimneys often have spiralling baffles around them. Suggest what effect this has on the wind and why it is necessary.

fig 28

KEY WORDS
forced vibration • natural frequency • resonance

 Research on Tacoma Bridge collapse.

A2.5 Resonance in strings

- The natural frequency of a vibrating string depends on its length, mass and tension.
- A node is a point on a vibrating string having zero displacement.
- An antinode is a point on a vibrating string having maximum displacement.

- The frequency of a vibrating string depends on the number of nodes.
- A string can have different modes of vibration depending on the number of nodes.
- The quality of a note depends on the modes of vibration.

Stationary waves in strings

When a tight string, such as a guitar string, is plucked the string starts to vibrate with a particular frequency. This is its natural or resonant frequency.

Consider a string fixed between two points. When it is plucked in the middle it vibrates as shown, fig 29.

The fixed points cannot vibrate and so must remain still. A point which does not vibrate is called a **node**. The centre of the string can vibrate with the largest amplitude.

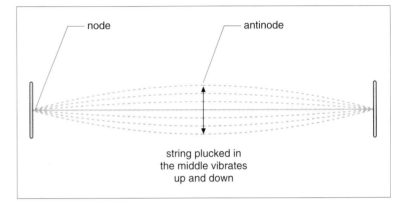

fig 29

All points on the string have their own amplitude. A point of maximum amplitude is known as an **antinode**. The wave, because it does not appear to travel along the string, is called a **stationary wave**.

a What type of wave, transverse or longitudinal, is produced when the string is plucked?

Other stationary waves are also produced when the string is plucked. The wave which has only one antinode is the wave which is vibrating at the string's resonant frequency. The note produced is the first **harmonic** (sometimes called the **fundamental** frequency).

b A string 1.2 m long is firmly fixed at each end. When plucked, it vibrates with only one antinode – the first harmonic. What is the wavelength of the note produced?

Harmonics

Fig 30 shows some of the other waves that can be produced when the string is plucked. Each wave

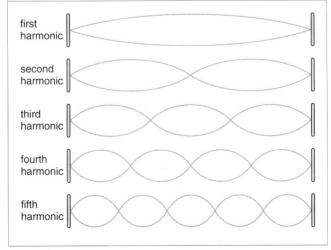

fig 30 | Harmonics

represents a different mode of vibration. Each time another antinode is present, so a higher frequency harmonic is produced.

c Paul plucks the middle C string of his guitar. It produces a first harmonic frequency of 261.6 Hz. What are the frequencies of the next two harmonics?

Quality

A tuning fork produces a pure note of just one frequency – the first harmonic. Other instruments which play the same note also produce other harmonics. The number of harmonics produced, and their relative amplitudes, result in complicated waveforms that gives each instrument its own characteristic sound or **quality**.

fig 31 | Fran Healy of Travis

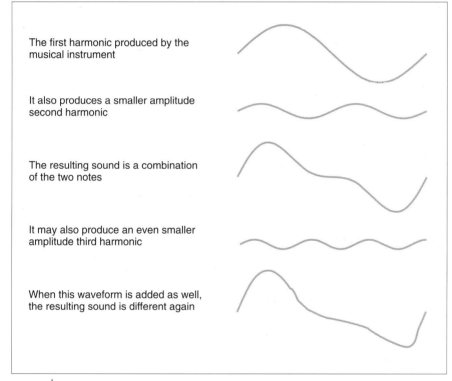

The first harmonic produced by the musical instrument

It also produces a smaller amplitude second harmonic

The resulting sound is a combination of the two notes

It may also produce an even smaller amplitude third harmonic

When this waveform is added as well, the resulting sound is different again

fig 32 | Adding different waveforms

Tuning

The note produced by a vibrating string depends on several factors. These can easily be seen by examining a guitar.

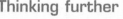

* The thicker and more massive the string, the lower the pitch of the note.
* The longer the string, the lower the pitch of the note.
* The tighter the string, the higher the pitch of the note.

fig 33

Thinking further

1 John plucks a fixed string at its mid point and listens to the note produced. He then plucks the same string a quarter of the way along its length. Describe how the note produced is different.

2 Fig 30 shows the different harmonics produced by a vibrating string. Plot a graph of frequency against

$$\frac{1}{\text{wavelength}}$$

for a vibrating string using the diagrams to help you.

KEY WORDS

antinode • fundamental • harmonic • node • quality • stationary wave

A2.6 Resonance in pipes

- The natural frequency of a vibrating air column depends on its length.

- Modes of vibration depend on whether the pipe in which the air is vibrating is a closed pipe or an open pipe.

Stationary waves in closed pipes

Everyone has at some time blown across the top of a bottle to produce a sound. The air in the bottle is forced to vibrate at its natural frequency. The air at the open top of the bottle can vibrate at its maximum amplitude, so at this point there is an antinode. The air at the bottom of the bottle is stationary, so at this point there is a node.

Although the wave produced is a longitudinal wave, we represent the displacement of the air by a transverse wave.

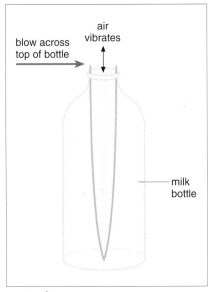

fig 34 | A stationary wave in a vertical bottle

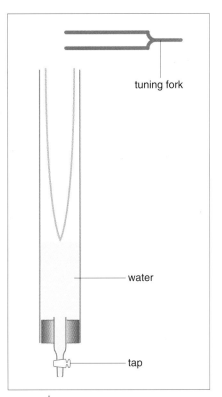

fig 35 | A resonance tube

If there is liquid left in the bottle, the frequency of the note produced is higher. The resonant frequency depends on the length of the vibrating air column.

In the laboratory we can investigate this using a long plastic tube from which water can be released. This arrangement is called a resonance tube.

A tuning fork produces a note above the tube. Compressions and rarefactions travel down the tube where they are reflected at the water surface. A stationary wave is produced in the tube.

When the water is released, a note is heard from the tube which increases in loudness, reaches a maximum, then becomes quieter again. The length of the air column which produces the loudest note is the resonant length.

a When a tuning fork vibrates with a frequency of 256 Hz above a resonance tube, the resonant length is 322 mm. What is the wavelength of the wave produced?

Stationary waves in open pipes

Some pipes are open at both ends. In this case, the air can vibrate with maximum ampli-tude at both ends, so there are antinodes at each end.

b A tuning fork vibrating with a frequency of 440 Hz produces resonance in an open tube 375 mm long. When a bung is placed in one end of the tube and the tuning fork held over the other no resonant note is heard. Explain why.

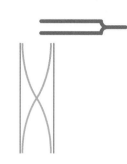

fig 36 | Stationary waves in a pipe open at both ends

Quality

Organ pipes can be either open or closed. They are very carefully made to allow certain modes of vibration to occur. As with vibrating strings, both **closed pipes** and **open pipes** have second and higher harmonics. These harmonics add to the fundamental note producing rich and varied sounds.

c Sketch the wave patterns for the second harmonic in a closed pipe and in an open pipe.

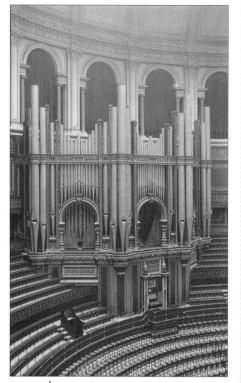

fig 37 |

Thinking further

◆ **1** A trombone player plays a note with the slide of his trombone fully extended. What happens to the pitch of the note as he shortens the length of the slide?

fig 38

◆ **2** Eight tuning forks are used in turn above a resonance tube. Their frequencies and the corresponding resonant lengths are shown in the table.

frequency in Hz	256	288	320	341	384	427	480	512
resonant length in mm	322	286	258	242	215	193	172	161

fig 39

Plot a graph of wavelength against $\dfrac{1}{\text{frequency}}$

Measure the gradient of the line. Comment on its significance.

A2.7 Interference (1)

> ## Key points
>
> - Interference is caused when two waves meet.
> - Constructive interference has a reinforcing effect.
> - Destructive interference has a cancelling effect.

Experience interference

In the laboratory, you can experience interference of sound using two loudspeakers, placed some distance apart, which are connected to the same signal generator. If you walk in a line parallel to the line joining the loudspeakers, you hear the sound become louder and quieter as you walk along the line. This effect repeats itself as you walk along the line.

In fig 40, Z is midway between the two loudspeakers. The distance from L_1 to Z (L_1Z) is the same as the distance from L_2 to Z (L_2Z). This means that the sound leaving the two loudspeakers reaches Z at exactly the same time. When the centre of a compression from L_1 reaches Z, so does the centre of a compression from L_2. The two waves arrive at Z in **phase** so the sound is loud. Similarly, if L_1X and L_2X are different by a distance equal to the wavelength of the sound, the two waves will again be in phase and the sound is louder.

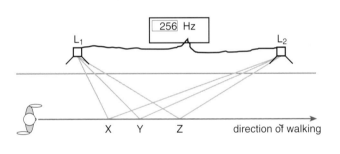

fig 40

At Y, however, the sound becomes quieter because the difference between L_1Y and L_2Y is half the wavelength of the soundwave. This means that the centre of a compression from L_1 arrives at the same time as the centre of a rarefaction from L_2. The two waves are exactly out of phase.

Moving along the line, several places are found where the waves are in phase and several where they are out of phase. Waves are in phase if the distances from the loudspeakers differ by an even number of half wavelengths, and are exactly out of phase if the **path difference** is an odd number of half wavelengths.

a Fig 40 shows a signal generator producing a note of 256 Hz. Point X is the nearest point to the centre, Z, where a loud note is heard. Calculate the path difference between L_1X and L_2X. The velocity of sound is 330 m/s.

b Calculate the path difference between L_1Y and L_2Y.

Constructive interference

When two waves are superimposed upon each other, the resulting wave is the arithmetic sum of the amplitudes of the two individual soundwaves. If the two waves are in phase, then the displacements are in the same direction. Peaks coincide and troughs coincide. **Constructive interference** is taking place. If the waves are sound waves, the loudness is greater than either of the individual sounds.

Destructive interference

If the two waves are exactly out of phase, then the displacements are in the opposite direction. Peaks coincide with troughs. **Destructive interference** is taking place. The resulting sound will be quieter than the louder of the two sources of sound.

Usually, waves will not be exactly in phase nor exactly out of phase. When this happens, the same rule applies. The wave produced is the arithmetic sum of the two.

Superposition

When two waves meet, one wave is superimposed on the other. This is known as **superposition**.

This principle is applied in radio transmission. A relatively low frequency wave representing the sound signal is superimposed upon a high frequency **carrier** wave. The human auditory range is typically between 20 Hz and 20 000 Hz and the radio carrier wave might have a frequency measured in thousands of megahertz. The resulting signal is transmitted and then the carrier wave is filtered out by the receiver. This type of radio transmission is known as **amplitude modulation (AM)**.

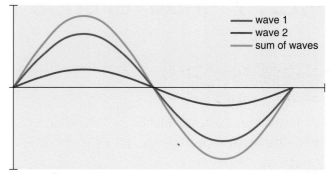

fig 41 | Constructive interference

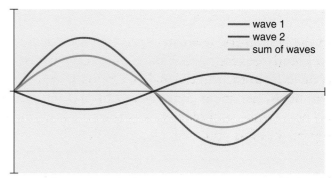

fig 42 | Destructive interference

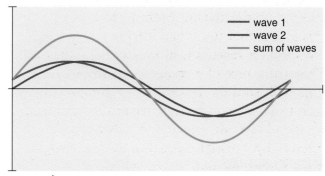

fig 43 | General interference

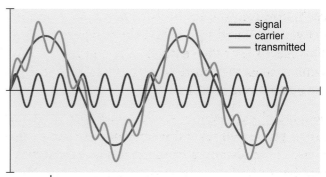

fig 44 | Amplitude modulation

Continued ▶

A2.7 Interference (2)

Beats

Two notes which are of only slightly different frequency produce an effect known as **beats**. The two waves go from being in phase to out of phase at regular intervals. This produces a pulsating note, the frequency of which is the difference between the two notes.

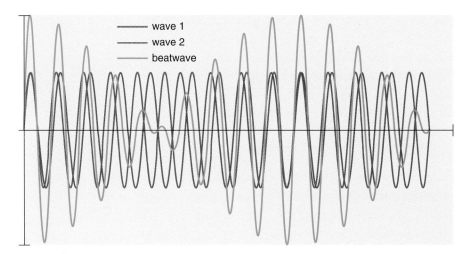

fig 45 | Beats

The principle of beats is used by instrument tuners. A tuning fork or another tuned instrument is sounded. The instrument to be tuned is played and beats are listened for. The tuning key or valve is then adjusted until the beat frequency reduces to zero.

c A piano tuner sounds a 440 Hz tuning fork as she tunes the A string. She hears a beat frequency of 6 Hz. When she tightens the string, the beat frequency increases. What was the original frequency of the A string? Explain your answer.

Interference of water waves

Interference of water waves can be seen in a ripple tank. Two ball ended dippers are attached to the vibrating bar to produce two sets of circular waves. Where two peaks or two troughs meet constructive interference takes place. Where a peak meets a trough, destructive interference takes place and the water remains still.

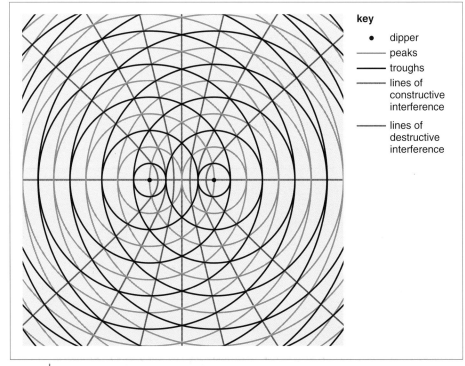

key

• dipper

— peaks

— troughs

— lines of constructive interference

— lines of destructive interference

fig 46 | Interference in ripple tank

Interference of electromagnetic waves

All electromagnetic waves are capable of interference. Visible light and microwaves produce interference effects which can be shown in the laboratory. Light from a laser is often used.

A single light source is used which is directed to two slits. This ensures that the waves have the same frequency and are in phase at their source.

The screen appears as a series of bright and dark bands. Where the light reaches the screen in phase, bright bands are seen but if the waves are exactly out of phase, no light is seen and the screen appears dark.

If a microwave transmitter is used, the same effect is evident but instead of a screen a microwave detector is moved along behind the metal plates.

d Explain why when showing the interference of microwaves, the gap between the metal plates is much larger than the width of the slit used to show interference of light.

One common example of interference effects in light is the coloured patterns produced by oil films and bubbles. The interference occurs between the light reflected from the two surfaces of the oil or bubble.

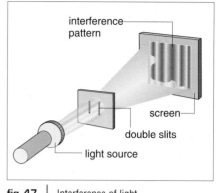

fig 47 | Interference of light

fig 49 | Coloured interference patterns in a bubble

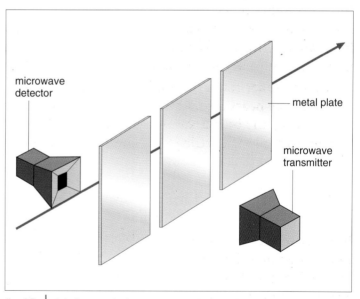

fig 48 | Interference of microwaves

Thinking further

◆ 1 Fig 50 represents an experiment to show interference of light. O represents the position of the central bright band and N the position of the first bright band from the centre. What is the significance of the path difference $S_1N - S_2N$?

Explain why the distance from the slits to the screen has to be relatively large.

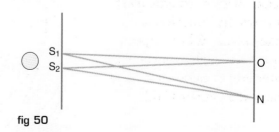

fig 50

— KEY WORDS —

amplitude modulation • beats • carrier • constructive interference • destructive interference • path difference • phase • superposition

A2.8 The nature of light

- Some properties of light can be explained by considering light to behave as a wave.
- Some properties of light can be explained by considering light to behave as a particle.

- This phenomenon is known as wave particle duality.

IDEAS AND EVIDENCE

History

Isaac Newton published his book *Opticks* in 1704. In it he wrote that 'Light is composed of tiny particles, or corpuscles, emitted by luminous bodies.' This was in contrast to the theory of Christian Huygens, who put forward the idea that light was a wave. The particle theory dominated the study of light until the 19th century when it was replaced by the wave theory of light and more recently the idea of the dual nature of light.

fig 51 | In order to position the white ball safely at the far end of the table, the snooker player needs to bounce it off the cushioned edges

Reflection and refraction

Reflection and refraction can both be explained by considering light as either a particle or a wave. Snooker players know how particles obey the laws of reflection as they use the cushion of the snooker table.

Children playing with a length of rope know how waves obey the laws of reflection. The child on the left moves her end of the rope up and down, the child on the right holds his end still. The wave travels along the rope and is reflected back.

Look at the model of refraction on page 53. The toy car moves in a straight line across the wooden floor until it goes onto the carpet at an angle. It slows down and changes direction. Refraction has taken place.

We are all familiar with waves at the seaside. They change their speed and direction as they enter regions of shallower water.

a Which model of light is the toy car demonstrating?

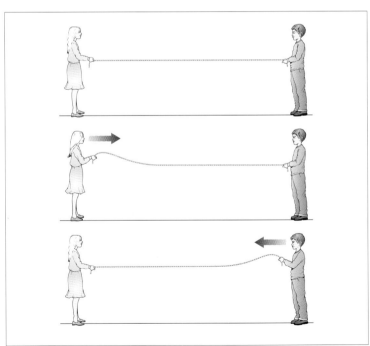

fig 52 | Using rope to show reflection

Diffraction and interference

Diffraction and interference can only be explained in terms of waves. Water waves spread out as they pass through an opening or at the edge of a promontory.

b What happens to particles as they pass through an opening? Fig 53 shows marbles being rolled towards openings in a metal sheet. Try the experiment and discuss whether diffraction occurs.

It was Thomas Young who helped to confirm the wave nature of light with his work on interference. The experiment with two slits and the resulting interference pattern (described in spread A2.7) was first performed by Young in 1803. Interference can only take place between waves.

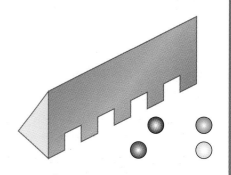

fig 53 | Marbles being rolled towards openings in a metal sheet

Light as a particle

The theory of this is well beyond the scope of GCSE physics, but the idea can be explained.

If light is shone on to a metal surface, electrons are ejected from the surface. This is called the photoelectric effect. If we assume that light is a wave, some of the features of the photoelectric effect are impossible to explain. In 1905, Einstein explained these features assuming light to consist of particles which he called photons. Once Einstein's ideas were confirmed, he won the Nobel prize for Physics.

Summary

phenomenon	explained by wave	explained by particle
reflection	✓	✓
refraction	✓	✓
diffraction	✓	✗
interference	✓	✗
photoelectric effect	✗	✓

fig 54

Light is sometimes a wave, sometimes a particle, sometimes both. This is the wave particle duality of light.

For a typical question on this topic see page 185 question 13.

Questions on processing waves

● **1** Which of the following statements are true and which are false?

A Light travels faster in a more dense material.

B The refractive index of blue light is less than the refractive index of yellow light.

C A convex lens converges light.

D Only real images are formed by convex lenses.

E The image formed by a projector is magnified and inverted.

F The image formed by a camera is diminished and inverted.

G Interference indicates that light behaves as a particle. *(7)*

● **2** The speed of light in air is 300 000 km/s. What is its speed in a material of refractive index 1.2? *(2)*

■ **3 a** Which part of the electromagnetic spectrum has a refractive index of 1.45 in glass? *(1)*

b Which part of the electromagnetic spectrum has a refractive index of 1.55 in glass? *(2)*

◆ **4** A 5 cm tall object is placed 20 cm away from a convex lens. The focal length of the lens is 8 cm. Draw a scale diagram to find the size, position and nature of the image formed. *(8)*

■ **5** The projectionist at the amateur cinema wants to make the picture on the screen larger. He moves the screen further away from the projector. The picture on the screen goes out of focus.

What must he do to the focusing lens to obtain a sharp image? *(2)*

● **6** Daniel holds a convex lens 35 cm above some screwed up pieces of paper on the outdoor barbecue. After a few moments, the paper catches fire.

a Explain why the paper catches fire. *(2)*

b What is the focal length of the lens? *(1)*

● **7** There is a choice of three convex lenses to use as a magnifying glass. Their focal lengths are 5 cm, 10 cm and 50 cm. Explain which one would be best to use. *(2)*

■ **8** Fig 55 shows light entering the eye of a person with long sight. The light does not focus properly on the retina at the back of the eye. Draw a diagram to show how a convex lens can help to focus the light on the retina. *(3)*

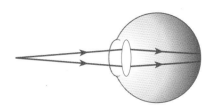

fig 55 | A long-sighted eye

■ **9** When a marching army reaches a bridge, the soldiers 'break step'. This means that they no longer march together in step. Use your ideas about resonance to suggest why they 'break step'. *(3)*

■ **10 a** Two strings on a guitar are the same length and at the same tension. One string produces a note much higher than the other when they are both plucked at their mid point. Explain why. *(1)*

◆ **b** One string produces a note (G) of frequency 392 Hz when plucked. What two things can the guitarist do to the string to make it sound a note (A) with a frequency of 440 Hz? *(2)*

◆ **c** Why does the G note produced from the guitar sound very different to the same G note produced from a violin? *(1)*

◆ **11** The length of air in a closed resonance tube is adjusted until the first harmonic from an unmarked tuning fork is heard. The length of the air column is measured as 25.8 cm. The velocity of sound is 330 m/s. Calculate the frequency of the tuning fork. *(3)*

◆ **12** A motorist is driving along a straight road. He knows that the road joins two towns which have radio transmitters which broadcast his favourite radio station at the same frequency of 200 kHz. As he listens to his car radio, he notices that the music becomes louder then quieter at regular distances. Use your ideas about interference to explain what is happening. *(3)*

IDEAS AND EVIDENCE

13 Many sunglasses are made from a polarising filter such as Polaroid™.

fig 56

Polarising filters reduce reflected glare from glass and water surfaces because reflected light has become polarised.

fig 57

If an object is looked at through a polarising filter, it appears less bright. A second filter placed in the path of the light displays interesting effects. In one position, the brightness is unaffected, but as it is rotated, it becomes dimmer until at 90° no light passes through the two filters.

| object viewed normally | object viewed through one polarising filter | object viewed through two parallel polarising filters | object viewed through two polarising filters at an angle | object viewed through two polarising filters at right angles |

fig 58 | Effect of polarising filters

We can imagine light as vibrating in all directions at right angles to the direction of travel. When the light becomes polarised, either by being reflected or by passing through a polarising filter, it only vibrates in one direction. The second polarising filter only allows vibrations through in one direction. This may not be the direction in which the light is vibrating.

One way of modelling the behaviour is to think of the polarising filter as being like a picket fence, fig 59.

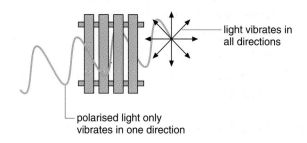

light vibrates in all directions

polarised light only vibrates in one direction

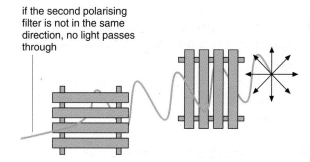

if the second polarising filter is not in the same direction, no light passes through

fig 59 | Model to explain polarisation

a What is the difference between light which has been reflected and light which has been transmitted? *(1)*

b Explain why polarising sunglasses reduce reflected glare. *(2)*

c Explain why polarising sunglasses still allow you to see things which are underwater. *(2)*

d Sometimes light behaves as a wave, sometimes it behaves as a particle. Use the information in the question and your ideas about light to explain whether polarisation supports the idea that light behaves as a wave or as a particle. *(5)*

A3 More about forces and energy

Introduction

A detailed knowledge of forces and energy is essential to an understanding of the physical world. Early civilizations developed simple 'machines' such as the ramp and the shaduf to raise heavy loads.

As scientists learned more so our machines have become more sophisticated. The development of electricity led to a giant leap forward in the application of physics for the benefit of us all. We now have machines capable of transferring huge amounts of energy, sufficient to send a rocket into space or to fuse tiny nuclei together, imitating the process that occurs in stars.

fig 1 | An Egyptian shaduf

You should already know quite a lot about forces and energy. In this Teaching block we are going to develop some of the ideas you have met before and introduce some more equations that will enable you to investigate the behaviour of moving objects more precisely.

Check-up

Have a go at the following questions. They will remind you what you should already know about forces and energy.

a   Explain how the shaduf in fig 1 allows the man to lift water from the well easily.

b   Saira runs 100 m in 12 s. Find her average speed.

c   A train pulls away from a station and accelerates at 0.5 m/s^2 for 1 minute. How fast is it travelling after 1 minute?

d   Tim has a mass of 75 kg. What is his weight?

e   An aeroplane slows down as it comes in to land. What can you say about the forces acting on it?

f   i   Find the kinetic energy of a car of mass 1200 kg when travelling at 20 m/s.

    ii   The brakes are applied and the car stops in 60 m. Find the braking force.

g   Explain why a free-fall parachutist reaches a terminal velocity.

h   Explain three ways of reducing heat loss from a house.

i   A 250 W machine does 160 J of useful work every second. Find its efficiency.

Contents of the Teaching block

This Teaching block is divided into seven double page spreads.

A3.1 Linear motion

We recall that a negative acceleration is a deceleration and how to calculate acceleration and displacement from a velocity–time graph. Equations to describe motion with uniform acceleration are introduced and used to solve various problems.

A3.2 Projectile motion

An object projected horizontally in the Earth's gravitational field follows a parabolic path. It has, in the absence of friction, a constant horizontal velocity and a steadily increasing vertical velocity.

A3.3 Momentum

The momentum of an object is equal to its mass multiplied by its velocity. The principle of Conservation of Momentum can be applied to many types of collision, from snooker balls to cars.

A3.4 Rockets

Rockets travel into space so need to carry their own supply of oxygen as well as fuel. We can apply the principle of Conservation of Momentum to explain how rockets and jet engines work.

fig 2

A3.5 Car crashes

We see that if the time of impact can be increased the forces that act are reduced. This reduces the risk of injury to the occupants. Safety features such as crumple zones, air bags and safety straps are discussed.

A3.6 Measuring heat

The energy transferred when an object changes temperature depends on its mass, what it is made of and the amount the temperature changes. The specific heat capacity of a substance is the energy required to change the temperature of unit mass by one degree.

A3.7 Efficiency

Efficiency is the ratio of the useful energy output to the total energy input. No device is 100% efficient; energy is always wasted, usually as heat. We evaluate the efficiency of various energy transfer devices.

fig 3

A3.1 Linear motion

Speeding up and slowing down

If the velocity of an object is *increasing* we say it is accelerating.

If the velocity of an object is *decreasing* we say it is decelerating. Retardation is another word for deceleration.

$$\text{acceleration} = \frac{\text{final velocity} - \text{initial velocity}}{\text{time}}$$

This means that if an object is slowing down, or decelerating, its acceleration is *negative*.

fig 4

a A car accelerates from 10 m/s to 20 m/s in 8 s. Calculate its acceleration.

b When travelling at 20 m/s the car brakes, stopping in 10 s. Calculate its deceleration.

Velocity–time graphs

Acceleration (and deceleration) can also be found from the gradient of a velocity–time graph.

Displacement can be found from the area between a velocity–time graph and the time axis, taking into account positive and negative velocities.

c Tom throws a ball straight upwards and catches it again 4 s later.
   i Draw a velocity–time graph and use it to find the maximum height of the ball.
   ii What is the displacement of the ball?
   iii How does your graph show this?

Motion with constant acceleration

When objects are moving with constant (uniform) acceleration in a straight line there are some equations we can use. These equations involve five symbols: $u\ v\ a\ s\ t$.

u = initial velocity (in m/s)
v = final velocity (in m/s)
a = acceleration (in m/s^2)
s = displacement (in m)
t = time (in s)

$$\text{average velocity} = \frac{\text{displacement}}{\text{time}},$$

or
$$\frac{(u + v)}{2} = \frac{s}{t}$$

Rearranging this gives
$$s = \frac{(u + v)}{2}\, t \qquad (1)$$

$$\text{acceleration} = \frac{\text{change of velocity}}{\text{time}}, \qquad (1)$$

$$\text{or} \qquad a = \frac{v - u}{t}$$

Rearranging this gives $\qquad v = u + at \qquad (2)$

Substituting the value
of v from equation (2)
in equation (1) gives $\qquad s = ut + \frac{1}{2}at^2 \qquad (3)$

From mathematics we know that
$v^2 - u^2 = (v + u)(v - u)$

Using equations (1)
and (2) it can be
shown that $\qquad v^2 = u^2 + 2as \qquad (4)$

d Show how to obtain equations (3) and (4) from equations (1) and (2).

e An aircraft is taking off. Starting from rest, it accelerates at $2\,\text{m/s}^2$ for 30 s. What speed does it reach? How far does it travel along the runway?

fig 5

Vertical motion

Equations (1) to (4) can be applied to vertical motion. If we ignore air resistance, all objects:
* accelerate at $10\,\text{m/s}^2$ when moving *down*
* decelerate at $10\,\text{m/s}^2$ (accelerate at $-10\,\text{m/s}^2$) when moving *up*
* have zero velocity at the highest point.

f Ben throws a ball vertically upwards at 12 m/s. Find
  i how high it goes
  ii how long it takes to reach this height
  iii the time it takes to return to Ben's hands.

Thinking further

■ **1** A train approaching a station decelerates steadily at $0.5\,\text{m/s}^2$. How would you describe its acceleration? If it was moving at 50 m/s before applying the brakes, how long will it take to stop?

■ **2** The second stage of a rocket increases its speed from 450 m/s to 750 m/s in 150 s. Find its acceleration.

◆ **3** Find the distance travelled by a train in the first minute of its journey if it has a constant acceleration of $0.32\,\text{m/s}^2$.

◆ **4** A stone is dropped from the top of a cliff 125 m high.
  a Find the time it takes to reach the foot of the cliff.
  b With what speed does it strike the ground?
  c A second stone is *thrown* down from the cliff top. With what speed is it thrown if it reaches the bottom in 4 s?

Data logger with light gates to produce velocity–time graphs. *Verify equations of motion.*

A3.2 Projectile motion

fig 6

> ### Key points
>
> - An object thrown horizontally in the Earth's gravitational field describes a parabolic path.
> - In the absence of friction a projectile has a constant horizontal velocity.
> - The vertical velocity of the projectile increases steadily due to the effect of gravity.

Moving sideways

If a stone is thrown sideways from the top of a cliff with a velocity of 5 m/s it follows a curved path called a **parabola**. The moving object is called a **projectile**.

If two similar balls are released simultaneously – one dropped vertically downwards and the other projected sideways – both land together. If illuminated by a stroboscope flashing regularly and photographed using a camera with an open shutter, the motion of the two balls can be seen in more detail.

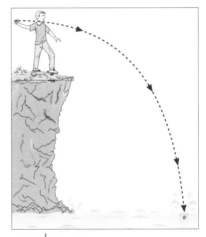

fig 7 | Parabolic path

fig 8 | Multiflash photograph of two falling balls

If we ignore air resistance we can treat the downwards and sideways motions separately.

- Downwards – the stone is acted on by the pull of gravity, so it has an acceleration of 10 m/s^2 vertically downwards.
- Sideways – no forces act on the stone in a sideways direction, so it travels with a constant velocity of 5 m/s. This means it moves 5 m horizontally every second.

The combination of these two motions gives the parabolic path shown in fig 9. The greater the horizontal velocity given to the stone, the further away from the cliff it lands.

a A stone released from a cliff takes 3 s to reach the water. How far away from the cliff will it land if it is given a sideways velocity of **i** 5 m/s, **ii** 10 m/s, **iii** 20 m/s?

In spread 6.1 we learned that Newton suggested that if the sideways velocity could be made big enough a cannonball could be fired from a high mountain and hit you in the back some time later. Due to curvature of the Earth, the cannonball would be constantly falling to Earth but never reaching it, so it would go into orbit.

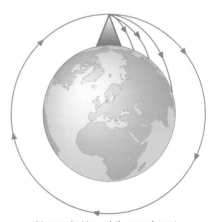

Newton's 'thought' experiment

fig 0

More about projectiles

For a stone thrown horizontally from the top of a cliff, we can use the equation $s = ut + \frac{1}{2}at^2$ to calculate the vertical distance fallen by the stone each second. The stone has no vertical velocity initially because it is thrown sideways. This means that $u = 0$.

We can calculate the distance the stone falls in 1, 2, 3 and 4 s. The stone travels further in each second as it goes faster, as we saw in fig 8.

We can also calculate the horizontal distance travelled after 1, 2, 3 and 4 s if the stone is given a sideways velocity of 5 m/s. If we draw a graph of the vertical distance against the horizontal distance moved, plotting points every second, it looks similar to the red line in fig 10.

b Check that you agree with the values plotted.

c The graph for a stone dropped straight down has been added in blue. What do you notice?

d Find the time the stone would take to reach the sea if it were thrown with a horizontal velocity of 10 m/s.

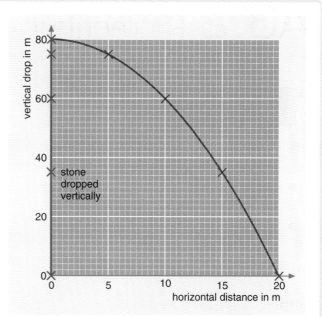

fig 10 | Graph of projectile motion and vertical fall

e How would the graph change if the stone were thrown with a horizontal velocity of 10 m/s?

──▷▷ Taking it further ▷▷──

Ball games

In many ball games the ball follows a parabolic path. In a rally in tennis the ball rises under gravity, slowing down until it reaches its highest point, and then accelerates downwards. In the absence of air resistance it travels the same distance each second sideways throughout.

f The ball should be hit at an angle of 45° to have the maximum **range** (i.e. to travel the greatest horizontal distance). Explain why.

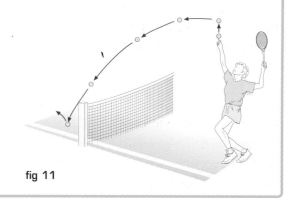

fig 11

Thinking further

■ **1** Harry is playing darts. He aims his dart straight at the bull's eye. Why does he miss it? Draw a diagram to show the path of the dart.

■ **2** A ball thrown down from a window takes 0.5 s to reach the ground. Find the time it will take if the ball is thrown sideways at 8 m/s.

◆ **3** Toby threw a ball with a sideways velocity of 15 m/s from the top of a 45 m high tower.

a Calculate the time the ball took to reach the ground.

b How far from the foot of the tower did the ball land?

◆ **4** A plane flying horizontally at 100 m/s is to drop supplies to a small village cut off by floods. The plane is flying at a height of 500 m. How far away from the selected target area should the plane's captain release the package, if it is to land on the correct spot?

┌─ **KEY WORDS** ─────────────
│ parabola • projectile • range
└────────────────────────────

 Find out more about Newton's ideas on the Solar System.

 Discuss the application of projectile motion in ball games and athletics.

A3.3 Momentum

> ## Key points
>
> - Momentum = mass × velocity. It is measured in kg m/s (or N s).
> - Momentum is a vector quantity.
> - Force = rate of change of momentum.
> - Impulse = force × time = change in momentum.
>
> - The total momentum before a collision always equals the total momentum after a collision, as long as no external force acts.
> - Momentum conservation can be applied to many practical situations.

What is momentum?

momentum = mass × velocity

Velocity is a vector so momentum is a vector too. This means that direction is important when calculating momentum.

a Calculate the momentum of a 1000 kg car travelling at 20 m/s.

b What is the momentum of an athlete of mass 65 kg running at 8 m/s?

Force = rate of change of momentum

Using the symbols introduced in spread A3.1,

$$\text{acceleration, } a = \frac{v - u}{t}$$

We can write $F = ma$ as $F = m\dfrac{(v - u)}{t}$ or $F = \dfrac{mv - mu}{t}$ (1)

force = rate of change of momentum

The **impulse** of a force is equal to the force multiplied by the time for which it acts; impulse = $F \times t$.

$Ft = mv - mu$ (2),   impulse = change in momentum

The unit of Ft is N s so the unit of momentum can be kg m/s or N s.

Equation (2) shows that the longer a force acts, the greater the change in momentum so the greater the final velocity. This is why we 'follow through' when kicking or hitting a ball. We explained this in terms of $F = ma$ in spread 2.6, but it is perhaps easier to understand by considering $Ft = mv - mu$.

c Ravi kicks a football of mass 1 kg with a force of 80 N. His foot is in contact with the ball for 0.1 s. What velocity does the ball gain? How would this change if Ravi kept his foot in contact with the ball for 0.01 s?

fig 12

Collisions

The total momentum before a collision always equals the total momentum after the collision (as long as no external force acts). This is the principle of **Conservation of Momentum.**

An understanding of momentum is useful when playing games such as snooker and pool. Consider two balls moving towards each other (fig 13).

We have given anything moving to the right a positive velocity and anything moving to the left a negative velocity.

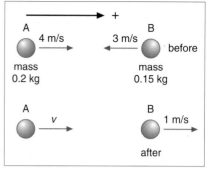

fig 13

total momentum before collision = total momentum after collision
$$(0.2 \times 4) + (0.15 \times -3) = (0.2 \times v) + (0.15 \times 1)$$
$$0.8 - 0.45 = 0.2v + 0.15$$
$$v = 1 \text{ m/s (i.e. to the right)}$$

d Fig 14 shows two cars colliding. After impact both cars are stationary. Find the velocity of the heavier car before the crash.

e Two trolleys collide and stick together (fig 15). Find their common velocity after impact.

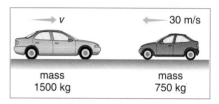

fig 14

Explosions

A gun moves backwards a little – **recoils** – when it is fired. Momentum is conserved. The initial momentum is zero so the total momentum *after* firing the gun must also be zero. The momentum gained by the bullet in a forwards direction is equal to the momentum gained by the gun in a backwards direction.

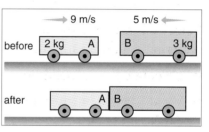

fig 15

Thinking further

◆ **1** Chris stepped off a boat onto a jetty but the boat moved away from the jetty and he landed in the water. Explain why this happened.

◆ **2** A bullet of mass 0.01 kg is fired into a sandbag of mass 0.39 kg hanging from a tree. The sandbag (with the bullet embedded in it) then moved at 10 m/s. What was the velocity of the bullet?

◆ **3** An alpha particle moving at 1×10^7 m/s collides with a stationary proton. After collision the alpha particle moves in the same direction at 0.5×10^7 m/s. The alpha particle's mass is four times that of the proton. Calculate the speed of the proton.

◆ **4** Sally jumps off a wall. Her mass is 50 kg and she lands with a speed of 5 m/s. Compare the force making her decelerate if she bends her knees and stops in 1 s, with the force if she forgets to bend her knees and stops in 0.01 s.

KEY WORDS

conservation of momentum • impulse • momentum • recoils

Application of momentum ideas to various sports.

A3.4 Rockets and jets

Simple rocket design

The action of a **rocket** can be demonstrated by blowing up a balloon and suddenly releasing it. The balloon whizzes around the room in the direction shown. The air escaping from the open end of the balloon gives a force on the balloon in the opposite direction. This is an application of Newton's Third Law (spread 2.4).

A rocket travels outside the Earth's atmosphere so has to carry its own **fuel** supply and **oxygen** for the fuel to burn.

The gases are forced out of the back of the rocket at high speed – about 2000 m/s.

fig 16

Jet engines

The **jet turbine** engine of an aeroplane works in a similar way to the rocket.

A jet engine does not travel in space so it does not need to carry its own oxygen supply. *Thrust SSC*, the car in which Andy Green broke Richard Nobel's land speed record in 1997, was powered by a jet engine.

fig 18 | A jet engine

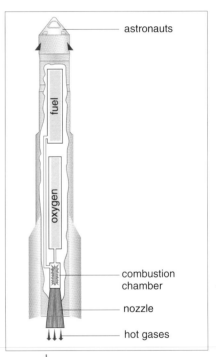

fig 17 | A rocket

Air sucked in at the front of a jet engine is compressed and becomes very hot. This ignites the fuel and increases the pressure of the gases. The hot gases are forced out backwards at high speed providing a forward thrust on the engine.

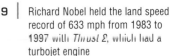

fig 19 | Richard Nobel held the land speed record of 633 mph from 1983 to 1997 with *Thrust 2*, which had a turbojet engine

How a rocket works

The motion of the rocket can be explained using the principle of Conservation of Momentum. Before the rocket lifts off the total momentum is zero (there is no motion). After lift off, the total momentum is still zero but the momentum of the exhaust gases backwards is equal to the momentum of the rocket forwards. Since the mass of the gases expelled each second is much less than the mass of the rocket, the initial speed of the rocket is small.

fig 20

a The acceleration of the rocket increases as it climbs. Why?

Spacecraft can travel large distances without burning any fuel. This makes long journeys possible.

b When a rocket is travelling at a constant velocity in a region of space where gravity can be ignored the rocket motors do not need to be working. Explain why.

c The rocket motors are turned on. They burn 25 kg of fuel in one second. The gases produced from this fuel are ejected backwards at 2000 m/s. The mass of the rocket at this time is 25 000 kg. By how much is the speed of the rocket increasing at this time?

Thinking further

■ **1** An aeroplane powered by jet engines cannot fly in space but a rocket can. Why?

■ **2 a** A model water rocket is made from a plastic lemonade bottle and a bicycle pump as shown in fig 21. Air is pumped into the bottle. Eventually the bung is forced out and the 'rocket' rises. Explain why the rocket rises.

◆ **b i** The unbalanced force on the water rocket at lift-off is 40 N and the mass of the bottle and water is 0.8 kg. Find its initial acceleration.

ii How will the acceleration change during the flight?

◆ **3** Use momentum ideas to explain why the balloon moves in the direction shown in fig 16.

◆ **4** A rocket uses 1600 kg of fuel and oxygen each second. The exhaust gases have a velocity of 800 m/s. Calculate the thrust.

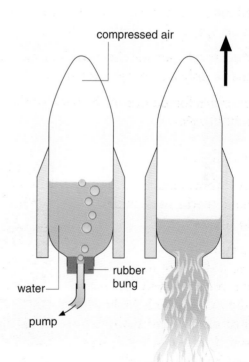

compressed air

water

rubber bung

pump

fig 21

KEY WORDS

fuel • jet turbine • oxygen • rocket

 Look up data on rockets in current use.

 Find out about the record breaking 'Thrust' jet propelled car.

 Find out more about jet engines

A3.5 Car crashes

> ### Key points
>
> - When vehicles collide the occupants can be injured due to the rapid deceleration.
> - If the deceleration is spread over a longer time the forces acting on the occupants are reduced.
> - Cars are designed so that they stop more slowly in the event of a crash. Crumple zones, air bags and seat belts all help to keep the occupants safe.

Collisions

When vehicles are in a **collision** they are brought to rest rapidly. This means that the occupants are also stopped very suddenly. The rapid deceleration means that there is a large force on them that can cause serious injury.

If the occupants are not wearing **seat belts** they may be thrown through the windscreen at high speed. They are not attached to the car so are not slowed down by the impact, as there is no force on them. According to Newton's First Law objects continue to move at the same velocity unless a force acts on them.

fig 22

Stopping slowly

$$\text{acceleration} = \frac{\text{change in velocity}}{\text{time}}$$

Deceleration is a negative acceleration.

If the time taken to stop is increased, the deceleration becomes less. This means that the forces on the people in the vehicles are reduced so they are less likely to be seriously injured.

fig 23

a Two cars, both travelling at 70 mph, are involved in a head-on crash. Explain why there is a greater risk of serious injury than if the cars had been travelling at 30 mph.

We can see the advantage of stopping slowly from
- $F = ma$.

This tells us that force, F, is proportional to acceleration, a.
- $Ft = mv - mu$ (met in spread A2.3). This shows that if the time, t, is increased the force, F, is decreased

Designed for safety

Crumple zones

The front and back of a car are designed to crumple in the event of a collision; these are called **crumple zones**. This means that the car takes longer to stop so the forces on the passengers are reduced.

The passenger compartment however, is built rigidly to withstand an impact without buckling, keeping the passengers safe.

Air bags

Air bags are installed in front of the driver (usually in the centre of the steering wheel) and front seat passenger. They are designed to inflate if the car decelerates very rapidly so that the driver and passenger are protected from hitting the steering wheel and dashboard.

fig 24

Seat belts

Seat belts are designed to stretch. The person is stopped more gradually, reducing their deceleration and hence the force acting on the person. If the seat belt did not stretch it would prevent the person being thrown through the windscreen but there would be a large force on them, sufficient to break bones and damage internal organs.

b Why would the force be large if the seat belt did not stretch?

c The harness of a child's car seat has several wide straps. Suggest why the straps are wide.

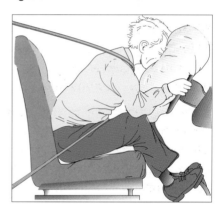
fig 25

Thinking further

■ **1 a** Why should you wear a seat belt in a car?
 b Why is it safer for the driver if the back seat passengers also wear seat belts?

■ **2** Cars are designed so that the passenger compartment is stronger than the engine compartment. How does this reduce injury in an accident?

◆ **3** Explain how an air bag works.

◆ **4** A car of mass 1000 kg is travelling at 20 m/s when it crashes into a stationary van of mass 1500 kg. The two vehicles become locked together.

a Find their speed immediately after the collision.

b Calculate the kinetic energy of the moving car just before the crash.

c Calculate the kinetic energy of the two vehicles immediately after the crash.

d Calculate the kinetic energy lost by the car.

e The driver of the car has a mass of 50 kg. How much kinetic energy does she lose?

f She moves 2 m during the crash. Calculate the average force on her from the seat belt. Comment on your answer.

KEY WORDS

air bags • collisions • crumple zones • seat belts

A3.6 Measuring heat

Key points

- Specific heat capacity is the energy required to raise the temperature of unit mass of a substance by one degree.
- When an object is heated the energy transferred is equal to mass × specific heat capacity × temperature change.
- In many processes energy is ultimately dissipated as heat.
- This thermal energy is spread so thinly throughout the surroundings that it cannot be transferred into other useful forms of energy.

Specific heat capacity

Reena is heating some water in a kettle to make a hot drink. The water and the kettle get hotter because they receive energy.

fig 26

The energy needed to heat the water depends on:

- the mass being heated
- the substance being heated.
- the temperature rise required

The amount of energy required to heat unit mass of a substance by one degree is called the **specific heat capacity** of the substance. It is measured in J/kg °C.

For instance, the specific heat capacity of water, *c*, is 4200 J/kg °C.

- 1 kg of water requires 4200 J of energy to raise its temperature by 1 °C.
- *m* kg of water requires ($m \times 4200$) J of energy to raise its temperature by 1 °C.
- *m* kg of water requires ($m \times 4200 \times \theta$) J of energy to raise its temperature by θ °C.

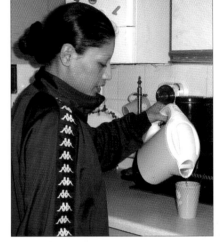

The energy transferred is equal to mass × specific heat capacity × temperature change.

$$Q = m \times c \times \theta$$

a Calculate the energy transferred when 3 kg of water are heated from 20 °C to 100 °C.

The material of the kettle does not require as much energy to heat it as the water. For instance, the specific heat capacity of copper is only 380 J/kg °C (see fig 27).

b Calculate the energy transferred when 3 kg of copper are heated from 20 °C to 100 °C.

c Calculate the energy transferred when 1.5 kg of water at 10 °C is boiled in a copper kettle of mass 1 kg.

d Cheaper saucepans are often made from aluminium. Why is it *not* the best material to use?

substance	specific heat capacity in J/kg °C
aluminium	880
copper	380
lead	126
iron	450
water	4200

fig 27

Molecular mass and specific heat capacity

Materials having the lowest specific heat capacity have the largest atoms or molecules. For instance, lead atoms are more massive than copper atoms, so there are fewer atoms in a kilogram of lead than a kilogram of copper. Each atom requires roughly the same amount of energy to raise its temperature by one degree, so lead has a lower specific heat capacity than copper.

Measuring specific heat capacity

The specific heat capacity, c, of a solid or a liquid can be found using the apparatus shown in figs 28 and 29.

The liquid is in a plastic container that has a *very* low specific heat capacity. This means that the energy needed to heat the container can be ignored.

- The mass, m, of the solid or liquid is found.
- The initial temperature is recorded.
- The heater is switched on for a known time, t.
- The ammeter and voltmeter readings, I and V, are noted.
- After the heater is switched off, the *highest* temperature reached is recorded.
- Energy supplied = VIt.
- Energy transferred = $mc\theta$, where θ = rise in temperature.
- Assuming, the **insulation** is perfect, $VIt = mc\theta$, so c can be found.
- **e** The insulation cannot really be perfect. What effect will this have on the value obtained for specific heat capacity?

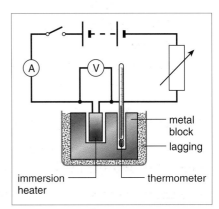

metal block
lagging
immersion heater
thermometer

fig 28

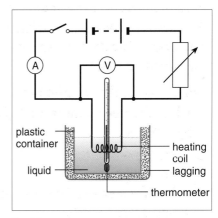

plastic container
heating coil
liquid
lagging
thermometer

fig 29

Energy dissipation

All hot objects, such as a hot drink, eventually cool down and reach the same temperature as their surroundings. The thermal energy lost from the hot drink is **dissipated** (spread out) in the surrounding room causing a *very small* increase in its temperature. This energy is spread so thinly that it cannot be recovered.

Thinking further

Use the information given in fig 27.

■ **1** Which requires more energy, heating a 4 kg block of iron by 5 °C or a 3 kg block of lead by 20 °C?

■ **2** Why is water used to cool car engines?

◆ **3** Tom and Claire are eating treacle pudding. Tom eats some treacle first and burns his mouth. Claire starts by eating the sponge; this seems much cooler. Explain.

◆ **4** A well-insulated 2 kg block of iron is heated using a 50 W immersion heater for 10 minutes. Its temperature rises by 30 °C. Find the specific heat capacity of iron.

KEY WORDS
dissipated • insulation • specific heat capacity

 Measuring specific heat capacity.

A3.7 Efficiency

Energy transfer devices

In the experiments to measure specific heat capacity in spread A3.6 we assumed that the energy transfer process was perfect. In fact this is never true; some of the input energy is always transferred into non-useful forms, often heat, that is dissipated in the surroundings.

Ramps were probably one of the earliest energy transfer devices but they are very inefficient. Ramps were almost certainly used to haul stones into place when the pyramids were built in Egypt.

fig 30 | Ramps helped the builders of the pyramids

Steam engines made use of the high pressure of steam to propel the engines but they only had an **efficiency** of about 8%.

A car engine converts chemical energy (from the fuel) to kinetic energy. But only about 25% of the chemical energy supplied is used to propel the car; the rest is wasted as heat.

fig 31 | A steam engine

Steam and car engines are examples of **heat engines**. These *depend upon* a rise in temperature in order to work, so much energy is transferred to the surroundings as heat. This means that the efficiency of heat engines is always low.

Any device with moving parts wastes energy as heat because of friction. Lubrication reduces the energy wasted.

a Explain why oiling a machine makes it more efficient.

Water power

James Joule is said to have spent his honeymoon measuring the temperature difference between the water at the top and bottom of a waterfall. He detected a small temperature rise at the bottom.

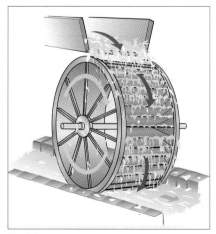

fig 32

b Explain why he detected a temperature rise.

Suppose a waterfall is 120 m high. 500 kg of water flow over it every second. 70% of the gravitational potential energy available is converted into thermal energy.

c Calculate the gravitational potential energy of the water at the top of the waterfall each second.

d Calculate the thermal energy produced each second.

e Find the difference in temperature between the water at the top and bottom of the waterfall.
(Specific heat capacity of water = 4200 J/kg °C)

f How would the temperature difference change if the flow rate were halved? Explain your answer.

fig 33

The kinetic energy of falling water has often been used to power machinery or to generate electricity.

The rotation produced by water falling onto a **water wheel** was used for a wide variety of jobs, from grinding corn to operating hammers and other equipment in a forge. Now the kinetic energy of falling water is used to turn a **turbine** to operate a generator in a hydroelectric power station. This is a renewable energy source.

Calculating efficiency

$$\text{efficiency} = \frac{\text{useful work or energy output}}{\text{total energy input}}$$

Efficiency is often expressed as a percentage.

$$\frac{\text{percentage}}{\text{efficiency}} = \frac{\text{useful energy output}}{\text{total energy input}} \times 100$$

(Note: Efficiency must always be less than 1, or less than 100%.)

g A 2 kW electric hoist raises a load of 600 N to a height of 90 m in 1 minute. Calculate its efficiency.

Scientists and engineers always try to improve the efficiency of energy transfer processes when designing equipment. This is to make sure that:

• we do not waste our valuable energy resources

• the equipment is cheaper to operate.

KEY WORDS

efficiency • heat engine • ramp • turbine • water wheel

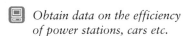 *Obtain data on the efficiency of power stations, cars etc.*

Thinking further

■ **1** A 500 W electric winch is used to raise materials on a building site. The winch takes 100 s to raise a load of 800 N through a height of 20 m. Find its efficiency.
Why is the efficiency low?

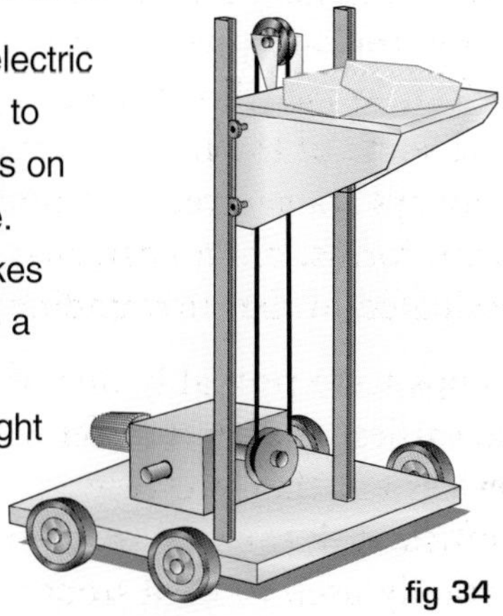

fig 34

■ **2** List the advantages and disadvantages of three renewable energy sources.

◆ **3** A water mill has an efficiency of 40%. 2000 kg of water moving at a speed of 2 m/s strikes the water wheel each second. Calculate the maximum output power of the water mill.

◆ **4** A team of engineers is employed by a car manufacturer to design the engine for a new small car. They cannot agree on whether it should be powered by a petrol engine or an electric motor. Discuss the factors they should consider in deciding.

Questions on forces and energy

● **1** Choose one word or phrase from the list to describe the following conditions.

acceleration • energy • heat • jet • parabola • rocket • straight line • temperature

a Increase in velocity.

b How hot something is.

c Path taken by a stone thrown out of a window.

d Something that moves out of the Earth's atmosphere. *(4)*

2 A speeding motorist is travelling at a constant speed of 40 m/s on a motorway. He passes a stationary police car which immediately gives chase, accelerating at a steady rate of 2.5 m/s² until it reaches a constant speed of 50 m/s.

■ **a** How long does the police car take to reach a speed of 50 m/s? *(3)*

◆ **b i** How far does the police car travel while accelerating? *(3)*

◆ **ii** How far does the speeding motorist travel in this time? *(2)*

■ **c** Draw a speed–time graph for each car, on the same axes, to show their motion. Label the graph for the speeding motorist, S and that for the police car, P. *(5)*

◆ **d** Use your graph to verify your answer to **b i**. *(2)*

◆ **e** How long does the police car take to catch up with the motorist? *(4)*

■ **3 a** How much energy is needed to heat 2 kg of copper from 20 °C to 520 °C? *(3)*

b A night storage heater contains 70 kg of concrete. It is warmed from 10 °C to 40 °C during the night when electricity is cheap.

■ **i** How much energy is required to do this? *(3)*

◆ **ii** The storage heater releases heat during the day. Why is concrete a better material than copper to use for this purpose? *(3)*

(specific heat capacity of copper = 380 J/kg °C
specific heat capacity of concrete = 800 J/kg °C)

■ **c** What physical properties should the materials used to insulate a house possess? *(3)*

4 A car driver has a mass of 80 kg.

■ **a** What is his kinetic energy when travelling at 20 m/s? *(3)*

◆ **b** On average, when braking, the car stops in a distance of 160 m. Find the force on the driver when braking from a speed of 20 m/s. *(3)*

◆ **c** In an accident the car stops in 1.6 m. Find the force on the driver now if he was travelling at 20 m/s. *(2)*

◆ **d** The speed of the car is doubled. What effect does this have on your answer to **c**? Explain. *(2)*

◆ **e** Cars are designed so that the passenger compartment is stronger than the engine compartment. How does this reduce injury in an accident? *(3)*

5 On take-off the burning gases gives a Saturn V rocket a forward thrust of 33×10^6 N. The mass of the rocket is 3×10^6 kg.

● **a i** Draw a diagram to show the forces acting on the rocket. Name each force and state its magnitude. *(3)*

■ **ii** What is the *resultant* force acting on the rocket? *(1)*

◆ **iii** Calculate the initial acceleration of the rocket. *(3)*

b After take-off the rocket burns 14 000 kg of fuel per second.

■ **i** How much mass has the rocket lost after 2 minutes? *(2)*

■ **ii** What is its mass after 2 minutes? *(1)*

◆ **iii** Calculate a value for the acceleration of the rocket after 2 minutes. *(3)*

◆ **iv** Why is your answer to **iii** likely to be too small? *(1)*

● **6 a** Distinguish between renewable and non-renewable energy sources. Give two examples of each. *(4)*

b Discuss the advantages and disadvantages of the energy sources you have named. *(8)*

7 Jade is investigating the performance of an electric kettle. Her results are given in the table below.

mass of water in kg	time to boil in s	energy supplied to kettle in kJ
0.5	90	200
1.0	150	380
1.5	205	540

fig 35

Initial temperature of water = 20 °C
Specific heat capacity of water = 4200 J/kg °C

■ **a** Calculate the energy used to heat the water in each experiment. *(6)*

◆ **b** Calculate the efficiency in each experiment. *(6)*

◆ **c** Why doesn't the time taken to boil double when the mass of water is doubled? *(2)*

◆ **d** Give two reasons why the energy used to heat the water is always less than the energy supplied to the kettle. *(2)*

◆ **e** Comment on the values obtained for the efficiency. *(3)*

◆ **8** Wayne tested Fiona's reaction time by holding the top of a 30 cm ruler so that it hung vertically with Fiona's fingers close to, but not touching, the zero mark at the bottom of the ruler. Without warning Wayne let go of the ruler. Fiona caught it at the 12.8 cm mark.

a What value does this give for her reaction time? *(3)*

b Why is this value likely to be less than it would be in a real situation? *(2)*

IDEAS AND EVIDENCE

9 Read the following passage about physics in sport and then answer the questions that follow.

Top-class athletes are forever breaking records. This is not only the result of better training methods. Clever use of physics helps shave those vital thousandths of a second off personal best times. The soles of their running shoes, the fabric of their kit and the surface of the track all make a difference to an athlete's performance. Detecting false starts and precise timing are important too, when you're going for gold. And it's all down to science in the end. The application of science to sport is guaranteed to improve performance.

To break records on the track everything possible is done to reduce air resistance, from the design of the kit to the position of the athletes' bodies during a race.

Good 100 m runners now accelerate to about 12 m/s in 2 s and then travel at a nearly constant speed. Compare the pictures of Roger Bannister running the first sub-four minute mile in 1953 and Cathy Freeman running in the 2000 Sydney Olympics.

fig 36 | Roger Bannister

fig 37 | Cathy Freeman (centre)

a Give three things an athlete can do to reduce air resistance. *(3)*

b How has physics made it possible to detect false starts accurately? *(2)*

c Suggest two properties that the running track should possess. *(2)*

d Why is different footwear needed for different events? *(2)*

e **i** Calculate the initial acceleration of the 100 m runner mentioned in the passage. *(3)*

　　ii Why did he stop accelerating? *(3)*

f **i** If the 100 m runner referred to in e has a mass of 60 kg, what is his kinetic energy after 2 s? *(3)*

　　ii Estimate the power he develops in his legs at the start. *(3)*

　　iii His body produces about twice this power. What happens to the rest? *(3)*

　　iv How could the power wasted be reduced? *(2)*

Glossary (TB1-8)

A

acceleration (2.4) rate of increase of velocity

acid rain (8.6) rain containing sulphurous acid (e.g. caused by coal-burning power stations), which damages stonework and wildlife

activity (5.3) number of disintegrations, per second or per minute, in a radioactive source

aerial (4.3) a device for receiving or transmitting radio signals

air resistance (2.5) retarding force on an object moving through the air

alpha particle (5.1) a helium nucleus (2 protons and 2 neutrons); it is emitted when some radioactive nuclei decay

alternating current (a.c.) (7.4) frequent change of direction of an electric current or voltage

alternator (8.4) generator of alternating current

ammeter (1.2) instrument used to measure electric current

ampere (A) (1.2) unit of electric current

amplitude (3.2) the maximum displacement of a wave from its rest position

antineutrino (5.1) a small particle emitted when a neutron changes into a proton and an electron

apparent depth (3.6) the depth a dense transparent object appears to be – effect caused by refraction

asteroid (6.1) one of many small rocks orbiting the Sun between Mars and Jupiter

asthenosphere (4.8) a layer of flowing mantle on which continental plates move

atomic number (5.1) the number of protons in the nucleus of an atom

B

background radiation (5.1) radioactivity that is always present around us

bacteria (5.5) simple organisms, some of which cause disease

balanced (2.6) state of equilibrium

becquerel (Bq) (5.3) unit of radioactivity equal to one decay every second

beta particle (5.1) a high-speed electron emitted when some radioactive nuclei decay

Big Bang (6.3) the explosion by which scientists believe the Universe began expanding

Big Crunch (6.3) one possible future for the Universe – the reverse of the Big Bang

black dwarf (6.2) a faded white dwarf (see **white dwarf**)

black hole (6.2) part of space with such a large pull of gravity that not even light can escape

blue supergiant (6.2) large star with short life

braking distance (2.9) distance moved by a car in stopping after the brakes are applied

C

cancer (5.4) tumours which grow out of control, eventually killing normal tissue

carbon brushes (8.2) conduct current to and from the coil in electric motors and generators

catapult (effect) (8.1) resultant force on an electrical conductor in a magnetic field that makes the conductor move

centripetal force (6.1) force on an object moving in a circle which acts towards the centre of the circle

charge (7.1) property of some sub-atomic particles; product of electric current and time ($Q = It$)

circuit breaker (7.5) automatic switch which 'trips' (turns off) if the current exceeds a specified value; can be reset by turning the switch on

coal-burning power station (8.6) power station where electricity is generated by burning coal to produce steam.

combined heat and power (CHP) (2.12) heat normally wasted from power stations is used to heat nearby houses and factories

comet (6.1) small ice lumps, which orbit the Sun in a very elongated elliptical orbit

compression (3.1) part of a longitudinal wave where the particles are closer together than normal

concave (3.3) curving inwards

conduction (thermal) (2.11) the way in which thermal energy is transferred in solids

conductor (electric) (7.1) a material that allows an electric current to pass

conservation of energy (8.3) principle that energy cannot be created or destroyed

constructive boundary (4.8) boundary between separating plates where lithosphere is being formed

continental drift (4.7) the theory which accounts for the movement of the continents over a long time

convection (2.11) the way in which thermal energy is transferred in fluids (liquids and gases)

convection current (2.11) movement of a fluid due to convection

conventional current (7.3) direction of current from positive to negative around a circuit

converge (3.3) to come towards a point

convex (3.3) curving outwards

core (4.7) the central part of the Earth

coulomb (C) (7.3) unit of electric charge; charge due to a current of 1 A passing for 1s

couple (2.1) two equal forces acting in opposite directions a distance apart

critical angle (4.4) the angle of incidence which produces an angle of refraction of 90° as light passes into a less dense medium

crumple zone (2.7) front or rear of a car designed to buckle and bend in an accident

crust (4.7) the outer layer of the Earth

cumulative (5.6) increasing by repeated addition

D

daughter nuclide (5.3) an isotope produced as a result of radioactive decay

decay (5.3) the splitting of a radioactive nucleus with the emission of ionising radiation

deceleration (2.4) slowing down; negative acceleration

degraded (energy) (2.12) energy that is so spread out it cannot be transferred into other useful forms

destructive boundary (4.8) boundaries between colliding plates where lithosphere is being destroyed

diffraction (3.7) the spreading out of a wave as it passes through an opening of a similar size (or smaller than) its wavelength

diffuse (3.4) spreading out in many directions or scattering

digital signal (4.4) signal which is either off or on so any small variations are not taken into account

diode (1.1) electrical component that conducts current in one direction only

direct current (d.c.) (7.4) current or voltage due to charge flow in one direction

displacement (2.3) straight line distance between two points

dissipate (1.1) change into non-useful form, waste (energy)

diverge (3.3) to go away from a point

DNA (5.6) deoxyribonucleic acid – a molecule which carries coded genetic information

Doppler effect (6.3) waves from moving objects appear to have shorter or longer wavelengths

double insulation (7.5) describes an electrical appliance having no electrical connections to the case so no earth connection is needed

drag (2.5) frictional force opposing the motion of an object through a fluid

dynamo (8.4) current generator

E

earth (wire) (7.4) part of household wiring that only carries a current if there is a fault, breaking the fuse

earthquake (4.6) this occurs where rocks break suddenly at a fault

echo (3.4) the reflection of sound

echolocation (4.5) using echoes to measure distance and hence find invisible objects

eddy current (8.5) current induced (e.g. in a transformer core) causing energy loss

electric current (1.1, 7.3) rate of flow of electric charge

electric shock (7.5) symptoms that follow the passage of an electric current through the body

electromagnetic wave (3.1) wave propagated as a periodic disturbance of the electromagnetic field

electrostatic precipitator (7.2) electrostatic device fitted to the chimneys of power stations and factories to reduce pollution

electron (1.1, 7.1) negatively charged particle

endoscope (4.4) used to look inside the body, consisting of a lighted optical fibre and a viewing device

energy (1.1, 2.8, 7.4) the ability to do work

energy efficiency (2.12) ratio of the useful energy output to the total energy input of a machine

epicentre (4.6) a point on the Earth's surface immediately above the focus of an earthquake

equilibrium (2.1) state that exists when a system is not changing (e.g. when forces are balanced)

exciter (8.6) d.c. generator providing current for the rotating electromagnets in a power station

F

Faraday's Law (8.3) the induced voltage is proportional to the rate of cutting magnetic field lines

fault (4.6) point of fracture of rock strata due to forces acting

filament (lamp) (1.3) very thin wire (in a lamp) heated to a high temperature by an electric power source so that it emits light

film badge (5.2) worn by people who work with ionising radiation to measure their exposure to radiation

Fleming's left-hand rule (8.1) rule for the direction of the force on a current-carrying conductor in a magnetic field

Fleming's right-hand rule (8.3) rule for the direction of the induced current when a conductor moves in a magnetic field

fluorescent (4.1) the emission of light by certain substances when struck by light or electrons

focus (4.6) the origin of an earthquake

focus (of mirror and lens) (3.3) the point to which rays of light converge or from which they diverge

follow through (2.7) practice of keeping the racquet, club etc. in contact with the ball for as long as possible to give it maximum velocity

force (2.1, 7.1) a push or pull exerted by one object on another

fossil fuel (8.6) fuel produced by the slow decay of dead things

frequency (3.2, 7.4) the number of complete waves passing a point in one second

friction (2.5, 7.1) contact force opposing the motion of one object sliding past another

friction compensated (2.7) the raising of one end of a runway so that the gravitational force down the slope is exactly equal to the friction force up the slope

fuel (8.6) substance burned to provide a source of energy

fuse (7.4) thin piece of wire which melts if the current through it is too high

G

gamma ray (4.3, 5.1) most energetic and penetrating electromagnetic radiation emitted in nuclear decay

gas-fired (power station) (8.6) power station in which the fuel used is gas

Geiger-Müller tube (5.2) a detector of radioactivity

generator (8.4) device that uses mechanical energy to produce electricity

geo-stationary orbit (6.1) a satellite in orbit above the equator taking 24 hours for each orbit

glancing angle (3.4) the angle between a ray of light and the incident surface

global warming (8.6) the heating of the Earth due to man-made causes such as the greenhouse effect

gradient (2.2) measure of steepness; often related to graphs, it is the tangent of the angle between a line and the x-axis

gravitational field strength (2.5) force acting on unit mass due to gravity; on Earth it is 10N/kg

gravitational potential energy (2.8) energy due to the Earth's gravitational pull on an object and its position above the ground ($= mgh$)

gravity (2.4, 6.1) attractive force between masses (e.g. an object and Earth)

greenhouse effect (8.6) trapping of the Sun's rays beneath gas layers in the atmosphere, causing global warming

H

half-life (5.3) the time taken for half the nuclei in a sample of radioactive material to decay

hertz (Hz) (3.2) the unit of frequency (one oscillation per second)

hydroelectric (power) (8.6) use of the kinetic energy of falling water to produce electricity

I

image (3.6) a reproduction of an object formed by a lens or mirror

incident ray (3.4) ray of light travelling towards a reflecting or refracting surface

induced current (8.3) current produced when a conductor cuts a magnetic field

induced voltage (8.3) voltage produced when a conductor cuts a magnetic field

induction (7.1) appearance of a voltage across a conductor when it moves with respect to a magnetic field

inert (7.2) non reactive

infrared (4.1) part of the electromagnetic spectrum with wavelength just longer than visible light

insulated (thermally) (2.12) surrounded by a material that does not readily transfer thermal energy

insulator (electrical) (7.1) material that does not allow an electric current to pass through it

insulator (thermal) (2.11) material that does not readily transfer thermal energy

ion (7.3) an atom that has gained or lost electrons

ionisation (5.2) the addition or removal of electrons from an atom

ionosphere (4.3) a layer of the upper atmosphere able to reflect long- and medium-wave radio waves

iron core (8.2) on which a coil of wire is wound to increase the magnetic field

isotope (5.1, 6.2) an atom of an element having a different mass number but the same atomic number

J

joule (J) (2.8) unit of energy; 1J = 1N m or 1kg m/s

K

kilowatt (kW) (7.4) one thousand watts

kilowatt-hour (kWh) (7.6) commercial unit of electricity (= kW × hours)

kinetic energy (2.8) energy possessed by a moving object ($= 1/2mv^2$)

L

L (love) waves (4.6) waves which travels through the surface of the Earth

laminated (8.5) thin sheets of iron used to make the core of a transformer, reducing eddy currents

lava (4.7) molten material which is extruded onto the Earth's surface

Lenz's Law (8.3) the direction of an induced current always opposes the change that produced it

leverage (2.1) increasing the turning effect of a force by increasing its distance from the pivot

lift (2.5) upward force on the wing of an aeroplane

light dependent resistor (LDR) (1.1) a resistor whose resistance decreases when the light level increases

light emitting diode (LED) (1.1) a diode that emits light when it is conducting a current

lightning (7.2) discharge between a charged thundercloud and Earth

lithosphere (4.7) the outer part of the mantle and lower part of the crust of the Earth

live (wire) (7.4) a high-voltage wire, with brown insulation, that carries electric current to mains appliances

longitudinal wave (3.1) a wave whose vibrations are parallel to its direction of travel

loudspeaker (8.1) a device which changes electricity to sound

lymphocyte (5.6) a type of white blood cell

M

machine (2.12) a device that enables a task to be done more easily

magma (4.7) molten rock

magnetic field (8.1) region around a magnet in which there is a magnetic force

mantle (4.7) the layer of the Earth below the crust

mass number (5.1) the total number of protons and neutrons in the nucleus of an atom

metamorphism (4.8) the action of heat and pressure on rocks, which then changes their original state

microwave (4.3) part of the electromagnetic spectrum – wavelength at the short end of radio waves

milliamp (mA) (1.3) one thousandth of an ampere

moment (2.1) turning effect of a force (see also torque)

motor (8.2) a device which uses electricity to produce motion

mutation (5.6) alterations in genetic material which change the cell or virus

mutual induction (8.4) voltage induced in a coil of wire by a changing magnetic field in an adjacent coil

National Grid (8.7) nationwide supply network carrying electricity from power stations to consumers

nebulae (6.2) clouds of gas and dust in space

neutral (wire) (7.4) wire, with blue insulation, kept at 0 V, which provides the return path for mains electric current

neutron (7.1) uncharged particle present in the nucleus of an atom

neutron star (6.2) a small, dense collapsed star

newton (N) (2.8) unit of force; a force of 1 N gives a 1 kg mass an acceleration of 1m/s^2

newton metre (Nm) (2.1) unit used for the moment of a force (force × distance) Nm

no-parallax (3.6) the lining up of object and image

normal (3.4) a line at right angles to a surface

nuclear (power) (8.6) the use of nuclear energy (from fission) to produce electricity

nuclear fusion (6.2) the joining together of light nuclei with the release of energy

nucleus (7.1) the central part of an atom containing protons and neutrons

nuclide (5.1) another name for isotope

ohm (Ω) (1.2) unit of electrical resistance; ohm = volt/ampere

ohmic (1.3) an electrical conductor that obeys Ohm's Law

Ohm's Law (1.3) at constant temperature, the voltage across a conductor is proportional to the current in it

oil-fired (power station) (8.6) power station in which the fuel used is oil

optical fibres (4.4) very thin glass fibres that light passes along by total internal reflection

order of magnitude (3.7) an indication of the size of a number according to its power of ten

P

P (primary) waves (4.6) longitudinal waves from an earthquake

parallel (circuit) (1.2) components connected across the same two points

parent nuclide (5.3) an isotope which undergoes radioactive decay

pay-back period (2.11) time taken to recoup the cost of installing thermal insulation from the savings made on fuel bills

photocopier (7.2) device that uses electrostatics to print a copy of a document

pivot (2.1) point at which a lever is balanced

plane (3.3) a flat surface

planet (6.1) a body which orbits the Sun or any other star, seen only by reflected light

plate (4.8) one of the sections into which the Earth's crust is divided

polar orbit (6.1) a satellite in orbit over the North and South poles of the Earth

pollution (8.6) damage to the environment from man-made causes

power (2.8, 7.4) rate of transfer of energy

power (rating) (7.4) power output of a device when working normally

power loss (8.7) difference between the input and output power of a device

primary (8.5) the input coil of a transformer

prism (4.4) a regular-shaped block of glass or other dense transparent material

proton (7.1) positively charged particle present in the nucleus of an atom

protostar (6.2) a new star formed from collapsing gas and dust

pulse (3.3) a single short burst of sound or other wave

Q

quasar (6.3) very bright distant object giving out large amounts of energy

R

radar (4.3) the use of reflected radio waves to measure distance or locate objects

radial (magnetic) field (8.2) magnetic field in the space between the curved poles of a magnet and an iron core that is aligned with the centre of the core

radiation (5.2) energy which travels as rays, waves, or particles

radiation (thermal) (2.11) part of the electromagnetic spectrum adjacent to red light (infrared)

radiation burns (5.6) caused by exposure to radioactivity, similar to heat burns but take longer to heal

radiation sickness (5.6) sickness caused by exposure to radioactivity

radio (4.1) a band of the electromagnetic spectrum, which is mainly used for communication

radiocarbon dating (5.5) using the activity of carbon-14 atoms in a sample to determine its age

radioisotope (5.1) an isotope which decays by emitting ionising radiation

rarefaction (3.1) part of a longitudinal wave where the particles are further apart than normal

reaction (force) (2.5) force on an object resting on a surface that is perpendicular to that surface

reaction time (2.9) time taken by the

brain to respond to a signal (also called thinking time)

real depth (3.6) the actual depth of a dense transparent object

real image (3.6) an image that can be projected onto a screen

red giant (6.2) an average-sized star that expands at the end of its life

red shift (6.3) when a galaxy is moving away from us, the light appears redder than usual

red supergiant (6.2) a large blue supergiant which expands at the end of its life

reflected ray (3.4) ray of light which is travelling away from a mirror

refraction (3.5) the change in direction of light as it passes from one transparent material to another of different density

renewable source (8.6) source of electricity that does not get used up (e.g. wind) or is quickly replaced (e.g. biomass)

repel (7.1) two objects that move away from each other, such as like poles of a magnet

residual current device (RCD) (7.5) detects a very small change in the current in the live and neutral wires of an appliance and breaks the circuit immediately

resistance (1.1) opposition of a circuit component to the flow of charge; ratio of voltage across a component to the current in it

resultant (force) (2.6) single force which equals the sum of two or more other forces

retardation (2.4) see deceleration

reverberation (3.4) the repeated reflection of sound

ring main (7.4) a parallel circuit used to connect 13 A power points in a house

ripple tank (3.3) a shallow tank of water used to illustrate wave phenomena

S

S (secondary) waves (4.6) transverse waves from an earthquake

satellite (1.3, 6.1) an object in orbit around a larger object

scalar (2.3) quantity having magnitude (size) but no direction

sea-floor spreading (4.8) the moving apart of two plates where new crust is created by magma from the mantle

seat belt (2.7) restraint on car occupant to reduce injury in case of accident

secondary (8.5) the output coil of a transformer

seismic waves (4.6) the collective name for L waves, P waves and S waves

seismometer (4.6) an instrument used to measure Earth tremors

semiconductor (1.3) material able to conduct charge to some extent – less than a metal but more than an insulator

series (circuit) (1.2) components connected end to end in a circuit

short circuit (7.5) the by-passing of part of a circuit by a stray wire, reducing the resistance and increasing the current

slip rings (8.4) rings that (with carbon brushes) conduct current to and from the coil in an a.c. generator

Solar System (6.1) the Sun and everything circling around it

sonar (4.5) the use of sound waves and their echoes to measure distance or locate objects

spark counter (5.2) device which sparks when air is ionised, so is used to detect alpha radiation

spectrum (4.1) the distribution of energy emitted from sources arranged in order of wavelength

speed (2.2, 3.2) rate of change of distance (distance/time)

split-ring commutator (8.2) split ring that keeps the forces on the coil of an electric motor in the same direction producing continuous rotation

step-down (transformer) (8.5) transformer that reduces voltage

step-up (transformer) (8.5) transformer that increases voltage

sterilise (5.5) make free from bacteria or other micro-organisms

stopping distance (2.9) distance a vehicle travels from the time the driver sees an obstruction to

coming to rest (= braking distance + thinking distance)

streamlined (2.6) shaped to offer the least possible resistance to motion

stroboscope (3.3) instrument used to observe moving objects by making them appear stationary

substation (8.7) where transformers are used to successively step-down voltages from the National Grid for local use

subduction zones (4.8) areas where the oceanic plate descends beneath the continental plate

superheated steam (8.6) high temperature steam produced by boiling water at high pressure in a power station

supernova (6.2) an explosion of a large star at the end of its life

supernova remnants (6.2) glowing cloud of gas thrown out from a supernova

T

tangent (2.2) straight line that just touches a curve

tectonic (4.8) relating to, causing, or resulting from structural deformation of the Earth's crust

tension (2.5) a force in a stretched object

terminal velocity (2.10) the velocity of a falling body when the air resistance, acting upwards, is equal in magnitude to the weight, acting downwards

thermistor (1,1, 4.2) an electronic component whose resistance changes with temperature

thermograph (4.2) a picture formed by recording differing temperatures

thinking distance (2.9) how far a car travels before the brakes are applied, while the driver is still reacting

thinking time (2.9) see reaction time

thrust (2.5) force spread over an area; push or pull due to a rocket engine

toner (7.2) powdered ink used to produce a print in a photocopier

torque (2.1) the turning effect, or moment, of a force, especially a couple

total internal reflection (4.4) reflection inside a material when the angle of incidence exceeds the critical angle

tracer (5.4) a radioisotope introduced into a system so that its path can be followed

transformer (8.5) device used to increase or decrease alternating voltages

transmission (8.7) movement from one place to another (e.g. electricity via the National Grid)

transverse wave (3.1) a wave whose vibrations are at right angles to its direction of travel

trench (4.8) formed when one of the Earth's plates moves up and over another

turns ratio (8.5) ratio of the number of turns on the primary coil of a transformer to the number on the secondary coil

ultrasound (4.5) sound of high frequency – above 20 000 Hz – which is inaudible to humans

ultraviolet (2.6, 4.1) part of the electromagnetic spectrum with wavelength just shorter than visible light

unbalanced (2.6) system not in equilibrium, having a resultant force or moment

Van de Graaff generator (7.1) machine which produces a very high voltage by electrostatic means

variable resistor (1.1) resistor whose resistance can be changed

vector (2.3) quantity having magnitude (size) and direction

velocity (2.3, 3.2) the rate of change of distance with time in a straight line (displacement/time)

vibration (3.1) the to and fro motion of a particle or of an elastic solid about an equilibrium position

virtual image (3.6) an image which cannot be projected onto a screen – no light passes through it

visible light (4.1) the region of the electromagnetic spectrum to which our eyes are sensitive

volcanic ash (4.7) molten rock blasted out from volcanoes

volt (V) (1.2) unit of voltage (1 V = 1 J/C)

voltage (1.2) energy converted in an electrical component when unit

charge passes through it (= energy/charge)

voltmeter (1.2) instrument used to measure voltage

watt (w) (2.8, 7.4) unit of power equal to 1 joule/second

wavefront (3.3) the instantaneous position of a wave at right angles to its direction of motion

wavelength (3.2) the distance between two successive points of identical displacement on a wave

weight (2.1) force on an object due to gravitational attraction (= *mg*)

white dwarf (6.2) a small star which has collapsed when its fuel has run out

work (2.8) work is done when a force moves in the direction of the force; work done = energy transferred = force × distance moved in the direction of the force

X-rays (4.1) high energy, penetrating electromagnetic waves of short wavelength

Glossary (TBA1-3)

A

air bag (A3.5) installed in cars; designed to inflate if the car decelerates rapidly, protecting the occupants

amplitude modulation (A2.7) changing a radio wave's amplitude by the addition of a signal wave

AND (gate) (A1.1) a circuit with two inputs that gives a 'high' output only when both inputs are 'high'

antinode (A2.5) a point on a stationary wave with maximum amplitude

B

beats (A2.7) phenomenon which occurs when two notes of close but different frequencies are sounded together

binary code (A1.5) a digital counting system using only two digits, 0 and 1

bistable (A1.5) a switching circuit with two stable states

bit (A1.5) short for binary digit

C

carrier (A2.7) a radio wave onto which is added a signal wave

chip (A1.3) a small piece of semiconducting material (usually silicon) which contains millions of circuit elements, and forms an integrated circuit (IC)

closed pipe (A2.6) a tube, in which air is vibrating, closed off at one end

collisions (A3.5) impacts between two or more objects

condenser (A2.3) a system of lenses which collects light to focus it

conservation (of momentum) (A3.3) if no external force acts, the total momentum of a system before a collision equals the total momentum afterwards

constructive interference (A2.7) a reinforcement of waves to produce a larger amplitude

crumple zones (A3.5) areas at the front and rear of a car that are designed to buckle in a crash so that the car takes longer to stop and the force on the occupants is reduced

D

destructive interference (A2.7) a cancellation of waves to produce a smaller amplitude

digital (A1.5) able to take only a certain number of values, such as 0 and 1 in logic circuits

diminished (A2.2) as applied to an image which is smaller than the object

dispersion (A2.1) the spreading out of a ray of light into a wider beam as it is refracted to produce a spectrum

dissipated (A3.6) scattered or spread out

E

efficiency (A3.7) ratio of the useful energy output to the total energy input in an energy transfer process

erect (A2.3) as applied to an image which is the same way up as the object

F

flip-flop (A1.5) another name for a bistable switching circuit

focal length (A2.2) the distance between the optical centre and the focal point

focal point (A2.2) the point through which rays parallel and near to the principal axis pass after refraction at a convex lens

forced vibration

forced vibration (A2.4) an externally applied vibration which causes another object to vibrate

fuel (A3.4) source of energy

fundamental (A2.5) the main natural frequency of vibration of a string or air column

G

gate (A1.1) an electric circuit that can be either 'on' or 'off' in response to certain input signals

H

harmonic (A2.5) a multiple of the fundamental frequency which occurs when a string or air column vibrates

heat engine (A3.7) machine that depends on a rise in temperature in order to work

I

impulse (A3.3) the product of a force and the time for which it acts

input (A1.3) anything that goes into an electronic circuit

insulation (thermal) (A3.6) use of a material that is a bad conductor of heat to reduce energy loss or gain from an object

inverted (A2.2) as applied to an image which is upside down compared to the object

inverter (A1.1) a device that reverses an input signal (see NOT gate)

J

jet turbine (A3.4) an engine in which the exhaust gases from burnt fuel leave in one direction propelling the object attached to the jet turbine in the opposite direction

L

latch (A1.5) a bistable circuit with only one output that remains switched on even when the original signal is switched off

logic (gate) (A1.1) decision making circuit that uses electronic switches (see gate)

M

magnified (A2.3) as applied to an image which is larger than the object

moisture sensor (A1.2) a device that detects the presence of water, producing a related electric signal

momentum (A3.3) the product of the mass and velocity of an object

N

NAND (gate) (A1.4) equivalent to an AND gate with a NOT gate; the output is 'high' as long as both inputs are *not* 'high'

natural frequency (A2.4) the frequency with which any object can be made to vibrate with maximum amplitude

node (A2.5) a point on a stationary wave with zero amplitude

NOR (gate) (A1.4) equivalent to an OR gate with a NOT gate; the output is 'high' when neither input is 'high'

NOT (gate) (A1.1) a circuit with one input that is the reverse of the output; when the input is 'high' the output is 'low' and vice versa

O

open pipe (A2.6) a tube in which air is vibrating open at both ends

optical centre (A2.2) the centre of a convex lens through which we consider light to be undeviated as it passes

OR (gate)

OR (gate) (A1.1) a circuit with two inputs that gives a 'high' output when either of its inputs is 'high'

output (A1.3) anything that comes out of an electronic circuit

oxygen (A3.4) an element essential for combustion

P

parabola (A3.2) a curved path as followed by an object thrown horizontally on Earth

path difference (A2.7) the difference in the distance travelled by two waves

phase (A2.7) the amount by which the points of identical displacement of two waves differ

potential divider (A1.6) two resistors, or a single resistor which can be tapped at any point along its length, connected so that part of the voltage across the whole can be obtained

principal axis (A2.2) the line joining the focal points of a convex lens passing through the optical centre

processor (A1.3) something that changes the input of an electronic circuit in a specific way

projectile (A3.2) an object thrown upwards at an angle or projected horizontally near the Earth's surface

proportional (A2.1) when a straight line graph passes through the origin, the two variables are said to be proportional in that the y-variable is a constant multiple of the x-variable

Q

quality (A2.5) what a note from a particular instrument sounds like as a result of different harmonics

R

ramp (A3.7) sloping surface that aids movement from one level to another

Random Access Memory (RAM) (A1.5) computer memory containing millions of bistables

range (A3.2) the horizontal displacement of a projectile

real (A2.2) as applied to an image which can be projected onto a screen

recoils (A3.3) moves backwards, as, for example, a gun does when fired

reed relay (A1.2) two easily magnetised strips of nickel-iron, or reeds, activated by a current in a surrounding coil, which make and break a circuit very rapidly

refractive index (A2.1) the ratio of the speed of light in a vacuum to the speed of light in the material

relay (A1.2) an electromagnetic switch that uses a small current to turn on a larger one

reset (A1.5) an input signal to a bistable circuit that restores it to its original state

resonance (A2.4) the vibration of an object at its natural frequency

rocket (A3.4) a jet engine which carries its own oxygen supply so it can travel into space

S

seat belts (A3.5) restraints worn by the occupants of a car to reduce injury in a crash

sensitivity control (A1.7) a variable resistor used in a potential divider to adjust the external condition that changes the input to a logic gate

sensor (A1.1) a device that reacts to an input energy, such as light, and produces a related electrical signal

specific heat capacity (A3.6) energy required to raise the temperature of unit mass of a substance by one degree

stationary wave (A2.5) a wave which exhibits nodes and antinodes formed by the reflection and superposition of one wave upon itself

superposition (A2.7) the addition of two waves to produce a wave whose instantaneous displacement is the arithmetic sum of each individual displacement

system (A1.3) a group of electronic components, consisting of input, processor and output, working together to do something useful

T

truth table (A1.1) a table summarising the way in which the output of a system of logic gates varies depending on the state of the inputs

turbine (A3.7) a device, powered by water or steam, that produces rotation

WXYZ

water wheel (A3.7) wheel turned by the kinetic energy of water

Writing good extended answers

All GCSE Science papers have questions where you must answer with a series of linked sentences. These questions are called **extended** and **continuous writing**.

At least 25% of the marks in your examination are awarded for these questions requiring longer answers. Most candidates do not do as well on these as on other types of question. It is well worth practising to get better at this.

Here are two examples of typical long answer questions. Some help is given to show you how to answer the first one.

1 **The output from a power station is** [4 + 1] **connected to a step-up transformer. The transformer is connected to transmission lines. Explain why a step-up transformer is needed.**

Before starting to answer this question think carefully what the question is asking you to do. You are asked to *explain why a step-up transformer* is needed. You are *not* asked about other stages in the process of generating electricity and delivering it to our homes. There are four marks for content (shown by the 4 in brackets) so you must make at least four different points and they must be put into a correct order.

In the table below are some of the points you might make. Some of the points are wrong, some are correct but not relevant to the answer, and some are needed in a good answer.

■ Go through each of the statements and decide which should be included.

■ To get a good answer the statements have to be put in the correct order. Write them out in the correct order.

2 **A 10 000 m runner gets very hot and** [3 + 1] **sweaty. How does sweating help him to lose energy?**

This time you must use your ideas about heat transfer to explain why the runner loses energy. Make a list of relevant points. Then select the key points and put them in a logical order so that when you write them out you have a clear, concise answer that explains why the runner loses energy.

Marks are now awarded for **quality of written communication** in this type of question. In the questions above there are marks for content and one mark the examiner can add for the quality of written communication. This can be awarded for any of the following:

■ The correct use of sentences with capital letter, verb and full stop.

■ The correct use and spelling of scientific words.

■ The correct use of scientific terms e.g. conduction, convection, radiation.

■ Putting events in the correct and logical order to ensure communication.

Your longer answers will improve if you remember what you have done on this page.

a step-up transformer increases the voltage	the coils of a transformer are wound on an iron core
increasing the voltage increases the resistance	increasing the voltage reduces the current
cables have resistance	the smaller the current the less energy lost
electricity is produced by electromagnetic induction	a step-up transformer has more turns on the secondary than the primary coil
transmission lines form part of the National Grid	power loss = I^2R
the power lines get hot	transformers only work with alternating current
a step-up transformer increases the current	voltage flows along the wires

Drawing line graphs

Many GCSE Science papers have a question requiring you to draw and use line graphs. You will probably draw a line graph for your Sc1 coursework.

- On Foundation tier written papers the axes and scales will be given to you. One or two of the points may have already been plotted. All of the points will fit on a straight line or curve. There may be an anomalous point.

- On Higher tier papers you may have to choose scales and axes. For coursework, you will have to choose scales and axes.

Here are some results from an experiment to find out how the voltage across a resistor changes when the current through it changes.

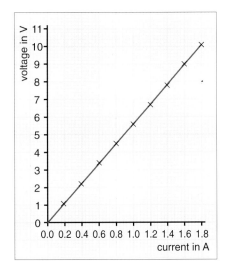

current in A	0.2	0.4	0.6	0.8	1.0	1.2	1.4	1.6	1.8
voltage in V	1.1	2.2	3.4	4.5	5.6	6.7	7.8	9.0	10.1

The independent variable is the current. This is the one changed step by step during the experiment. It goes on the horizontal or x-axis. The dependent variable is the voltage. It depends on the variable changed during the experiment. It goes on the vertical or y-axis.

Before starting to draw a graph you will need a sharp pencil, a 30 cm ruler and a piece of 2 mm graph paper. Use a ruler to draw the axes and label them. Now choose suitable scales. The graph should be as large as possible by using sensible scales based on numbers easily divisible into 10 such as 1, 2, or 5. Most graph paper has nine large squares along its shorter side. Use this as the x-axis and make each large square 0.2 A. On the y-axis, make each large square 1.0 V. The graph should start at zero. If you draw a graph which does not more than half fill the grid in any direction, you will lose a mark in an examination.

Now plot the points carefully marking each point with a small cross. You will lose one or two marks if you plot points wrongly. When you draw the best line, remember that science results come from experiments and are not exactly right but are as good as our equipment allows. Lines may not be exactly straight, but the points may lie very close to a straight line. Use a ruler to draw the best straight line you can. Never join dot to dot. Think about whether the graph will go through the origin. Try to have as many points above the line as below the line. Sometimes with experimental results there are anomalous points. You should then draw your best line to miss these points.

Sometimes the points lie close to a curve. If this is the case, do not join dot to dot and do not try to draw a straight line. Think about whether the graph will go through the origin. Draw a single smooth line missing out any anomalous point.

Here are a set of results from an experiment to find out how the amount of gamma radiation passing through lead sheets depends on the thickness of lead. Use this data to draw a graph.

thickness of lead in mm	2	3	4	6	8	10	15	20
count rate in counts per minute	25 005	11 010	4992	3304	1496	998	489	284

Index

X, Y, Z